DISTANT LANDS

Tales of a Solo Traveler

KEITH WILKINSON

outskirts press

Distant Lands
Tales of a Solo Traveler
All Rights Reserved.
Copyright © 2017 Keith Wilkinson
v3.0

The opinions expressed in this manuscript are solely the opinions of the author and do not represent the opinions or thoughts of the publisher. The author has represented and warranted full ownership and/or legal right to publish all the materials in this book.

This book may not be reproduced, transmitted, or stored in whole or in part by any means, including graphic, electronic, or mechanical without the express written consent of the publisher except in the case of brief quotations embodied in critical articles and reviews.

Outskirts Press, Inc.
http://www.outskirtspress.com

ISBN: 978-1-4787-8970-3

Cover & Interior Photo © 2017 Garland Keith Wilkinson . All rights reserved - used with permission.

Outskirts Press and the "OP" logo are trademarks belonging to Outskirts Press, Inc.

PRINTED IN THE UNITED STATES OF AMERICA

Contents

Introduction..i

Part One: 2010 Living with Locals—Lessons in Culture 1
   1. Nepal in Transition..3
   2. Indian Summer 12
   3. India and Nepal Again—Strengthening Ties........................26

Part Two: 2011 Third Trip around the World:
Rhine to the Mekong 53
   1. Germany—Lure of the Lorelei 55
   2. Istanbul--Off to the Races 60
   3. Exploring the Gulf States 69
   4. Briefly Nepal before a Month in India..................................75
   5. Thanksgiving in Nepal 92

Part Three: 2012 Multiple Deserts,
Weddings and the White House... 123
   1. The Deserts of Egypt..125
   2. India—Wedding Negotiations..135
   3. North India—Himalaya Highs, Trance and Dalai Lama......140
   4. Marathon of Weddings...148

    5. The Pushkar/Nimaj Weddings..159
    6. "It Ain't Over Until It's Over!"..172
    7. A Sad Christmas and a Happy New Year! 177
    8. Sympathy in Nepal and Mountain Village........................182
    9. Inauguration of a President 190

Part Four: 2013 Rafting the Himalayas,
Whales in the Desert, Camels in India **195**
    1. Rafting Nepal; Hot Days in India..197
    2. Whales in the Desert 212
    3. Qatar, Oasis of Wealth 224
    4. Nepal for Dashain 227
    5. Utter Pradesh 234
    6. India Birthday 238

Part Five: Fourth Trip around the World—Istanbul to Tokyo **247**
    1. A Night in a Turkish Fire Station..249
    2. Nepal with a Friend from India 257
    3. A Month in India 264
    4. Small Village Project and 75th Birthday!...........................281
    5. Staying with Tokyo Friends 290

Part Six: 2015 Holi Festival and Earthquake **297**
    1. Bangalore in the South to Manali in the North 299
    2. Holi Celebration and My Hair turns Pink!.......................310
    3. Nepal's Earthquake Leads to Return Visits 326
    4. Surprise Birthday Trip 340

Part Seven: 2016 Turkey, Terror and Turning 77 .... **345**
    1. Ramadan with Family in East Turkey 347
    2. Days of Calm before the Storm 367
    3. Nepal's Mountain Villages and
       a Tale of Indian Villages Abandoned by Love....................383

Acknowledgements 393
Postscript 397

Introduction

Travel gets into your blood. I confess to being smitten. I love being with people of various cultures and experiencing life with them first-hand.

In the two years leading up to age 70, I had made consecutive solo trips around the world. I hardly knew what I was doing on that first trip, other than exploring without a lot of pre-planning or control over events. The spontaneity of that style of travel seemed to suit me well, though it did get a bit overwhelming at times. It allowed me flexibility to meet people and accept them on their own terms. Surprising for me was how easy it was to meet and make new friends. As I entered each new country, it was only a matter of hours or a day at most before I was invited to experience some adventure or other, or to meet friends or family. In the process, I developed a number of close friendships, especially in four of the more challenging countries I visited—Nepal, India, Turkey and Egypt. In the case of Nepal, I spent an entire month, last time, living with a Nepali family. In the case of India, I found myself virtually adopted into a family through a deep friendship with a young man. In Turkey over the past two years, I've forged an abiding friendship, leading last year to a week spent in the far eastern village near the Armenian border. With these involvements, I experienced life as lived in its daily expression—celebrating festivals, weddings and birthdays.

I mourned with the families in the loss of loved ones, celebrated the births of babies and endured the trials of nature and political upheaval. These friendships led to additional trips and triggered two additional around-the-world solo journeys.

Turning 70 did not signal the end of my travel. In fact it opened the door for more unique and varied experiences, more than ever before in my lifetime. This account spans those seven years of travel experiences, including two additional trips around the world, plus multiple visits to certain countries. The account is based on journals and blogs, and covers my travel from ages 70 to 77. I offer it as testimony that travel does not need to be age-limiting. The essence of healthy living, I believe, is living out one's dreams, whatever they may be. It is reaching for one's stars. Whenever travel becomes out of the question for me, I hope never to cease the journey of living. For me, travel is the adventure of a lifetime. Hopefully, it has made me a better human being.

These recorded adventures include treks in mountains and jungles, visits to small villages, participation in sacrificial activities during festivals, learning local customs, involvements in a marathons of weddings, honoring deceased family members, celebrating birthdays and simply experiencing the ordinary routines of daily living, eating, sleeping and surviving. There were times when I got overwhelmed from being immersed for weeks or months in an unfamiliar culture. There were times I became exhausted by the very ordeals of travel, whether by bus, train, motorcycle, dugout or on foot. I managed to endure demonstrations, riots and a military coup. I visited ghostly abandoned villages, sweltered in over-crowded cities, and prayed in temples, churches and mosques. The list goes on, but you get the idea.

The most important discovery for me in these journeys has been that we each share one important aspect of being which should bind us all together—our humanity.

It is in that spirit that I invite the reader to join me for seven years' worth of journeys to distant lands. One day, in my meditative reading, I found this bit of ancient wisdom which inspired the title for this book, *"Like cold water to a weary soul is good news from a **distant land**." Proverbs 25:25 Holy Bible NIV.*

Let's start with a riot in Kathmandu. Hardly good news!

Part One
2010 Living with Locals—Lessons in Culture

"The world is a book, and those who do not travel read only a page." –St. Augustine

1

Nepal in Transition

Thursday 6 May 2010

Kathmandu: Riots and Paralysis

American Airlines' longest flight is from Chicago to Delhi, taking fourteen and a half hours to fly with no rest for me upon arrival there, for I spend a restless night in the airport waiting to catch a flight to Kathmandu early in the morning. Yet I am refreshed by my excitement at seeing the magnificent view below as we descend over verdant mountains, lightly shrouded in fog to land on Kathmandu's very short runway. Outside the terminal, I am eagerly greeted by four lovely friends, come to airport to receive me with big hugs all around, adorning my neck with colorful garlands of fragrant flowers and informing me that a general strike is in progress and that no vehicles are being allowed on the streets of Kathmandu! Our only option is to walk from the airport to my friend's house, some three miles away. Walking isn't that bad for me really, having spent nearly two days in transit on planes and in airports. In fact, I welcome it as a good way to stretch my legs. We take time to stop along the way to rest, giving us a chance to catch up on the events surrounding us, as we enjoy cold 7-Ups all around.

Distant Lands

Nepali Friends

As to the strike, it seems that the three leading political parties—the Maoists, the Communists and the Congress parties are at odds about governance in the country. The country had kicked out its king by the time I had made my second trip to Nepal and now they can't agree on a constitution. The strike has paralyzed the entire nation. Nothing is moving. The streets are filled with demonstrators. For the most part the demonstrations have been relatively peaceful–consisting mostly chants, flag waving and the display of signs for their various causes. As with any such demonstrations however, acts of violence can and do occur. It helps that my four friends are with me to provide the necessary escort to navigate our way through the melee. We encounter a Communist demonstration or two as we walk. My friends tell me that most tourists remain stuck in their hotels and that businesses are closed—banks, restaurants, and others, making travel nearly impossible, except from airport to airport. The strike is costing the country literally millions of dollars in lost tourist income. Here I am, once again, in the middle of it all.

Nepal in Transition

Right now we really can't go anywhere. We hunker down and spend the next two days taking walks along the back streets. Manish says that we might be able to venture out as far as the perimeter of the city toward a mountainous area and this is what we do. It is refreshing to be outside and the two days gives me a chance to recover from jet lag. From the heights, we look down on the city where we see numerous demonstrations still in progress. Newari people live at this side of Kathmandu. They are the ancient farmers and traders of Nepal. We stop at a place for snacks and engage in a pool game, much to the amusement of the local youth, who obviously are much more skilled than we.

According to the news reports we receive by the end of the second day, the strike has ended. Perhaps we can now proceed with some caution with our plans for travel. One of these friends happens to carry a Maoist membership card, which may prove useful in case we are stopped in one of the Maoist-prone areas, which include much of the countryside outside the main cities. Having the card does not necessarily mean that he ascribes to their views, but it allows him to function in those areas. We make a plan to go to Bandipur tomorrow. Power outages occur much of the day and night in Kathmandu, challenging me to keep up my travel blog on a daily basis. However, I'm happy to be in Nepal. It is a great place to visit and the people here are wonderful. It is good to be among friends. Too bad the country is unable to benefit from stable governance. However, that could just as easily be said of other parts of the world!

Return to Bandipur

We mount bikes, the four of us—Raju, Sonu, Manish and I—and head toward Bandipur, an ancient village built at the crest of a mountain some 130 kilometers from Kathmandu. I had visited there in October and wanted to return. Traffic out of Kathmandu is its usual chaotic mess. I cover my face with a bandana in an effort to keep out some of the dust and smog from smoke-spewing vehicles. There are no pollution controls here! Once over the pass leading out of the Kathmandu Valley, it is a matter of descending along a rapidly flowing river. The road hugs the side of the mountain, subject to occasional, if not frequent, landslides as well as multiple traffic mishaps. One false move and you find yourself over the side plunging thousands of feet into a whitewater river below. Along the way, we stop at a favorite place to eat fish, freshly caught from the nearby river. Oh, is it good eating! The fish are fried crisp and served along with fresh cucumber, salted and washed down with favorite drinks. From there, we stop off at a resort built next to the river, which has a large swimming pool. The water is refreshing after enduring the dust and smog of Kathmandu and well worth our taking the extra time spent. After all, why be in a hurry? Following the refreshing swim, we bike on toward Bandipur, first crossing the river where we ascend along a different river valley. We take a turn-off at the edge of one of the small villages and take a winding road making our way to the top of a mountain. The sun is just setting. The bikes strain to make the steep climb. Once we arrive at the top, we park our bikes outside the village which allows no vehicles inside. It is a great concept!

Unfortunately, the power goes off after we arrive. Still, we manage to enjoy our dinner at the sidewalk cafe just below the room we have rented. The room turns out to be the very same one we had rented last time, painted a bright blue, trimmed in yellow and with a balcony overlooking the main street lined with medieval-style buildings. Ancient Bandipur was once an important stop on prosperous trade routes from China to India. We enjoy the ambience of a leisurely dinner eaten in the dark, with only occasional light provided by our mobile phones. When you are with friends, there is little need to hurry dinner. In fact, we take a full three hours to eat and enjoy good-natured bantering back and forth. Bandipur loves to welcome its guests. However, there is one important caveat—visitors must be quiet after 9 p.m. There are no police here, I'm told, so one has the idea that if there were problems the villagers have their own ways of dealing with them. We are careful to respect their wishes and move up to our room before the curfew to sit on the balcony for a time, just to look up at the stars made the more brilliant by the absence of light pollution.

Siddha Cave is located down the mountain from Bandipur about halfway. The steps leading down are sometimes a bit steep for me, giving the front-side leg muscles a good workout. In many ways, going down is harder than going up. The day becomes quite hot by the time we reach the opening. The cave turns out to be much bigger than I had expected. A guide there maintains vigil and is the one who takes us inside to explore its various chambers hanging with stalactite and stalagmite formations. Some of the cave chambers are quite slippery and we use a rope provided to pull ourselves up some of the more difficult inclines. Deep in the cave, we come to an enormously deep abyss that one can descend by ladder. We are told it requires another hour or so for further exploration, but we decide it is too much for us, as we weren't prepared for serious cave exploration.

Once outside, we regroup and head on down to the bottom of the mountain, instead of climbing back up. We stop for rest there and have lunch at a place called "Helen and Rocky's" in a small cluster of housing just off the highway. After lunch, we catch a bus to the next village in order to arrange for transportation back up the mountain to Bandipur. A Jeep-like vehicle, which is seriously overloaded with passengers and looking not too capable, is all that is available, but we book passage on it anyway. With no other place to ride, Manish and I climb on the top, while the others squeeze inside. I wish I had a picture of this weird-looking contraption. The truck doesn't have the usual petrol tank but instead uses some kind of canister with a line to a pressure pump near the motor requiring thorough pumping to make it work. Fully overloaded by now, we lurch our way forward with hisses and groans and volumes of smoke billowing from the exhaust. The strange vehicle continues to groan its way up the various grades toward the top of the mountain. About a third of the way, it suddenly bellows, hisses and stops dead in its tracks. We all unload while they pump and prime

Distant Lands

and try starting it again, but to no avail. Meanwhile a few drops of rain start to fall on us and soon turns into a first-class downpour, sending us scurrying to find shelter under the porch of a nearby farm house, huddling under overhanging eaves to wait while another vehicle is summoned from below. When it finally arrives, we squeeze our sweaty, wet bodies together under a small canopy at the back of a truck. Duly packed in, the truck lurches and groans its way up the mountain. This part of our jaunt is becoming a sweaty, wet and miserable experience.

When we reach the guest house, we waste no time heading for the shower! Refreshed and with dry clothes, we go once again for dinner at the sidewalk cafe, anticipating a chicken dinner of a rooster that Manish had selected earlier from a local man and arranged with the manager to have it dressed and cooked for our dinner. It is now being prepared as we wait. Again, we sit on the street and enjoy animated conversations about the day's ventures and finish once again on the balcony above.

We head today toward another village, called Daman, which they tell me is atop a much higher mountain and quite some distance away, first stopping at a waterfall located just off the road not far from Bandipur, a beautiful falls with water rushing over rock outcroppings. The guys insist that I get into the water to experience for myself the feel of the cascading water flowing over me. I'm game. Following local custom, I strip to my underwear and make my way tentatively into the water over the slippery rocks. Once under the falls, I enjoy the thrill of the rushing waters, while the others take pictures, one of which I post on Facebook, a discreet one of course. The water is a bit cold at first, but nice. After some time, I dry off a little—who thought to bring a towel? We resume our journey, to be joined by another friend, Deepak, at a juncture of highways that will lead us to Daman, a cavalcade of three motorbikes and five guys. We begin an ascent up a steep grade, stopping to eat wild berries that a lady has gathered from mountain trees for sale by the roadside. Once we crest the high pass, we descend into a beautiful valley, laced with terraced farms with crops of potatoes and cabbages. One of the guys calls out for us to stop so he can harvest and prepare marijuana from the many plants that grow freely along the sides of roads. He takes a smoke before going on. We cross to the far side of the valley and climb once again until we reach the village of Daman high up the mountain, where we arrive just before dark, arranging a room in an old lodge teetering on the side of the mountain. The air by now has grown noticeably colder, making us shiver.

Breakfast is taken at a nearby tower, which we climb in order to gain a spectacular view of the high peaks of the Himalayas off in the distance. The day is a bit hazy, yet we get a few clear glimpses of the peaks. At a man-made reservoir we stop for a lunch of fish and drinks. The paved road plays out, to an unpaved and rough road ascending toward a new pass to lead us back to Kathmandu. Things begin to unravel. One of the bikes breaks down. We try towing it up the steep grade, using one of the other bikes but that proves too much for the bike and it also breaks down. A couple of the guys set out to walk to a village to arrange for a truck to be sent to haul the bikes to a shop. After a couple of hours the truck arrives and we load the bikes but then the truck breaks down as well! This is fast becoming a jinxed day! With only one working bike remaining, Manish instructs his brother Sonu to take me back to Kathmandu while the others remain with the broken bikes. When we arrive back in Kathmandu, we are told to call a friend to come for them. It is dark by the time we arrive to make the call. The others do not return until well after midnight.

Visiting a Buddhist Monastery
Manish has heard me express interest in learning about Buddhism, so he suggests we visit a remote Buddhist monastery to the east of Kathmandu some 60 or 70 kilometers away. This time we travel, just the two of us. Clearing Kathmandu's impossible traffic, we zip along an open road through old villages, such as Thimi, with its ancient buildings and streets filled with bazaars selling everything imaginable. We

Distant Lands

climb a range of mountains. Manish points out the large statue of the Hindu god Shiva standing stately at the edge of the mountain facing the valley below. We continue through valleys and up steep grades until the road cuts off toward the monastery, at a most difficult ascent. This road is steep and quite rough, embedded with sharp stones causing the motorcycle to bounce about. I hang on as tightly as possible. The monastery compound consists of beautifully adorned buildings and grounds, kept immaculately clean much in contrast to the roads, streets and rivers elsewhere in Nepal. Beautiful flowers accent Tibetan-style buildings and fill nearby gardens. Most everything is shut down for lunch as we arrive at noon. We park and walk to an area on the backside where they sell curios and snacks to rest there until 1:00 p.m. when things will reopen. We finish our snacks and I hear chants, drums and the sound of Tibetan horns emanating from a building nearby, where I walk to discover a group of about 15 monks conducting afternoon prayer rituals, and slip inside through an open door to sit quietly on the floor, so as not to disturb. I snap a shot with my camera, but the light flashes much brighter than I expected, making me somewhat embarrassed. I fear that I have disrupted the solemn atmosphere of the ritual. A monk next to me, playing a drum, gestures toward me, which I interpret to mean "no photos, please." However he continues the gesture, only this time he is motioning my attention toward the lama sitting at the front leading the ceremony. I sit frozen for a few seconds trying to be as inconspicuous as possible but the lama makes eye contact and motions for me to come and sit beside him on the dais, the small platform from which he is leading. I cautiously move there. Without missing a beat, he continues the ritual making no further acknowledgement of my presence. Here I am, sitting front and center at a Buddhist monastery during their worship experience. The enveloping sounds become quite haunting, and amazingly beautiful, deep sounds of drums drowned out by the bellowing sounds of long Tibetan prayer horns. I begin to feel vibrations coursing through my body. Shorter horns break through with sharper sounds and the crescendos of drum and horns become interspersed with the chants by the monks reading from ancient scripts penned on small cards, resting on stands in front of their seated figures. I sit transfixed. Manish comes to a side window to see what has happened to me and motions that we should get going, so I quietly as possible, slip away as the chants continue. I wanted to stay longer.

For my last night in Nepal, Manish and friends take me to a rooftop restaurant where we revel in recounting days spent together. They are anxious to know when I might return. We hear a commotion in the street below us and see taxis starting to block a key intersection, creating total gridlock. It is a protest concerning the arrest of a couple of drivers, we learn. Perhaps it is an appropriate send-off for me by experiencing another demonstration. I had arrived during demonstrations and now I leave with another small one in progress, par for the course in these travels.

We take an alternate route home, arriving about 2:00 a.m.

2

Indian Summer

Sunday 16 May Pushkar, India
Hot Days in Rajasthan
The heat is most oppressive in Delhi at this time of year at about 112 degrees. I had arranged to stay at the YMCA in New Delhi and hoped to meet up with my nephew's fiancée for dinner but when I called she begged off saying her mother was ill and that they are soon to leave for south India. I tell her I understand and we enjoy chatting for a few moments by phone.

Trains are fully booked, so I settle for bus transportation instead for my trip to Ajmer and Pushkar. I go early to the Bikaner House bus terminal to purchase a ticket to Jaipur on a large air-conditioned bus made for comfortable travel. I will arrange for another bus once I get to Jaipur and continue my trip on to Ajmer. My friend Suresh, quite anxious for me to come, peppers with me a stream of texts asking for my arrival time, which remains fluid depending on the buses. We arrive in Jaipur about 12:30 p.m. to a crowded and chaotic terminal, like most in India. The heat in Jaipur is even more oppressive. I have only enough time to buy a bottle of water and grab a fried chili wrapped in a newspaper, before boarding the bus to Ajmer, which is not air-conditioned. By now it surely must be 117 degrees, not a good time to be on a crowded Indian bus, while eating a fiery hot chili pepper and drinking water, by now as hot as the day itself. The wind from the open windows is much too hot to be left open. I think to myself, what other idiot would be traveling like this? Only a devil from Hell could enjoy this heat. Perhaps the devil and I are related, a thought making me laugh at myself. When Suresh calls again, I tell him I will arrive in Ajmer by 4:00 pm. And he tells me he will come by motorbike to take me the 15 or so kilometers on to Pushkar. I step off the bus in Ajmer and spot him making his way through the crowd, excited to greet one another. Indian hospitality being what it is, we stop for tea, hot tea of course. I dream of a cold glass of iced tea, American style. Suresh suggests we wait due to the heat until sundown to make the last leg of the trip. I nix that idea, ready to get this part of travel over with. We pile my luggage on top of ourselves and head into the stifling heat toward Pushkar, arranging a couple of nights in a guest house, fortunately with air-conditioning. Unfortunately the power is out, leaving me nothing to do but sweat. In the evening Suresh comes to take me to his family home where I greet the family and have dinner. A place is made for us to sit rooftop, where I am served dinner. In India it is the custom for the honored guest to be fed first, while everyone else sits around and watches the guest eat. The food is good, but Indian food takes some getting used to and I eat it slowly, with all eyes on me. After the first plateful, I am full, but Suresh advises me that I must take more! When I make a comment about being the only one eating, his mother brings food for him, so he can join me and we eat in the presence of his mother, a sister and her husband, and another friend who has joined us.

Magnificent Udaipur

We plan to travel in celebration of Suresh's completion of his recent studies. He suggests we visit the cities of Udaipur and Jodhpur in Rajasthan, which requires hiring a car with air conditioning. Suresh asks if we can also include his friend Navneet, who has also finished his studies as well. I agree that it is a good idea for the three of us to travel together. Udaipur is quite some distance away, though the roads prove to be fairly good. Indian traffic, however, is enough to make even the strongest Western heart stop beating. Along the way, we stop for chai to watch a monkey, tethered nearby, jump around catching biscuits thrown by customers. Between jumps the monkey squats and stares intently at us with penetrating eyes as if to suggest, that were it not for a slight reshuffling of our respective DNAs, we could be the ones tethered and jumping for biscuits, while he could be sitting and drinking chai. Darwin could be proud of this monkey.

Reaching Udaipur late in the afternoon, we make our way through busy streets to the oldest part of the city and its narrow winding streets, to a hotel located high above on a bluff across from the palace, for which Udaipur is famous. Suresh uses his best negotiating skills to obtain a room for us at a reasonable price, with a large enough bed sufficient for the three of us. In the cooler part of the evening, we take our time to explore the city.

Our morning gets off to an adventurous start, when Suresh goes to the toilet. Toilets here are outfitted with water lines for cleansing, typical to this part of the world. Suresh grabs the knob to turn off the water line and the whole thing comes loose, showering him with a fast stream of water which quickly floods the floor. Navneet and I, hearing the commotion, rush to open the door only to be met by a cascading flood pouring into the room. I yell for Navneet to alert the hotel staff while I grab our bags and clothes from the floor and with Suresh still trying to get the water stopped. The staff comes running and yelling, to find Suresh still on the toilet trying frantically to stop the water. I move our clothes across the hall to a room which is not locked. They finally get the water source turned off. By now the room is completely flooded. Mops are brought, while Suresh gets himself clothed. The whole episode is a tale not soon forgotten, to be told later. The hotel staff kindly allows us to use the room across the hall, while they clean and repair ours, making for an auspicious start to our day.

While the repairs are being made, we visit the city and the beautiful lake for which Udaipur is famous, including a large Hindu temple. At the end of the day, we select a nice restaurant recommended to us by the hotel staff. A fully uniformed doorman ushers us to seats near the lounge. We order several appetizers, despite high prices, spring rolls, cheese balls and onion rings. Our entrée is elegantly served by waiters, transferring food from serving carts to individual plates, impressing Navneet who had never seen anything like it before. Our bill reflected the ambience, which we justify as making up for our auspicious morning with the flooding toilet. Later we speculate just how much each nibble had cost us.

Some days are like that, a mixture of the unexpected and a bit of elegance thrown in to make them memorable.

A Hot Day in Jodhpur
The road out of Udaipur leads us over arid mountains on a small paved road, winding its way through small rural and scenic villages. We stop to photograph elephants at work. Remote villages are always interesting to me. I would love to have time enough to chronicle their daily activities, but we press on toward Jodhpur. May is the driest and hottest month in Rajasthan and the landscape by now is parched by an overbearing sun. We put up for the night in a hotel, after much wrangling over price by Suresh. The ride has been wearying and we retire early.

Jodhpur Palace is located at the outskirts of the city atop a bluff with a view of the famous fort in the distance. The palace was designed by a British architect and constructed in 1929 making it one of the more modern structures to be seen in India. The day is quite hot by the time we buy tickets and make our way through the courtyard to the elegant structure. Various rooms are furnished elegantly, with pictures showing the ruling Maharaja in his finest regalia.

Because of the heat, I am ready to return to Pushkar. It has been too much to bear. I veto visiting the old, historic fort because it would involve too much walking outside, however Navneet wants to visit the zoo, and I reluctantly agree. As I feared, all the animals are hunkered inside to avoid the heat and we see only the rear end of one bear and a few birds. The zoo is not that well presented in any case. Disappointed, we head back toward Pushkar at mid-morning. We had considered stopping in the village of Jethana on the way to visit Suresh's uncle, but his mother who was visiting there at the time was already by now on her way back to Pushkar.

May is not the best time to visit Rajasthan. Just imagine Phoenix in the summer.

Poojas at the Lake
Suresh, being Brahmin, serves as a priest at the sacred lake in Pushkar, arising early each morning to assist devotees with prayers, who come to the lake for ceremonial bathing. I fulfill a promise and join him there. He wants to lead me through a prayer ceremony, which he does, praying for good health, good life and prosperity for me and my family. There are incenses and offerings of flowers, coconuts and sweets to accompany the prayers along with the scattering of rose petals in the lake. I dip my hands in the water ceremonially but do not do the full bathing. The various gods Shiva, Vishnu, Krishna are mentioned and we do an action to block bad karma along with an action to invite good karma as we throw petals over our shoulders and scatter others into the lake. The prayers are followed by requests for donations to the Brahmins, who run the temples who also provide food for the participating families and charity for others. These rituals have been going on for thousands of years, making Hinduism one of the oldest religions in the world. I respect the exercise, though I follow my own understandings in matters of faith.

For breakfast, Suresh's mother has fried vegetables—potato, onion, chilies in a batter making for a wonderful snack. His father brings sweets and Suresh gives me shirts and native attire to wear. They can't do enough for me; such is their affection and hospitality.

We stop to visit Navneet's shop. He along his brothers sells women's and girls' clothing, a small shop on the street near the Brahma Temple. A cow wanders in and Navneet gently shoos it out. Cows are sacred here and wander the streets at will, sometimes entering the shops. Cows have the right-of-way.

Suresh arranges a very small car for us to go the small village of Jethana, that we had bypassed coming in. The car is designed to comfortably carry about four adults. Suresh didn't tell me that we would stop in Ajmer on the way to pick up his uncle and family to give them a lift back to the village after they had been shopping, which makes us now *ten* people, eight of whom are adults. We cram everyone plus merchandise into the tiny car. How we all fit in, I'll never know. Suresh straddles the gear shift, while I sit in front on the passenger side. He has to stand each time the driver makes the shift making it an overly friendly gesture. Being overloaded is too much for the air-conditioner for this small car to function, so we roll down the window and sweat as we go. Uncle promises a shower once we arrive in Jethana and certainly it will be needed. Despite rough roads and being packed like sardines in a can, we manage to arrive there. Jethana's extremely narrow streets justify the use of a small car. I sense the eyes of villagers on us as we approach the house, a narrow two story affair with steep narrow steps leading up to two rooms and a kitchen above. We remove our shoes of course and gather in the main bedroom to sit on a large bed, while water is brought along with chai and snacks. Uncle then invites Suresh and me downstairs to shower in a room where there is a bucket of water. Uncle is quite friendly, though he speaks no English. He gestures for me to strip and ushers me to where the water is. It is the custom to shower in one's underwear for modesty. As I start splashing water on myself Uncle comes to show how I must wash inside. There's nothing quite like a demonstration! When I finish showering he gives me a towel to dry off, while Suresh takes his shower. After the shower, he ushers me back to the bedroom upstairs, where I comb my hair and get dressed in fresh clothes. Uncle invites us to stay the night.

Suresh talks about staying the night also, but agrees to leave the decision to me. I tell him that we can think about it, trying not to be too abrupt about my desire to return. We also visit his oldest uncle who is in bad health, recovering from abdominal surgery, perhaps from cancer, a man of skin and bones, but says he is feeling a little better. Chai is served. The family members attending him are quite curious about me as an American and ask if I have any American currency to show them. At first I say I don't but then remember that I had secreted away a $100 bill in my wallet for use in emergencies. I produce it and they pass it around eagerly examining it as if it were a million dollars. Suresh says I should give the uncle a 100 rupee note as a gesture of good will, along with some advice about his health. I present the money as a gesture of respect but fall short on the advice. We return to the other uncle's house.

Dinner is served on the rooftop where it is a little cooler when the sun sets. As the honored guest I am once again served first, seated before a small stool which serves as a table. Grandma, grandpa, uncle, aunt, sister and the cousins seat themselves in front of me to watch every nuance of my eating. I am still getting used to Indian food and find it uncomfortable to eat when all eyes upon me. I manage to get it down, whereupon my plate is piled high again. I clear about three-fourths of that plate and mercifully the others are then allowed to eat.

My camera batteries have gone dead giving me the excuse to tell Suresh that we should go back to Pushkar tonight. I promise the family that I will stay some other night.

We return to Pushkar.

My daily ritual is to take early morning walks around the dry lake. The lake had been drained so that algae and other problems can be disposed of. Early worshippers are busy at the many temples, bathing in concrete *Ghats* (tanks) filled with water for that purpose, while the lake is dry. Suresh tells me of dreams to build a small house apart from the multi-family dwelling, with a room reserved for him and his younger brother Kamal, and for me when I come. With all the relatives around, he desires a place apart. Since the multi-family house has been in the family some 200 years, rights to ownership are valid only if they live there, if I understand it correctly.

We hang out in my air-conditioned room most of the hottest part of the day. Mercifully the power does not go off this time. After dinner, we hire a car and his brother Kamal, Navneet, Suresh and I to go to Ajmer to shop. I had promised to buy him a pair of jeans and a shirt, which we find at a popular men's shop, busy with young men trying on jeans and shirts. Most do not bother to wait for changing rooms and just make changes in the store. We buy a nice pair of jeans and a purple shirt.

Love and Marriage
Suresh comes early to my room and we spend time talking. He expresses a deep affection for me and talks again of providing a small room for my use when I visit. He tells me about his best friend and how much the two of us mean to him. He speaks of marriage as the fulfillment of his life destiny and responsibility to the family for providing children. It is more common than not, in this realm of arranged marriages, that some of the deepest affections are reserved for close friends. His friendship has been passionate and intense from the time I first visited last fall and it seems only to have grown with time.

Distant Lands

Suresh and Keith

We visit his best friend Mohit's house one afternoon, but he is not home, and the only person at home is his grandfather, a stately self-assured man in his 80s, a retired pharmacist, equivalent to being a doctor there. They live in a large house not far from the Mela arena. Mohit later tells me he hopes one day to start his own retail business on the lower floor facing the street. I really like the grandfather. We hit it off immediately.

A dust storm has descended on the city, bringing a cool front giving some relief from the heat. The sky grows dark from the dust sending shopkeepers scurrying to secure their wares. Drops of rain fall from the sky filled with dust, like drops of mud. They splash on me as I hurry back to my room. I need to shower but just as I begin, the power goes off leaving me in total darkness. Suresh comes to take me to dinner and finds me stumbling around in the dark trying to get dressed. He offers the light of his mobile phone to help me find my clothes. We feel our way up dark stairs at his house and eat by candle light. The air by now has cooled and the sky is clear. Suresh, Navneet and I spend the rest of the evening in my room, teasing each other and enjoying life together like a bunch of giddy school boys.

Leaving Pushkar
Suresh's mother prepares a feast for my last dinner with them. His father presents me with a garland of flowers and his mother applies the *tikka* blessing to my forehead. It is time to go. Suresh is despondent about my leaving and keeps saying "I can't live without you!" I don't know quite how to respond. I board a large bus filled with all kinds of burlap bundles stacked in the aisles. The odor of the burlap is so overpowering that it causes my sinuses to stop up. The bus has no springs and we bounce and jog our way roughly to Ajmer by a roundabout road which takes over 45 minutes. There is no bus station for the transfer; the bus just stops along a street. When I ask where to locate my overnight bus to Delhi, the driver simply gestures in the direction where several buses are parked, but none of these is the right one for Delhi. Frantically I pull my luggage through the crowds searching, fearing that I will miss the connection. Another person directs me to a parking lot filled with buses, but none of these is the right one either. I grow frustrated, sweat pouring off me in the hot air of the night. Finally, someone directs me to the right bus, located farther down the road some distance. The ride turns out to be miserable as we roar through the night toward Delhi, arriving the next morning at 6:00 a.m. I am let out along a rock-strewn road somewhere in Old Delhi. I have no idea where I am. I hail a rickshaw driver who agrees to take me to New Delhi and helps me locate a cheap hotel. I check into the USA Hotel, somewhat less than a two star one, but I am happy just to be "somewhere." Next time I vow to take the train.

Teamwork in Small Villages
One of the main reasons I came to India this time is to meet up with a team from my city for a special project working in small villages in north India. I receive a call from my host, apologizing for a problem

Distant Lands

in making contact with me earlier. He suggests that I come to a private guest house in Delhi and wait there for the arrival of the group. I make my way to the guest house by Metro. The group from America isn't due until tonight, so I hire a rickshaw to take me to a mall and knock around there for a time. It is a modern mall and I do enjoy some KFC for lunch. Mostly I just walk around and look.

At the guest house we make preparation for our work, before departing to Utter Pradesh in two vehicles, with luggage tied to the top. Most of the group had not been to India before. It is fun to watch their reactions to the traffic. The hotel we check into is an upgrade from what I normally use, even though it is necessary for two of us to share a bed, while a third guy sleeps on a pallet on the floor. The project involves medical and educational surveys in the small villages, along with interactions with local people. Translators are assigned to each of us to assist with communication. After some days of preparation, the teams separate into pairs to go separate ways by buses to the outlying areas, to then walk small roads and trails to the more remote rural villages. It is quite an experience. Upon entering a village, we are generally greeted with curiosity and welcomed to someone's home for chai. In one village, a man is working at a sewing machine, part of India's prevalent fabric cottage industry. He invites us into his home and serves chai to my partner. With the aid of the translator, we talk as children gather at doors and windows, staring bright-eyed at these strangers from afar. Women look on, but stay busy with chores. The crowd soon swells to forty people or more. We tell stories and inquire concerning their livelihoods. I tell of my growing up on a farm in Oklahoma and speak of animals and crops we raised. It is a good experience, sharing mutual experiences. The man invites me to stay at his house anytime I come to India. My friend jokes with me in English that the man doesn't know what he's asking, because I might just do it! True. I take him to be sincere in welcoming me anytime, and I would enjoy it. We walk around the village, often seeing boys swimming in ponds with the buffaloes.

Indian Summer

Village Boys Swimming

We spend days like this, sharing experiences, gathering stories and equipping local leaders to provide assistance, inspiration and hope to the people there. It is an educational experience for our group as well.

The Taj Mahal
The project concludes with a training event for our local hosts and we return to Delhi to stay the night in the private guest house, leaving the next morning early to catch a train to Agra, so the group can visit the Taj Mahal. It will be my second time there but this time with the benefit of a guide to shepherd us through India's most iconic landmark. The Taj Mahal is always busy with tourists. Security is tight. We tease our leader about his thorough shakedown by the security officer in the screening process. An archway provides an opening to the actual Taj, making a visual frame for a visitor's first glimpse of the white marble building in the distance, inspiringly beautiful by its symmetry. We are in complete awe of its architectural beauty, as most first-time visitors. We take photos from that location before proceeding to the Taj itself,

removing shoes before ascending the steps to the building itself. The Taj is a mausoleum for a bride who died early. Her remorseful husband had it constructed in her honor. She is buried deep in the crypt, below the replica of the crypt viewed by visitors.

Taj Mahal

Following our visit, the group visits a carpet mill where intricate carpets are being woven by hand. Several purchase pieces to be shipped back to the USA. While everyone is involved with the carpets, my translator arrives at the door and motions for me to come outside. He has come with a friend of his on a motorbike and they invite me to join them for a ride around Agra. Since I was not interested in carpets, having purchased some before, I agreed to go with them, though it is extremely hot as we buzz through the city. They show me places that the others do not get to see. It is my kind of travel. We visit a craft shop specializing in the white marble for which Agra is famous. We buzz along busy streets and into an old section of the city, ending up at a friend's shop to see shoes being made in a cottage industry. We sit on the floor and drink chai. They present me with a pair of sandals newly manufactured by hand. Unfortunately, I have no money with me and can offer only a US one dollar bill, which I autograph and present to be framed and hang in their shop. I explain that in the U.S., many shops and restaurants frame the "first" dollar made. I hope it meant something to them, although I'm sure they would have preferred more substantial money from a visiting "rich American." My friend introduces me to another friend of his, a young man in the unusual predicament of being Christian living with his family who is Hindu and facing a difficult decision, because his family will soon select a Hindu wife for him for which he has little say. He wonders what to do. Mixed marriages across religious lines are very rare and usually contentious.

When we catch up with the group, they are visiting Agra's famous Red Fort offering a dramatic view of the Taj Mahal from a distance and famous historically for its role during in the rebellion called "The Mutiny," which occurred the 1800s when Indian rebels nearly threw off British rule, but fell short and were put down brutally. We return by train at night to the warm guest house in Delhi, with a single fan to stir the air.

Return
We catch the long flight back through Chicago, arriving in Oklahoma City at sunrise. I am greeted by my son-in-law Rick and grandchildren Olivia and Zachary. Everything looks refreshingly green compared to sun-baked India. I am struck by the open spaces and marvel at the lack of crowds. I ignore a month's worth of mail and take a refreshing shower, glad to be home once more.

It isn't long before I begin missing my friends back in Nepal and India.

3

India and Nepal Again—Strengthening Ties

It was true. It didn't take long to begin missing my friends in distant lands. We had kept in daily contact through Facebook and emails and always there was the question "When are you coming again?" In a matter of just four months, I am busy making plans to return again to Nepal and India.

Sunday 24 October 2010

A Room for Me in Pushkar
My host family in India is creating a room for me during my stay for a full month in Pushkar. Their dwelling is some 200 years old and part of a temple complex on the lake at Pushkar. Pushkar is considered one of India's holiest cities, small by comparison to most cities in India, a town of about 18,000 people. However, the population swells into hundreds of thousands during the famous Camel Fair, which will begin next month!

The room is located on the rooftop courtyard, offering a view of the sacred lake, a room used for years only for storage. Workmen busily clear and clean the concrete walls of centuries of grime, amazingly transforming it into a beautiful room, painted a pleasing lavender, with a carpet on the floor, providing a gathering place for the family. I spent last night there for the first time, shared with five Indian family

India and Nepal Again—Strengthening Ties

members. It is the way of India; one is to never alone! Last night, for a time, I counted no fewer than twelve in the room! It is a lovely and loving family and they make me feel included; I feel at home.

The dwelling is multi-family, with several extended families sharing the three-story structure, constructed around an open atrium. Each family has a small room assigned to them, sharing an open space for cooking, with small enclosures for showers and places to wash clothes. The rooftop is a special place, where I love being, with its view of the lake. Suresh warns me to watch out for the red monkeys, for they can run up behind a person and push him over the rail. Some of these monkeys are quite aggressive.

It is with anticipation that I return here, to hang out on the streets of Pushkar as people go about their daily business. I am now familiar enough that people speak to me by name as I walk the streets. I adapt to the vegetarian regimen for meals. Most everything is quite tasty, though just a little strange at times to my taste buds, but all is good. I drink only bottled mineral water, easily obtained from street markets.

Living with local people is my preferred way to learn the culture. Local hospitality is warm and welcoming. People are as curious about me as I am about them, and we learn from each other.

So, for now, I am quite happy to be here, joining young guys at a local gym to do workouts to keep myself in shape, necessary with all the eating. One 17 year-old asks me about my age. I tell him to reverse the numbers of his age 17, and he will know. I will be 71 in a few days. He seems a little surprised at first, and I have to admit, so am I. I am grateful for good health, which I consider a gift. I want to travel as long as I have it. So here I am.

But first, let me tell you about my visits to Chicago and Nepal before arriving now in India.

Distant Lands

Friday 1 October Chicago, USA

Friends and Family

Having only two days to prepare for a two month trip is hardly enough time but I make do, packing bags much more full than I like because I'm carrying gifts to people I have met before.

My first stop is Chicago. I plan to help my friend John celebrate his 70th birthday. We host a cook-out on the deck of his town house, with twelve of his closest friends invited. John presses me into service, putting me in charge of grilling the chicken. The evening is cool and pleasant and we have a nice time. I enjoy meeting his friends. One guy tells me that he is originally from Pakistan.

This time of year provides the best of fall with warm days and crisp, cool nights. On days while John is busy with other things, I go downtown by Chicago's "El" for walks through Millennium Park and downtown. Chicago is one of my favorite "big" cities. The air is clean and everything looks great. Buckingham fountain is one of the most impressive fountains anywhere.

Weekend in Chicago

My cousin Jerry Gooch contacts me and we set a lunch date for Saturday at Chicago Joe's to meet with Jerry and his family. We calculate that it has been at least 52 years since we saw each other last. Jerry is the youngest son of my mother's oldest brother and only about eight when we were last together. It is a delightful time getting re-acquainted over lunch with his family. We visit Palatine to meet his son Robert, working at an amusement park built by the Lego Corporation, called LEGOLAND. He works there as a manager of the amusement center. Robert shows me the large elaborate constructions made totally from the Lego blocks, featuring sites and scenes, ranging from Chicago's skyline to jungles complete with full-size tigers. We ride several rides together, enjoying a great time.

India and Nepal Again—Strengthening Ties

Nepal Land of Mountains and Mystery

I meet an interesting guy on my flight from Chicago to Nepal. He tells me he is from a village in western Nepal, now living in San Francisco, working in Silicon Valley on computer chips. He has a Ph. D. from Sanford. We enjoy talking about all things Nepali and about his life in America. He tells me he is now a U.S. citizen, a fine example of America benefitting from its immigrants.

My friend Manish and friends Deepak along with Manish's brother Sonu are on hand at the Kathmandu airport to greet me with garlands of yellow flowers. We drive to the apartment this time. The last time I visited, you may remember, we had to walk some miles because of the strikes in progress.

With little time for adjustment to jet lag, Manish announces that we will take motorcycles to the mountains to visit a special temple, leaving tomorrow morning. Our ride through the mountains is at times quite spectacular, that is, until the motorcycle I am riding develops a problem going up one of the mountains. We are forced to coast back down to a village by the river to spend the night, arranging a room at a local guest house; primitive but not too bad if you can handle a few bugs running across your legs at night.

With bike fixed—It was an air filter problem—we head back to the mountain, crossing the mountains in the daytime instead of at night. I would have missed the view and the road could have been dangerous. Cresting the top puts us in the clouds, which is quite chilly. I had not dressed warmly enough. Once we reach the other side, we descend to a beautiful valley, sprinkled with small villages. We stop to view a waterfall. After some time, we make it to the city of Dokhata, the jumping-off point for trekkers approaching Mt. Everest, which is another 21-day hike from here to the base camp, which we don't attempt of course. Instead we walk downhill to the ancient temple, where a stone god is supposed to have powers to herald bad events. When the stone, normally dry, starts to sweat, it is a sign that a disaster is to come. It had sweat 65 years ago, before an 8.2 magnitude earthquake hit the region. We still see the evidence of those landslides. Then in 1992 the stone sweat again; this time fourteen members of the Royal Family were massacred by a distraught family member. Fortunately we find it not sweating now. Being a non-Hindu, I am forbidden to enter the inner temple itself, but my friends do, bringing their offerings. I hope the sweating stone stays dry until we leave.

Returning over the high terrain, we arrive back in Kathmandu quite late, marking my fourth day with little sleep. I hope to get some rest before going to Chitwan National Park, our next venture.

The Jungles of Chitwan
The road to Chitwan National Park leads from the mountain pass out of Kathmandu, down the river valleys toward the Indian plain below, over the spectacular, if not a little scary at times road, clinging to the mountain side. Down below, the cascading river shows off white water turbulence, pouring over large boulders. The road is path of every kind of vehicle known to mankind, ranging from large, heavily burdened trucks to overcrowded buses, pedestrians and animals. It is the festival season. Joining the people stuffed inside and on top of the buses, are the sacrificial goats as well, some even being transported by motorcycles. The sacrifices for the Dashain Festival are due to begin soon.

The owners of the small roadside open-air restaurant recognize me from my previous trips. We eat fresh fish fried whole, making a crunchy snack.

An all-day jeep ride into the teeming jungle of Chitwan is not available at the time, so we opt instead for a dugout canoe to take down the river for a trek into the jungle on foot to visit a crocodile breeding center deep in the jungle. A guide and an oarsman to handle the canoe is provided. All is quiet along the river. It is serene and peaceful as we float quietly. We see birds—peacocks, storks, swallows and ibis. Crocodiles lazily sun themselves on the banks of the river, looking our way as we pass by at eye-level. We stop for a short trek to visit a rhino mother and her calf, cooling themselves in a small pond. The guide cautions us to be quiet. Rhinos have excellent hearing but poor eyesight. The rhinos flap their ears above the water, bodies happily submerged in the wet mud. The guide tells us that recently he saw a small croc perched on top of one of the rhinoceros.

We continue downriver to the departure point for the trek, where we head into the jungle on foot. Sonu is terrified, especially later when we encounter the tracks of a large tiger. The paw print is deeply impressed in the mud. The guide assures us the track is a few hours old. We follow the tiger tracks as we continue. A rhino startles us and we freeze in place, but it was running away from us through the underbrush. Had we been two minutes earlier, we might have had to face it as it crossed our trail!

Tiger Paw Print

Though we do not see a tiger but we do visit the crocodile farm, with different sizes of the species common to the area. Crocodiles are the great survivors of nature, surviving well over millions of years. The advent of man may become their ultimate challenge for future survival. It is one reason for the breeding farm.

Bandipur Mountain Village at Festival Time
It is festival time. The *Dashain* festival is in progress by the time we reach the ancient village of Bandipur for my third visit in two years. Everyone is dressed in their finest native attire. The morning brings a procession of sacrificial animals including chickens and goats, carried or led toward the mountaintop temple to be sacrificed. In the afternoon the procession reverses, with children and others bearing headless goats and chickens back to the houses for preparation for the feasts to soon begin. Families gather from for the sacrifices and feasting. Little children participate by carrying the chickens toward the temple for sacrifice.

Animal sacrifice is deeply embedded in many religions, either in present form or in their past. In some cases, animal sacrifices followed earlier traditions of human sacrifices. I learn that in former times, prisoners in Nepal who were scheduled for execution were held over until this festival to be executed as sacrifices. It is no longer the practice, of course.

The view of the Himalaya peaks from Bandipur is breathtaking, especially in the early morning when the air is clearer. What you first might think are clouds, are really peaks, rising above the clouds.

We relax today to observe the local traditions. It is important not overschedule travel and miss days like this. It is a rich experience and I consider myself most fortunate.

Temple by Cable Car
The temple called Manakamana is reached by cable car, spanning the

India and Nepal Again—Strengthening Ties

river and ascending the mountain. In the festival time it is a popular destination for the faithful. Provisions are made for goats and chickens to travel by cable up the mountain to be sacrificed. That's the way it works here. The line is long as we wait to board, with the sounds of chickens squawking and goats bleating. Do goats bleat? Sheep do. Perhaps there is another term for goats, but you get the idea.

A little girl carries two baskets of pigeons with her. The ride is almost straight up. Manish tells me he has taken hikers by the foot trail up the mountain, which he points out below us as we soar overhead. That which takes us twenty minutes took his well-conditioned hikers over five hours. I'm glad we chose to come by cable car.

A continuous din of hawkers selling offerings of flowers and food for use at the temple greets us as we make our way through. The streets are crowded with people leading or carrying goats. Steps lead to the temple courtyard, a scene out of the old days with sounds and commotions of rituals and incense filling the air. Trails of blood lead from the temple area where goats are being led to the place of sacrifice and carcasses are beign carried out in bags for the trip down the mountain. Manish's brother Sonu goes with me to the actual place of sacrifice. The floor literally oozes with blood. The faithful enter bare-footed, bringing their goats or other sacrifices. Knives swoosh slashing off heads as blood shoots everywhere. It is a gruesome scene to watch, but no one winces at the scene of great slaughter. I remind myself that we also slaughter animals in our culture, but discreetly away from eyesight so we don't wince as thousands of cattle, sheep and chickens are slaughtered daily for our food. We don't bother with rituals of thanksgiving to accompany the taking of life. Here at least, thanksgiving and offering are made before blood is spilt. One wonders which is the more gruesome.

Distant Lands

Temple Sacrifice Area

Once the sacrifice is done, the remaining carcasses are inserted into everything from plastic bags to canvas or fabric. The plastic bags contain the blood more successfully, while the others drip with it. We follow the trails of blood back toward the cable cars and down the mountains. Sacrifices like this go on for days. Each family then feasts on the roasted animals. Businesses and schools shut down for the festival. The normally-crowded highways are virtually clear, a strange sight for me as we make our way back to Kathmandu to spend the next days at home. Manish tells me he stopped doing the sacrifices some seven years ago, saying there had been enough killing. He continues to do the other ceremonies including the *tikka* blessings during *Dashain*.

It is raining today. With luck, I can finish my blogs before the power goes off.

Delhi India's Capital City
After multiple delays leaving Kathmandu, I reach Delhi's new Indira

India and Nepal Again—Strengthening Ties

Gandhi International Airport terminal, opened in time for the Commonwealth Games which occurred earlier this month. It is big, new and quite functional, joining several other Asian capital cities with new airport facilities. My friend Suresh from Pushkar takes an all-night bus ride to get to Delhi in order to meet me at the airport. He waits patiently during my three-hour delay to greet me with a big smile.

Delhi teems with millions of people. The streets of New Delhi are laid out in circular fashion, which helps traffic flow but a nightmare to navigate for the uninitiated. Our hotel is located in an older part of the city among crowded shops and small businesses. As usual, the traffic is dense and intense, with plenty of dust and smog to assault the nostrils.

I am happy to see Suresh again, planning to be his guest for an entire month. We spend a couple of days in Delhi knocking around, visiting several shops. I am to attend the wedding one of his friends in November.

Wednesday 27 October

Celebrating My Birthday in Jaipur

Jaipur, Rajasthan's capital city, a teeming city of millions is known as the Pink City for its pink-hued buildings. We decide to return here to celebrate my birthday. Last year, I arrived here from Nepal and Delhi on my birthday, having already celebrated early in the Himalayas with my Nepali friends and did not consider the prospect of spending my actual 70th birthday alone in a strange city to be a problem. My *tuk-tuk* driver felt otherwise. Without my knowing it, he arranged a birthday cake with candles which said "70," celebrated with the waiters and others at a rooftop cafe. I'd love to find Jamil again to thank him for the gesture, but finding a *tuk-tuk* driver here among thousands might be like finding the proverbial needle in a haystack. Still, I think of him and toast the stranger who made this traveler feel at home!

Distant Lands

The Diwali festival is fast approaching. Everyone buys new clothes for this festival and houses are decorated with lights. It is a festive occasion, reminding me a lot of Christmas time back home. Carolers even go around singing for people in their homes.

I enjoy staying with my host family in Pushkar. They have welcomed me as a member of their family. I value the richness of being with local people in their element, viewing life up close, helping me to better understand their traditions and practices. It is an incarnational way of traveling, adding understanding through experience.

Three Days in a Farming Village
The village of Jethana is some 30 kilometers away from Pushkar, which we reach by motorcycle, taking the short-cut through the country. Otherwise it is a 50 kilometer ride through heavy traffic on a highway. I'm on the bike with an uncle of Suresh's. The good thing about the short-cut is that it allows me to see the countryside, as we drive at a moderate speed through the arid land. Herdsmen tend herds of cattle and goats. There is farming and even some irrigation for growing crops for the table. Table is a poor choice of words, as most eat from plates on the floor. I like the countryside, because I began my life on a farm in northwest Oklahoma and this allows me to return to my roots in some ways. There are small clusters of dwellings here and there and an occasional small village. Eventually we arrive in Jethana, itself a relatively small village of concrete houses built close together. Many of Suresh's mother's family live here and it is where Suresh grew up and attended school, staying then with an uncle who runs a school. He had stayed there from the ages of 2 to 15. That uncle now has two young children of his own, ten year-old Mitty and four year-old Keshaw. We celebrate Mitty's 10th birthday on our first night here with cake, candles and birthday gifts. An aunt in the family has died, so we keep the celebration subdued out of respect. Keshaw is a bright four-year-old and proudly demonstrates his ability to print the English alphabet and ability to write numbers from 1 to 100. He finishes both tasks with speed.

India and Nepal Again—Strengthening Ties

Suresh plans to make a trip to Jaipur for two days to help a friend select clothes for a brother's impending wedding, so he leaves me in the care of his family, with instructions that my every need be met. The hospitality is gracious, but sometimes a bit confining, in the sense that one becomes almost a prisoner of hospitality! As the guest, I am invited to sit. It makes everyone nervous if I stand even for a moment. They constantly say "Sit, sit!" If I am sitting, pillows are brought for me to stretch out and recline. Food is brought in a never-ending procession. "Eat, eat!" I must watch television for entertainment. Watching Indian television is as mind-numbing as American television, only with less violence. Suresh has told them that I like to take walks, but custom declares that I never be alone on excursions from the home. I ask out of politeness if I can go for a walk. The whole family gets involved in the decision, and here that includes virtually the whole village. I am asked to wait in order to have chai and a snack to eat. An eighteen year-old relative is awakened from sleep and assigned to walk with me. Since he does not know that I had already had a snack, we walk only a short distance before he decides I should immediately visit another uncle's house for chai and something to eat. How could I possibly walk without eating? He does not speak English, so I have little way of challenging the notion, so we go to a second uncle's house where I am told again to "Sit, sit," while tea is brought, along with a snack. This is followed by a full-course meal for breakfast. OK, now maybe we can walk. I go for my shoes. "No, sit, sit!" It is the uncle instructing me to sit while he goes somewhere and promises to return in 30 minutes. OK, perhaps then we can walk. After an hour or so, he returns and lunch is brought. "Eat, eat!" My idea of walking is not getting very far. After eating, I must surely need to rest, being elderly and all, so pillows are brought for me to sleep. Finally at about 4:00 p.m., with me insisting on walking, Sonu, the eighteen year old, accompanies me, showing me the school where he went. We walk a short distance down a country road. "We turn around now," he announces. Surely that I've had enough walking for one day, he reasons, and so it goes. Actually all is good and these are wonderful people, wanting only to take care of my every need, except of course, my need to be move about or to be alone. In India, being alone is a vacuum to be filled. When I snack or sleep, a circle of people gather around to watch. I guess it beats watching television!

The bus stop at the edge of town is lined with a few shops, offering chai and sweets. It is the place where the men of the village gather to talk and banter, the worldwide phenomenon in smaller towns. Everyone soon knows me and I am welcomed with great curiosity. I drink tea and eat sweets without charge. Trucks amble by on the busy highway. At night, the only lights in the city are those of passing trucks, with only a few electric light bulbs burning. The night is for sleep. We retire to the roof where the monkeys scamper about. I look at the stars and explain which are stars and planets. It may seem strange to prefer the night sky to television, but the sky is so much more interesting.

In some ways, it is a return to a boyhood long since gone. All we had was our family and the night sky. We had the sounds of distant neighbors and the low of cattle at night. In the summers, we slept out under these same stars. Here the only difference is that I am sleeping on a rooftop.

Life is good when we allow it to be. Really, I am happy here.

Diwali Festival and President's Visit
Diwali is in full swing in Pushkar, the festival of lights. Houses are festooned with lights and streets are decorated. Families gather at homes around altars to pray and give blessings. Fireworks light the night sky. The noise of firecrackers is quite deafening, especially at night. The poor dogs are beside themselves. Walking or riding bikes through the streets become dangerous affair as kids throw fireworks at random. The big ones are called "Atom bombs" which deafen the ears. I put cotton in both ears. We buy an ample supply in Ajmer to explode at night, sparklers, flower fountains, as well as atom bombs. Today, one of the

India and Nepal Again—Strengthening Ties

atom bombs goes off in my hand, leaving me with a swollen index finger as a result. It blows a ring from my fingers. With immersion in cold water and ice, it is OK now. I will tell you more about that ring in the next installment.

Everyone dresses in new clothes for Diwali. Last night I wore a new shirt and new slacks. Today, I am wearing the traditional Indian dress, a long tunic with pajama legs. It is all black, prompting some to call me Keith Khan, saying I am Muslim. It will be an outfit to wear in the Middle East next time I travel there. The streets fill with a parade of people showing off new clothes and greeting friends. It is their version of Easter Parade down Fifth Avenue in New York of the last century, with a few significant differences of course. No matter the finery, the cows still leave their deposits on the streets and one must watch where one steps. Some of the cow deposits are decorated with flowers, making small altars. Monkeys scamper about on the roof tops.

I am paraded up and down the streets with various friends, who want to show off their visitor from America. We are received into numerous homes, as sweets and other goodies are brought. One household even gives me money as a gift.

There is much astir about the visit of President Obama to India. He is in Mumbai now and will be in Delhi. Residents of Ajmer are quite excited as an agreement is announced that establishes Ajmer as a "smart city," with the promise of technological assistance. Obama is well regarded, referred to affectionately by my friends as "OM-Baba." It is significant for them that he has chosen to visit India, the world's largest democracy and vital to our interests in Asia. He may be president, but I doubt he enjoys a greater celebrity status than I have in Pushkar!

Once Diwali is finished, it will be time for the Camel Fair and the wedding of a friend. I can anticipate more days of wonder, provided I don't blow another finger off.

Distant Lands

Curse of the Turquoise Ring

I meet Helen, a sprightly 80 year-old lady from Scotland (I'm guessing her age!) and we go for a pleasant walk together. I find her to be quite knowledgeable and experienced as a traveler. I delight to hear her Scottish brogue as she rolls the "r's" with ease. Along the way, she points out at silver shop, which she encourages me to browse without pressure to buy, a rare find, for if you show interest in any object, the owners hound you until you buy or follow you if you don't. Generally, I choose not to look and just walk on.

A turquoise ring interests me. It is from Tibet and offered at a reasonable price, so I buy it. When I return, Suresh is quite perplexed that I have bought something without his assistance. "You must return it and I will buy one which is suitable for you." I decline his offer and choose to keep the ring. He warns me that it will bring me bad luck.

A few hours later, we are popping fireworks, as previously alluded to, near one of the temples. Apparently it is no sacrilege to rattle the chambers of the gods with such noise. One of the "atom bombs" goes off prematurely in my hand, injuring my finger, blowing the turquoise ring to the ground. I do not miss the ring at first, because I seek relief for my injured index finger. Toothpaste is brought to apply to the finger, but I insist that we find cold water or ice in which to submerge it. My finger is more bruised than burned. While applying the ice to it, I discover that the ring is missing. I tell Suresh who goes to search for it, and as usual the whole family and half of Pushkar get involved. The ring is found, bent and blackened. "See," he says, "the ring is cursed."

Later we visit his friend Mohit's house. Mohit and brothers are gone at the moment but we meet a young couple with an infant, apparently one of the many relatives, though the relationship is not explained to me. I am welcomed and offered food. As we take our leave, the infant wiggles and falls from his mother's arms to the marble floor, cutting his lip. Suresh and the father grab up the infant and hop on the motorbike to rush him to the clinic. They return later and the boy turns out to be OK. Was this also the curse of the Turquoise ring?

The next day, I am hounded by young kids wanting me to take their photo and wanting to play with my camera. I was not sure that I trusted them, because children are sometimes used as thieves for lifting cameras and wallets from unsuspecting tourists, but I give in since others are present and I do take their photos. Upon return to my room, I discover that my mobile phone is missing.

I call Suresh on a back-up phone and tell him that I am missing my mobile phone. Since we had just come from where the boys were hanging all over me, I immediately suspect them. Suresh rushes to the street to look for my phone and again the whole family and half of Pushkar get involved. After he leaves, I continue searching around my room, when I luckily find the mobile. I had placed something over it. I send Suresh a text to tell him to stop searching and to come back. What I don't know is that he had already found the boys and accused them of taking my phone and was in the process of rushing them to the police station. The boys were in tears, of course. When he sees my text, he apologizes to them. I later have to apologize to the whole family. The stories of these mishaps spread like wildfire through Pushkar. People begin stopping me on the street the next day to inquire about my hand and wanting to know if I had found my mobile. It is all a great drama. "See," Suresh says again, "the ring." I decide put the cursed ring away.

Pushkar Population Explodes!
I survived the day yesterday without additional dramas. Apparently the curse had been satisfied and things have returned to normal. Or so, I think.

Already, the shops are loaded with new stock hanging from awnings and there are more tourists about. Indians come by the busload for ceremonial bathing at the *Ghats* at temples which ring the lake. I think

Distant Lands

I mentioned once before that there are 1000 temples in Pushkar, which works out to a temple per every 12 people of the permanent population.

Stories still circulate about my firecracker-exploded finger and the perceived loss of my mobile. Every movement I make seems monitored by family and friends to ensure my safety, or perhaps to guarantee that I don't do something totally crazy. We gather at a spot on one of the back streets to sit and watch people come and go, somewhat akin to the "spittin' and whittlin' clubs" of small-town America. The guys gather close around me to talk. Conversations are animated with gestures and loud in volume, surrounding me and talking at once. Anything that happens on the street is of immediate concern and interest to everyone else. Impromptu guides pop up to connect with tourists. Young women get called to and flirted by the young men on the street. Most women have learned to ignore them and go on their way. More and more, I begin missing a complete conversation in my own language. I've almost forgotten what it was like, lodged in the middle of the babble of Hindi surrounding me. Though I do pick up a few words, I never know how appropriate they may be in mixed company.

At times I question what brings me here. Is my need to know, or is it my need to feel connected. For whatever reason, here I am.

Who Is Shaking My Bed?
I awake to someone shaking my bed. Or so I think. I rise and look around, but I am the only person in the room. Has there been an earthquake? Sure enough, an earthquake has rattled me awake! It is a 4.5 one I learn later, part of a series of quakes recently. No buildings have collapsed on top of me, although I wonder if some are of doubtful construction. I ponder again if it has something to do with my turquoise ring. I decide that's ridiculous. I begin wearing the ring again. If nothing happens in the next 24 hours, I will feel vindicated.

I confess to moments of homesickness and yearn for conversations in my own language. I think about toilets that work, electricity that is dependable and potatoes and gravy, rather than rice and curry. These moments of nostalgia signal an approaching cultural overload. There is the Camel Fair and a wedding yet to come, after which I plan to have Thanksgiving at home with my family—potatoes, gravy, and all! I need to hang on a bit longer.

Pushkar Lake—Feeling Disconnected

Pushkar Lake at Dusk

It is just before sunset. The lake, normally bustling with people, is nearly empty. The setting is serene. I take the opportunity to take photos, since photos of bathers are strictly prohibited. After taking the photos, I sit for a time to let the beauty of the lake with the sounds of bells and distant chants surround me. It is a peaceful moment. One is often overwhelmed by the relentless noises of the city, with the constant beeping of horns, the loud shouts, the din of motors and people, animals and fireworks.

Distant Lands

I have begun to feel disconnected. For the first time, I am homesick, feeling increasingly more like an alien, a stranger in a strange land. Something is wrong and I do not quite understand what it is. When I return to the street, Suresh and friends all gather around me, talking loudly in a babble of language I don't understand. I break. I move close to Suresh's ear and shout, "This is what it sounds like to me." He is completely startled by my outburst, giving me a stricken look. I must pull away. I head back to the lake, to escape.

It is a Greta Garbo moment. I want to be alone. I find a place to sit alone and have it out with myself and with God. Why am I here? What is wrong? I feel adrift, without anchor. I have respect for the various religions and understand what drives people toward religious expression. I am not here to criticize or to reform. That is not the problem. I pray and speak alone to God in the inner recesses of my being. I need an anchor to regain the equilibrium that comes from faith. It hits me that the problem isn't my friends, or their ways of speaking. The problem is with me. In the hubbub of travel, with these many friends and host family, I have somehow lost connection with my spiritual anchor. After a time of meditation and repentance for my self-centered behavior, I return to the street and try to explain to my friend and host, the Brahmin Suresh. I apologize for being short with him and try to tell him what is happening with me. It is difficult for him to understand, yet he is sensitive and asks if perhaps we should go to the lake to pray. We walk together to stand together beside the still water. "May I get some incense?" he asks. I say "yes." With incense lighted, we each in our own spheres of faith begin to pray. We both understand God to be greater than either of us and more than our understanding. We walk together barefoot around the lake in a uniting moment. A burden is lifted and I am no longer a stranger, an alien. I am where I need to be. I am no longer homesick. It was like an epiphany of experiential learning, a small taste of what it must have been like for God to enter our strange culture to live among us as human.

Suresh and I are once again ourselves. Later, we find great fun by taking a late-night camel ride. All is well.

Pushkar Camel Fair Begins!
Today is opening day for the Pushkar Camel Fair. The Bedouins have set up camp with their camels at the edge of town. The streets are filled with people and vendors hawking all the wares one can imagine during a fair.

It rained heavily last night, something uncharacteristic for this time of the year and especially in a desert area. While the desert may have welcomed the rain, the streets have become soupy with mud and cow manure, mixed with the smells of raw garbage from the sewers. I will be glad for the dry weather to return. In my host's home, eight-days of marriage preparations have begun. A band of drummers arrives at the house while I eat breakfast and a procession forms as the family goes to temples for ceremonies and then return with much fanfare. The women of the household sit on mats and sing traditional songs. I will miss the actual wedding due to my return on November 24. However, I will take part of another wedding which is for the brother of Suresh's best friend Mohit. The groom has arrived from Delhi during the night and the preparations for his wedding are well underway. He tells me that he is delighted that I will be in attendance for the wedding parties.

Dancing Horses
Today's feature at the fair is dancing horses. The Bedouins come to buy and sell horses and to arrange for stud services. Along with the basics of this important agricultural industry, there are numerous performances. Horses are trained in dance routines, rearing on their hind legs on command. Contests of dancing horses take place in a small arena. The Mela Arena is quite large and many events take place simultaneously scattered across the grounds in smaller temporary enclosures. To get a view, you must push your way into a crowd and hope you are tall enough to see. Tourists generally have that advantage in that regard,

but some tourists rent a camel, parking it just right for a good view, seated above the crowd.

I decide to do that too with the one camel still available. I negotiate a price and get lifted to my luxury-seat high above ground for a perfect view of several horses going through routines before a panel of judges and an enthusiastic crowd. It is horse-day at the Camel Fair, along with the requisite dancing cobras, dancing girls and relentless hawkers. The crowds continue to swell. The hawkers grow more insistent. The risks of theft increase. Beginning tomorrow, I will not carry my mobile or wallet, only my camera and some identification of course. I may attach a rope to my camera to help secure it. I don't want a repeat of last year's theft, but aside from that risk, the fair is both fun and overwhelming at the same time.

At night there are the cultural dances. Suresh and I are ushered to the V.I.P. section where pallets and cushions are spread for us to lounge upon as we watch the programs of dances. Children's groups perform. Some not so well but as the evening progresses, the dances and routines get better.

Camel Caravans and Weddings
A policeman approaches this morning to ask if I want to sit on a camel without charge. I am doubtful, but he assures me there would be no cost. I am soon perched atop a camel with a good view of the arena. What I didn't know was that I have become part of a caravan of camels and camel carts for the benefit of Rajasthan Tourism. We form a camel caravan, making our way through town and out into the desert, being filmed as we go. Those of us lucky enough to have been here early make up the caravan for free. My camel is placed behind the bagpipes at the head of the line. A banner proclaiming "Rajasthan Tourism" leads the way, as we ride through the streets, followed by a line of camel carts carrying other people. We are being photographed amid cheers along the way, being filmed for a trailer advertising Rajasthan Tourism.

India and Nepal Again—Strengthening Ties

Camel Ride for Rajasthan Tourism

The caravan comes to a stop in the desert at a newly constructed stage, apparently being developed into a show area for the future, but right now is by itself out in the desert. Soon there is dancing and stories being told. Tourists are invited to the stage to dance, after which we pass through the camel camps on the way back to the arena. It is great fun at no charge! I do give a tip my camel driver.

For the past two nights, we have attended two different wedding parties for friends of Suresh. Indian weddings are elaborate affairs lasting several days with ceremony, food, and dancing. The bands are loud. The brides and grooms are attired in traditional wedding attire. Gifts are brought and spread before them. I present a ceremonial Native American Wedding tea pot I had bought. Other ceremonial offerings are made. The couple exchanges garlands of flowers instead of rings. The groom then moves through the crowd giving respect to the guests and in return, each gives money. Then there is food, lots of it. The wedding parties are huge. They are a prominent family in Pushkar and everything is quite elaborate, with many guests in attendance. I wear a traditional "Maharajah-style" Indian outfit, complete with a fancy turban. Two German guests, also friends of the family, are here to attend as well. We dance in an outdoor arena set up with tables of food to feed the group. The night air is cold and by the time we leave I am quite chilled but it is all fun. And, it is not over. We have several more days of wedding events to attend.

A Sea of People
The final day of the Pushkar Camel Fair has come. It is the day of the full moon when people come to Pushkar for the ceremonial bathing at the lake. It starts early. My friend Suresh is up at 2:00 a.m. to assist with the *Poojas*, the prayers offered. Already the streets are crowded. The night air is cold but still people come by the thousands for the bathing ceremonies. By daybreak, the crowd has swollen to hundreds of thousands, with people everywhere, making it nearly impossible to move through the crowds, pushing and shoving.

I go to the lake at 4:00 a.m. to watch families come. The air is cold and the water is cold but in they go or just splash the waters over themselves, shivering until they can change to dry clothes, done openly but with careful modesty. Suresh works continuously until 6:00 p.m. which is exhausting. At night we go to a wedding party but do not stay long. He has to have some sleep. Moving through the crowds each day makes me feel like an extra in a peasant-revolt movie scene, when the crowd charges forward with primitive pitchforks held high. I find myself swept along amidst the pitchforks and other farm instruments held high in the air, having been purchased from vendors, who have made them by hand. It is pandemonium. Once I make it through, I rejoin the two German friends, who are staying with the family where the wedding takes place. We spend the day observing the crowds safely on the rooftop from above.

When the fair ends, the crowds are gone and some rain comes. It is

India and Nepal Again—Strengthening Ties

much quieter now in Pushkar. My final full day arrives. I will catch the train for Delhi tomorrow to fly home. First there is one more night of wedding to attend.

Dancing in the Streets and Over the Top to Home!
The night before I leave India, we join the groom's wedding procession through the streets of Pushkar, one of the many ceremonies connected with an Indian wedding. We meet at the groom's family home. The groom is prepared and mounts a white horse. Drummers lead the way followed by a loud-speaker system with a keyboard, which in turn is followed by a full brass band. It is raining as we begin and has been raining most of the day. The streets have returned to their confused normal. Young girls hold large lamps formed on either side of the procession, powered by a generator that follows us through the winding streets. In between the bands and instruments, we create spaces enough to dance as we go. It gets frenetic at times, crazy at times, tender at times. People twirl rupee notes over the heads of the dancers to ward off evil it is believed, but also for a more practical purpose, in that the money is gathered up by the musicians for extra pay. All is done with good fun.

I dance with the groom's brothers, cousins, family members and friends. The two guys from Germany also join in, as do onlookers from the streets. I meet one couple from Istanbul, who are filming us and then join to dance with us. The procession lasts for over two hours, through the small streets so narrow, they cause everything to get snarled. We make our way around vegetable carts that get stuck in the way. The rain has made the streets soupy with mud and the ever-present cow manure but no one seems to care. We dance on muddying our fine Indian wedding attire. My ears may never be the same from the loudness of the music.

Once the procession ends, the groom goes to a hotel room. His bride has gone to Jaipur with her family. Tomorrow's ceremony will take place there and the groom will bring her back to Pushkar to his family

Distant Lands

home. Since she is gone, tradition does not allow for him to go to his home without her, so he has to take a hotel room for the night. We join him for late-night pizza and conversation. Other family members stay the night.

With this part of the wedding over, my time has run out. I say farewells to my host family, who are genuinely sad to see me go, begging me to stay longer, but I explain my need to be at our own festival of Thanksgiving, a time for our families to be together and I want to be with mine. Suresh, my friend and host, is especially sad. "How can we live without you?" It is hard to leave, for I have become a part of them. On the train from Ajmer to Delhi, the air is cold as it rattles through windows that won't close properly. Suresh has asked a lady to help me negotiate a taxi when I get to Delhi but she in turn finds a young man who speaks English to do it for her. The young man's uncle works for Air India and is meeting him and his mother when they arrive, so he works a deal for a taxi to take us all to the uncle's house for tea and then to take me on to the International Airport, at a third of what I would have paid otherwise and now I have made new friends. They also invite me to stay for a family member's wedding which takes place on December 2, but I tell them I must go

As we fly over Afghanistan on a clear night, I am miraculously able see Kabul clear enough to make out its streets. It is 1:40 a.m. and no one is about. The city is all lighted up, surprisingly I think. I see lights from one smaller city. Other than that all of Afghanistan is dark. I am reminded of Hosseini's books, "The Kite Runner," and "A Thousand Splendid Suns" both of which I recommend. I have just finished the latter. No one can understand the ordeals women face in many parts of the world without reading that book.

Chicago O'Hare seems almost vacant, especially by comparison with the crowds of India. We may have space but India has soul. That's what my travel is about—soul.

India and Nepal Again—Strengthening Ties

It is difficult to imagine that I wait almost a year before taking off again. This is to be my third around the world solo adventure. I have put off seeing my friends as long as I can. The bug has bitten again and I must go.

Part Two
2011 Third Trip around the World: Rhine to the Mekong

"For the smitten, travel never ends. Adventure beckons like a Siren's song. Restlessness stirs within the mind. Dreams form of faraway places. The bonds of friendship pull tighter on the heart. The world which seemed so large at one time no longer seems that far. Distance shrivels. My neighborhood expands." –My Journal

1

Germany—Lure of the Lorelei

Thursday 15 September 2011
Edmond Oklahoma, USA

Preparing To Go Again!
Once again, I set sights on travel around the world. Where it leads, I cannot know, yet it draws me. Maybe the writer of the Odyssey was right. *"There is nothing worse for mortal man than wandering."* The story of that wanderer of long ago remains one of mankind's oldest stories which still resonates today. For me, travel is a metaphor for life. We are each on a journey through life, a journey that never ends so long as there is breath. Beyond that we cannot yet know, except in the realm of faith.

Packing now is so much easier than the first time. I've learned to scale back to the bare essentials. One does not need the excess, which becomes a burden.

Let me assure you that I am not a wealthy traveler. I travel lightly and cheaply. Airplane fares consume the major part of my travel budget. What others spend on cruises and packaged travel for a week to ten days, I spend for an entire trip around the world of three or four months. It helps that I travel solo; it suits me well. I ask for the prayers and indulgence of my family, who are always much in my thoughts and heart wherever I am in in the world.

Koblenz, Germany

The Enchantments of Lorelei
My flight to Frankfurt is without drama, other than that faced by all airline passengers these days; seats set much too close together. The lady in front of me seems unable to get comfortable and continues to bang my knees with her seat at every opportunity. That said, I am happy to arrive at the Frankfurt airport on time Sunday morning. The weather is cool and cloudy in the early morning. My friend, Hank is on the way from Koblenz to pick me up and messages that he should arrive in a few minutes. On the autobahn northwest out of Frankfurt, we clip along at a cool 180kph (120 mph). Hank is a German driver, quite used to the pace, so I try not to worry too much about the breakneck speed. After some miles (kilometers), we *ausfahrt* (exit) the autobahn onto a two-lane road for a slower, less heart-quickening pace along the fabled Rhine River. The Rhine flows north from Switzerland. This section, known as the "Romantic Rhine," is a favorite destination of tourists from over the world. It has been peopled since the early arrival of humans in Europe, and like much of Europe, has been fought over during most of its history. The Rhine is the stuff of legends, most famous of which is the siren call of Lorelei, the beautiful temptress inhabiting an outcropping along a sharp turn in the river. Boat wrecks were common at this critical turn, attributed to the sailors' distraction by her beauty. We stop to hike to the heights above, where she in mythology beckoned those sailors. From these heights, one sees a grand view of the river. The air is bracing for me, having recently endured 100+ temperatures back home, during most of the summer.

Germany—Lure of the Lorelei

Hank at the Rhine

We bid the statue of Lorelei *auf wiedersehen* and continue our way along the river's edge, banked by grape vineyards. This is wine country. The Rhine is famous for its wines, especially its Rieslings. The city of Koblenz is a historic city of about 100,000. Hank's house is located at the edge of the part of town opposite the river, where we are welcomed by Hank's friends, William and Honjoerg, and by another guest of theirs, a student named Toby, recently come from Cologne. He is a student of classical guitar, which he displays for us with an impromptu concert before and after our dinner, exhibiting both talent and passion. He tells us that his professor, Roberto Aussel of Argentina, often comes here as well from where he now lives in Paris.

I had met Honjoerg, Hank's housemate, in India when we attended a wedding there. William, another housemate from Taiwan, prepares our dinner. The house is multi-storied with a small in a basement area, where I stay, while the others room on various floors above. They frequently host travelers coming to Koblenz.

Distant Lands

While the others are busy the next day at work, I take in the *Bundesgartenshchau 2011*, a garden show held annually in various cities around Germany, which happens to be hosted this year by Koblenz, making timing just right for me to attend. The show is being held on the lawn of a large fortification, dominating the Rhine valley below, adequately providing a festive place for the display of beautiful flowers. My ticket allows access to the garden show, the fort and the use of a cable car spanning the river, enabling me to visit Koblenz proper. Since the grounds of the show are packed on this Monday, I skip the crowds and take the cable across to the city. It is a spectacular ride down a steep slope and high above the river. I wander leisurely through the streets of the older part of the city. Much of Koblenz, like many cities in Germany, was largely destroyed in WWII. Many of the old buildings, including the magnificent cathedrals, have since been restored, so that this section of Koblenz retains much of its old medieval flavor, even if much of it is quite new. A large plaza offers outdoor restaurants, giving me places to sit and watch people. Germans are brisk walkers, displaying energy and love for the outdoors. Absent are the enormous physiques of fast-food consumers, typical of too many of today's Americans! After a brief lunch, I return to the fortress, spending time exploring the fort and its museums. A classical concert is in progress, featuring a lady with a fine soprano voice. In one pavilion, champion dahlia flower arrangements, having been judged, are on display for their beauty.

It is a good day. I walk toward home and along the way stop to visit with a man working in his yard. He offers me two apples, recently fallen from his tree.

After his work, Hank and I travel to Bad Emmes, an old spa and splendid hotel complex, favored by the Russian Czars who came to this resort in another era, leading to a long decline, but is now being restored to become a favorite destination for well-heeled tourists. A Russian church is located there as well.

Germany—Lure of the Lorelei

Cruising the Rhine

It is a beautiful morning. Hank suggests that I take a short cruise up the Rhine. Short-term cruises of two hours are available, he says, enough for me to enjoy a wonderful outing on the magical Rhine, seeing beautiful homes, hotels and castles that dot the banks along the way. The weather is perfect. Fall is just beginning here. In a few short weeks the foliage will be at its peak, making this a great time to visit the Rhineland of Germany. I am enjoying my brief stay here. River traffic on the Rhine is heavy at times, filled with barges and cruise ships. The Rhine is a popular with tourists who cruise from Switzerland to Rotterdam or vice versa, making stops along the way to explore the various castles and quaint towns lining the shores. This short cruise is pleasant and relaxing and I take photos along the way.

Hank joins me for lunch at a popular stand-up *brat* place where we order brats and fries for a German fast-food experience. Customers are a mix of laborers and businessmen in suits, who stand side by side, enjoying the fare.

We have dinner together, all of us, dining on German cuisine prepared by William. We are joined by Sandra, Honjoerg's girlfriend and her dog Rocky. Tomorrow being Hank's birthday, gives the group a perfect chance to celebrate with an early birthday dinner. Their landlord also invites us to join he and his wife at their beautiful house across the back yard, with a warm fire going in the fireplace. He tells me he is a retired forest aid-worker who traveled much of the world, including time in Afghanistan in the 60s and 70s and Southeast Asia, including the Philippines and parts of Africa, where he helped manage and develop forests. He is quite an interesting guy. We hit it off immediately, comparing our respective travel adventures. At 74, he is two years my senior. Hank and I stay long after the others leave, until after midnight, and toast Hank's actual birthday. It is a great evening and fun, adding a new friendship.

2

Two: Istanbul—Off to the Races

Thursday 22 September

Early Arrival in Istanbul

Hank and Honjoerg drive me beyond town some distance to a station to catch the "fast train," direct to the Frankfurt Airport, which arrives speedily in less than 30 minutes. Since it is dark, it is impossible for me to judge just how fast the countryside slips by, but I know that we are moving at top speed. Two and half hours after my departure aboard Lufthansa, I am in Istanbul, arriving at 2:20 a.m. local time. What does one do in Istanbul at 2:20 a.m.? I know that I am too early to check into the hostel I have reserved but book a shuttle to take me there anyway. The driver has difficulty finding my cheap hostel, not too uncommon in my method of travel, for the ones I select are often located in out-of-the way places. The driver searches up and down the narrow, winding streets of old Begoglu in these early morning hours. The location gets creepier and creepier as we go. Few people are out and about, and the ones that are, look like the kind who might slit your throat just as easily as to invite you home for dinner, with little way to tell the difference. My shuttle mate, a young business man from Macedonia here to teach businesses about computers, tells me he is on the way to the Sheraton, on his company's dime of course. He expresses sympathy for me as the driver lets me out at the small hostel, called

Two: Istanbul—Off to the Races

Cheers Midtown, but surprisingly confesses to me that he'd really like to be traveling like me. So much for the stuffy Sheraton! Ali is on night duty at the hostel and seems friendly enough. I am not surprised that he tells me I cannot check in now. He takes pity on me and offers to put a mattress on the kitchen floor downstairs for me to use until then. Check-in will not be available until noon. I help Ali pull the mattress from a storage closet and he finds sheets to spread over it. I assure him I will be fine. In a few minutes he comes to tell me that he has chatted with a lady friend, who shares work with him, telling me she feels sorry for me and offers the use of a room they use alternately during their sleepy all-night duty. I accept and move into the room for a few short hours of needed sleep. All is good.

The people in the room reserved for me appeal for a late check-out and the morning clerk grants their request, not knowing that I am present and waiting. I kill time exploring the area around Begoglu, and finally get to check in about 1:00 p.m. The room is nice even though towels are not yet available. Late in the afternoon I head for the historic Sultanahmet area where the Blue Mosque and *Hagias Sophia* are located and send a message to my friend Nurettin who tells me he is on the way. We meet up about five, just as a storm passes, blowing dust and the vendors' goods all over. He introduces me to his friends, one of whom invites us for dinner tomorrow night.

The Race is On!
Millions of tourists descend on the Sultanahmet area of Istanbul each day to visit the famous *Hagias Sophia* and the Blue Mosque. Both are incredible structures, especially the Hagias Sophia, built by the Byzantines in 637 and still standing despite frequent earthquakes that often hit the area. I had been through it on my last trip. The queue for tickets is so long that I decide to forego another visit just now. Perhaps I will catch an early morning visit, before cavalcades of air-conditioned buses disgorge hordes of tourists from the cruise ships lining the bay. Right now it is enough for me to wander about and see the people.

Distant Lands

Friday being the Muslim holy day allows numbers of local families to explore and picnic in the park, where they relax and watch little children at play. I locate a grassy slope and lie in the shade and relax. At times, being lazy is the best way to travel.

Nurettin Unal comes late Friday afternoon by motor cycle and tells me to hop on, for we are going to his house for the night and tomorrow we will participate in rowing competitions on the lake. There is no time to get anything from my hotel, such as a toothbrush, change of clothes or daily medications. I just hop on and away we go, using a helmet he has brought for me to wear. We zip through the heavy traffic to the other side of Istanbul to his new apartment. He married in June and has moved to a nice apartment, quite roomy by Istanbul standards. Nurettin competes internationally in swimming and works locally as a fireman. His new wife Sibel is a lawyer. I had met her before on my last trip. I first met Nurettin on a street corner in Perth, Australia where he had come for a swimming competition and was having trouble reading a map and had beckoned for me to help, and we have been friends ever since.

He treats me to a nice dinner of sea bass at a restaurant by the Marmara Sea. His apartment also has a nice view of the Marmara Sea. An older gentleman joins us there for tea and fruit and tells me he had worked previously in Canada as a cabinet maker, traveling the U.S., which he found quite interesting. He is now 76.

I sleep on a couch for the night.

Nurettin and I bike to a near-by lake, adjacent to the sea, where he will participate in a rowing competition with his recently formed team, composed of swimming buddies and others. This will be their first competition, though they have had little time to train before the event. Nurettin is optimistic and highly competitive and will give it his best. The events of the morning include mixed men and women teams. The teams, though competitive, remain loose, enjoying a lot of fun for this hobby event. Some wear silly hats to signify their team.

Rowing Competition

It is a fun group. Ali is a senior year medical student, Mostafa and Anil are first-year computer students, and swimmers. Another Ali works in the Prime Minister's service, if I understood correctly. The events are for 200 meters and with several runs. They place fifth out of eight, which for being beginners is not that bad. They actually win one race, causing lots of excitement.

The men's final event takes place in the afternoon. They have more work to do but they are determined to succeed. Government officials show up for photo opportunities to present the trophies. Techno music plays from loud speakers. The young people seem curious about me and frequently inquire about my travels. I take pictures of the races and the teams, which they want me to share. These are bright twenty-year-olds.

Nurettin Teaching Rowing Technique

Nurettin returns me to Begoglu late in the afternoon. I had earlier called the hotel to let them know I would be away last night, offering Ali the use my room. I have dinner at a Turkish sidewalk café, taking a water pipe of double apple, the traditional way for Middle Easterners to relax. The owner of the establishment comes to sit with me and chat. He is a curious home-spun philosopher. We discuss Greek and classical thought. He shares an ancient proverb: "Dream as if you will live forever, live as if you will die tomorrow."

Hanging Out in Old Istanbul
Istanbul is one of my favorite cities of the world. Few cities of the world have the charm, history and mystery as old Istanbul, founded on a promontory known as the Golden Horn of the Marmara Sea connecting the Dardanelles with the Bosporus. It is part of the sea route from the Black Sea to the Mediterranean. The promontory is uniquely suited as a great defensive position, surrounded on three sides by water. The Romans built a defensive wall around it and heavily fortified it.

Two: Istanbul—Off to the Races

The city was known as Constantinople then and served as the seat of the Roman Empire for centuries. Emperors were crowned here. It remained a strong redoubt for centuries against the wave of Mohammed and his followers who had swept the Middle East from the seventh century on. Constantinople's crowning edifice was the *Hagias Sophia* basilica, a magnificent structure for its time. It reigned for centuries as the largest church in all Christendom and today after 1500 centuries of war and earthquake, remains the world's fourth-largest church building. It is no longer a church, for in 1453 the Byzantine Empire fell to Sultan Mehmet who brought powerful siege guns to destroy the wall on its European land side. After the fall, the *Hagias Sophia* continued as a church for a time but later was remade into a mosque and is now a museum hosting literally thousands of visitors every day to marvel at its wonders. Mosaics from the Christian era are being carefully restored.

Interior of Hagias Sophia

I stick around Istanbul to experience this rich culture in an unhurried way. My days are simple. I take a tram to Sultanahmet, the old walled city, take tea at the Dervish cafe sometimes with an omelet and walk

Distant Lands

about visiting the shops and observing the people. A poster advertises an apartment for sale in Istanbul and I wonder what it would be like to live here. I stop at a nearby bookstore to buy Irfan Orga's *Portrait of a Turkish Family* to read. It details the life of a Turkish family during the prosperous but declining days of the last Sultan up to the outbreak of WWI which brought great economic and cultural ruin to Turkey. His is a tale of the struggle endured by that family. Sometimes I sit for periods of time on a park bench to read, soaking up the fall sun, a leisurely way to experience travel. How often we dream of quiet days with little or nothing to do except soak up nature, observe people and experience a rich culture. I know I am lucky in that regard. Of course, it has its downside. One is constantly barraged by young and engaging guys, with good language skills, who ask where are you from and inform you that a brother, cousin or uncle lives in America and could they please offer you a cup of tea, and oh by the way, my family has a carpet shop nearby with "no obligation--just visit." Sometimes I fall under their spell and go. I am given tea and soon carpets are being spread before me. In spite of my repeated protests, that I don't want to buy, they proceed unabashedly and at the end, when I do not buy, they become quite angry. So I have learned it is best not to go at all.

The sights, sounds and smells of each country are unique. Here the sounds that most resonate in my memory are the regular sounds of the Muslim prayer calls, ringing out from mosques several times each day, a cacophony of sound from early morning until evening, each mosque in response to the other. Strangely, there is another, the "hissing" sound made by luxury buses arriving with loads of tourist passengers, hissing as air-controlled comfort jets adjust to the roughness of the road, shielding passengers from undue jostling by the reality of rough pavement. Sitting near the square, you hear that constant "hissing." Another sound, absent, is the sound of barking dogs. I hear no dogs barking in Istanbul! Cats are abundant, yes, but I have yet to see or hear a dog. Apparently dogs are not welcomed in this culture. Cats reign supreme, scurrying stealthily about under the tables of the sidewalk cafes. As

Two: Istanbul—Off to the Races

to smells, what could be better than the smell of food being prepared by the numerous sidewalk cafés? Kebabs of meats, lamb and chicken braised for donner sandwiches. Baklavas and other sweets tempt. The city is fairly clean, absent fetid smells from sewers, as in India. The sky is mostly clear on these fall days.

Traveling Two Continents for a Dollar
I take a ferry across the Marmara Sea to its Asian side. It is my last day here. The cost of the fare is only a couple of Turkish Lira, a little over a dollar and not bad for crossing from one continent to another. The ferry berths near the train station at Kadikoy, where I disembark and walk to explore the area. I stop at a pub for tea, with only one customer, an older man sitting at the counter, who motions for me to sit with him. He speaks no English but seems to welcome my company and, if I understand his gestures and impromptu sign language correctly, tells me that I would be a welcome guest at his house should I ever return to Turkey. I point to numbers on my phone clock to indicate that I can't stay long, for I have to return to the ferry. You might have loved my imitation of a ferry crossing the sea and an airplane taking off, as I attempt to tell him I am flying to Bahrain. He seems more curious than amused by my descriptions, but we both enjoy the effort.

On my last night I decide to try a Turkish Haman (bath) for which Istanbul is famous. Public baths are a holdover from Roman times though the term has now passed into the vernacular as "Turkish bath." I had earlier spotted one near my hostel in operation since the 1440's. I enter through a door at street level and descend steps into a large room. This bath is frequented by locals and I find no one who speaks English. However the young attendant is able to quote a price, including a massage, both of which seem reasonable enough and welcome, having walked up and down the hills of Istanbul these past days. The attendant shows me to a private room for changing and gives me a wrap to be tucked around the waist. I am not quite sure where to begin, but find my way to the showers to clean off before entering marbled rooms with basins and fountains of water for a more thorough washing. A few men of various ages are about, so I judge what to do by watching them. There are marble basins at the perimeter of the room with dippers for splashing water over oneself. Water temperatures are controlled by mixing water from two spigots, one hot and one cold. The room is heated, relaxing me as I splash away. Both dry sauna and steam rooms are available. I'm sure I am a curiosity as the only Westerner there but by and large no one makes me feel out of place. Some of the men endure the famous scrubbing by attendants, who soap them down and use abrasive gloves to remove dead skin cells. I forego that part.

When I get too heated I head for cold showers to cool down. After an hour or so relaxing in the heat and water, I return to the main room, a cooler place. The attendant comes and drapes a large towel around my shoulders to keep me warm. After sitting awhile and drinking water, I am ready for the massage. At the massage room on the upper floor, I am motioned to lie on the massage table in the center of the room. The attendant is a young Uzbek, which is about all that I get from him as he speaks no English. He dribbles me with oil, unfortunately not heated and quite cold but otherwise pleasant as he applies his hands with skill. When he finishes, he covers me with a large towel and leaves me to sleep awhile, relaxed and feeling much better. Later I towel off and return to my hostel for a peaceful night's sleep.

3

Exploring the Gulf States

Friday 30 September

Brief Stop in Bahrain

Some countries get the briefest of my visits, due to being attached to travel schedules. Bahrain is one of those. It lies at the side of the Arabian Peninsula across from Iran. You have heard of it if you have kept up with the news of the "Arab Spring." There were riots a few months ago. I arrive during the early morning hours and the small nation seems quite peaceful. My gate is directly across from a Starbucks, tempting me with aroma of coffee, but I won't bother, since I would have to exchange money to buy it, so it is only the aromas that I enjoy.

Saturday 1 October

Dubai: The Pearl of the Gulf!

Dubai is an anomaly. It started as a small fishing village on the sandy stretches of beach by the Persian Sea when young divers brought up pearls from the oysters that thrived in an inlet now called "The Creek." Traders came to exploit a rich trade in pearls. Over the years it remained a nowhere place with nothing but the Arabian Desert inland. Eventually traders began to thrive on the rich trade in pearls, spices and precious jewels.

Distant Lands

By 1960, oil had been discovered in nearby Abu Dhabi, and with discovery of oil everything changed. Seven local emirates banded together to form the United Arab Emirates. Each emirate had its ruling sheik and one of the sheiks became the king. With oil came money, lots and lots of it. A World Trade Center was built, which until the 1990's, was the only a building worthy of tourist photos. It still functions but its tall-building status has been eclipsed by today's towering structures, especially that of the tallest building in the world, pointing like a needle puncturing the sky.

Development accelerated at a feverish pace in the 1990's, with skyscrapers and luxurious hotels being built as fast as construction permitted by the labor of thousands imported from India, Pakistan, and Southeast Asia, who worked in less than ideal conditions. Abu Dhabi had its oil but Dubai had sand in endless stretches and when space became limited they built sand spits into the sea. The Atlantis Hotel is built on one of these palm-designed islets. Two seven-star hotels cater luxuriously to guests with money to spare. Five-star hotels are now considered common as a class of hotels. Additional palm-frond-designed hotels are currently under construction.

Into this heady mix comes this solo traveler, arriving from Istanbul a city with thousands of years of culture and history. I am met by Alex, who is my new niece Jennifer's uncle, who lives and works here. Alex coordinates and manages forces of imported workers. He helped construct the sand islands for the hotels. He is a smart, skilled hard-worker from India. I had met Alex and his family at Jennifer and nephew Christopher's wedding earlier this summer in the U.S. Alex drops me at my hotel called The Dream Palace, a few stars short of five stars, but I have no desire to ruin my travel image by staying in luxurious accommodations, especially given the prices. This one is nice enough.

Toward dark Alex and his daughter Pryanka come to take me to the Atlantis Hotel to view it at night. It is a magnificent hotel. We tour around Dubai before going to their apartment for dinner with his lovely wife Ida, who welcomes me with warm hospitality. The Indian meal is delicious. It is good to be with them again. We pray together before Alex returns me to the Dream Palace.

It is not my usual thing to book a city tour, but Dubai is hardly a pedestrian city. Imagine Phoenix in the summer and add 70% humidity and you get an idea of what it is like outside. It does not take long for one to melt down in the wilting heat. The tour van takes a small group of us to a museum for a lesson in the history of Dubai. Across the way we view the clusters of skyscrapers and luxury hotels too numerous to mention, along with the world's tallest building. After visiting a museum, I exit the tour to spend time in a luxurious mall, which is permitted tour participants. It is cool inside. The mall boasts hundreds of stores and a giant aquarium. You can even snow ski here! It is ostentation without limits! However, a mall is a mall is a mall with the same stores, same displays and requisite food court with KFC, McDonald's and Burger King and a few other assortments. Except that the men wear white gowns and Arabic headdresses and the women wear black burqas with faces covered, you would think you were in a ritzy mall in New York, Dallas or Las Vegas. In fact, Dubai is sort of Las Vegas, Disney and New York all rolled into one!

The shining new Metro, which opened on September 9, 2009 at 9:09 a.m. and 9 seconds, efficiently sleek and new, returns me part way to my hotel, but I have to catch a bus from the mall to reach the station. How tacky is that!

Weekend in Dubai
It was a Friday when I arrived in Dubai. The weekend here includes Friday and Saturday with Friday being the holy day for Muslims. Other faiths follow suit using the same day for their day of worship. They are represented by the workers, who have come here from many parts of the world, Hindu, Buddhist and Christian, using Friday as their day of

worship, although most cannot practice it openly. You see no structures for them, but then a structure does not a temple or church make.

On Saturday, I continue my tour of the city to see the marvelous structures consisting mostly business and luxury tourist hotels. Villas costing millions and apartments beyond the reach of ordinary persons are abundant. The wealthy of Europe, America and the Middle East come here to spend the money they have come by due to worldwide appetites for oil and minerals, commerce or entertainment. Angelina Jolie has a place here, or so I'm told. I walk around a gold *souk* (market) tonight. Shop windows display more gold than Fort Knox, or so it seems. I gape in awe at a window displaying the biggest gold ring in the world, a huge band about two feet wide!

Dubai is an unnatural environment, getting its water comes from the sea. The water I drink has been desalinized from sea water, in a process of filtering through limestone, with a little sea water added back for taste. Without water this place could not exist. In fact, beginning in 2012 it reaches a threshold. In a few years a major crisis will occur, unless larger amounts can be processed. I am happy to read that plastic bags are required by law to become biodegradable by the end of the year.

Like all other places, Dubai depends on the world's interrelated global economy. The boom years are seeing some adjustment now to new realities, slowing the rate of growth more realistically, yet there is plenty of money here. The ruling sheiks have wisely invested their money back into their country's development. Some social reforms may be under way as well.

It is safe here with the crime rate is near zero, I am told, and surveillance is high. Traffic is monitored for speed. Speed limits on the two major highways are fast but fines for excesses are heavy. The one toll road is monitored and assessed by laser. There are a few concessions to other cultures in social structures. Alcohol is permitted in Dubai itself, but not in the adjacent cities nearby. If a person is caught, he goes to jail and gets his head shaved and receives 40 lashes.

One of the things I like, though, is the newspapers which report real news of world events and interest along with above average news reporting on television. I feel better informed here than when I am at home.

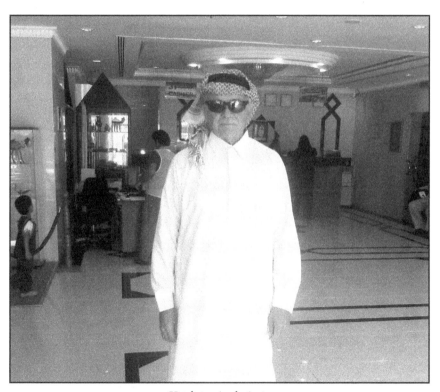

Keith in Arab Attire

If I were I able to speak Arabic, I might easily pass for a native, wearing the traditional white Arabic dress topped by the red-checkered Arab headdress. When outfitted this way, hotel staff shows me deference, greeting me with "Salaam." Waiters at restaurants rush to serve me and start speaking to me in Arabic, and as long as I don't open my mouth, I get away with it. Keeping one's mouth shut is probably good advice anyway.

Monday 3 October

Qatar

Qatar is my fourth Persian Gulf area kingdom to visit. The first was Oman in 2009 and now Bahrain, UAE and Qatar. Qatar is a sandy desert peninsula in the Persian Gulf next to Bahrain with the highest per capita income in the world. Its reserves of natural gas and oil are huge. The capital is Doha where the airport is located. I see nothing but sand between the airport and the city and its many new buildings and modern streets. The airport is expanding and Qatar Airways is a growing air carrier. Alas, I am only transitioning here, on the way to Kathmandu by Qatar Airways.

Alex took me to the Dubai Airport this morning. Before I left Alex and his family, I presented him a carton of mint tea as my gift. I had not looked carefully enough at the packaging until Alex informed me that it was really mint-flavored *tobacco* used in hookah pipes for smoking shisha. We laugh about my error. He returns it to me and tells me to take it with me to Kathmandu to give to someone who might make use of it. I try not to be embarrassed. One should examine one's purchases more carefully.

Dubai was only a brief visit but long enough. The climate is unbearable, soon to break with the coming of fall, which locals consider half-way pleasant. I hope so. Looking at temperatures back home makes me miss the fall there. No doubt I will find Nepal more to my liking.

4

Briefly Nepal before a Month in India

Thursday 6 October

Kite Flying in Kathmandu

Manish is sometimes the epitome of spontaneity, exclaiming with boyhood exuberance "Let's fly a kite." It is festival time in Kathmandu and off we go on motorbikes to a shop to buy kites, string and a string roller. We go to the roof of his rented house to prepare the kites and soon we are fully engaged in the competitive sport of kite cutting, fiercely competing with other kites flying high in the sky over the houses. He cuts down the highest flying one and goes after the others before his is cut loose, but he doesn't seem to mind that much. "I know someone is very happy they got it." All is in good fun. His niece and nephew, Pinkey and Vicky, get involved too.

I had arrived in Kathmandu last night after the flight from Dubai through Qatar, on a plane loaded with Nepalese heading home for the festival time to be with their families. Dashain is the most auspicious of the Nepali festivals, where goats are sacrificed and altars are prepared in the home. Houses are thoroughly cleaned in preparation for the visit of the goddess and *tikka* blessings are given to family members. I have experienced the full festival before, having spent a month here in 2009.

I met Manish the next day after my arrival, at the ancient Pashupatinath Temple, where he works as a guide. He spots me some distance away and comes running to give me a big hug of welcome before taking me by motorbike to his home to greet the family, his mother and father, returned after some time living apart. They are living in a new place from the last time I visited, his mother and father, who had been living apart, and his niece and nephew. I have dinner with them the night after flying the kites.

I had planned for a longer stay in Nepal, but Manish tells me he is booked to guide tourists on a trek for some days. I decide it best to rearrange my schedule to India and return next month when he will have time available to be with me. Next month he promises to take me to a remote part of Nepal. "Just wait and see," he says, "You will love it." I've learned to be flexible with my travel itinerary.

Saturday 8 October

Days in Delhi
Suresh greets me at the Delhi airport and we try out the new Metro system serving India's capital city, stopping at the Dwarka Mor station for a few days at home of Purashottam, his friend Mohit's elder brother, whose wedding I attended last November in Pushkar. He is away at work as a male nurse, but we gain entrance from a neighbor who has a key. Manu, as he is known, returns at night and we enjoy dinner together.

A festival is in full progress with effigies constructed in a square nearby representing demons to be burned later to the delight of children and adults. Fireworks go off everywhere. We make pallets on the floor for sleeping, the three of us as we retire for the night. Manu is delighted that I have chosen to stay at his house instead of at a hotel. A ceiling fan cools the night.

Briefly Nepal before a Month in India

I connect with Anita Raj and her lovely daughter Janetta for dinner at a Pizza Hut. They are my niece Jennifer's mother and sister. We enjoy pizza together and catch up retelling our experiences at the wedding of Jennifer and Christopher, my grandnephew, which took place last July in the USA. Anita is a school teacher at a Christian academy in Delhi. After dinner with them, Suresh and I join Manu and a friend's family for an Indian dinner I had promised to share with them, which follows immediately after having pizza. On top of that we share ice cream all around with the family and their two young sons. I am full to the brim by the time we finish, but this is India and these are the demands of hospitality.

Morning in Pushkar

Pushkar, India

I awaken in Pushkar to the sounds of clanging bells and cymbals, ringing out from the various temples surrounding the lake. Overhead monkeys screech from perches atop temple cupolas, making loud noises as one large male barks orders to underling monkeys, who are stripping green leaves for eating and who scamper noisily across loose

Distant Lands

sheets of corrugated metal used on roofs. Monkeys are literally the top caste in Pushkar.

The best times to walk is in the morning while the air is still cool from a night of desert air. I head toward the perimeter of this small city of about 18,000, greeted by beggars and temple sweepers as I walk. A holy man stops to touch the head of a sacred bull in a ceremonious gesture, moving the hand from the bull's forehead to their own.

Motorcycles thread their way through increasingly busy streets, the deep guttural sounds of those delivering milk from cans attached to either side, to the street markets. Small trucks enter loaded with fresh greens from the surrounding countryside for the outdoor stands, preparing to sell today's vegetables for cooking. A tower depicting the gods in powerful actions of triumph over evil foes stands guard over the entrance to the city. A statue of a benevolent Gandhi looks on from a pedestal of stone.

At the edge of the city, I take the street bound on either side by sand deposited by thousands of years of wind, which pile the small grains until they become large dunes. New houses are being built there. It is quiet this morning with few others out walking. When I come to the end of the street, a man counsels me to turn around to avoid the upcoming traffic of a busy street, but I am headed that way anyway. I thank him and walk beside the road with heavy trucks, motorbikes and occasional cars speeding past, near a shrine to Ganesh, the elephant-faced god, as an elderly man sweeps a stone clean of debris. A couple of guys on a camel cart invite me to join them at "no charge." I wonder where I might have gone had I taken them up on their offer.

I enter the city again amid the noise of traffic and vendors opening shops. Dust is stirred by women sweepers gathering the debris thrown by the people. At a juncture of streets Suresh and his cronies call to me and I join them for morning chai, to sit for a time as they joke among themselves. Someone points up the street as an apparition of flowing scarves and broad-brimmed hat, walking stick clicking on the street, floats toward us with high resolve. It is Helen from Scotland, a lady of mature years whom I had met last year. We greet each other and have more chai. Helen spends fall and winter months here to escape the weather there. "The cold of Scotland is not good for my joints. I can walk here," she exclaims with her Scottish brogue. She's always a delight and quite the confident traveler.

It is morning in Pushkar! My second day here has just begun.

Country Village
Relatives of Suresh invite me again to stay a couple of nights in Jethana, the farming village about 50 kilometers away. Three of his mother's brothers live there with their families and Suresh's grandfather and grandmother. I had made a short visit before. This time I go alone except, except with a cousin, Sonu, who accompanies me by bus from Ajmer. He is a nice young man of about nineteen or twenty, who works with his father as an electrician. I am happy for him to go with me, although his knowledge of English is very limited and we are able to have only a little conversation.

It is hot and crowded on the old rickety bus bouncing along up and down the back roads. A new highway is being built and we work our way around construction to arrive at the small village, sporting a few vendors of food, sweets and beverages at the bus stop. The vendors recognize me from previous visits and offer chai and samples of sweets. A stool is brought for me to sit on. A foreign visitor in Jethana is a rare occurrence and they are curious.

As we walk to the uncle's house up the street, little Mitty and Keshaw come running down the street to greet me. "Keith uncle," they yell, and a cluster of playmates and relatives crowd around me. I hear "Keith uncle" every few seconds for the rest of the day. Power is off, which is

Distant Lands

the norm during the daytime hours, so we head for the rooftop to escape the heat. New playmates appear eager to see the foreign guest and to seek the attention of Mitty's visiting "Keith uncle." When Suresh's uncle arrives from the school he runs, we sit on the roof and attempt to communicate, although his English is limited as well. Only Naman, a young cousin in his early teens, has a good enough command of English, which he amply displays non-stop for the rest of the day.

My allergies, that flared up earlier, go haywire in the small village. A painter has come to paint the house, mixing the fumes of the paint with the other allergens, sending me into a full reaction. I have to get out of the house. The grandmother, a wiry woman in her sixties, is a force to be reckoned with, strongly suggesting that I remove my shoes and rest in the bed. With no power in the small house it is stifling, so I put on my shoes and slip out when her back is turned, triggering a "guest has escaped" alarm. Sonu comes running to find me at the bus stop, where I had escaped to enjoy time with friends.

The only place I get the slightest cooling relief is outside on the street, sitting with a few small shop owners. My presence on the street seems to cause concern and I am ushered back into house in a friendly tug-of-war over the rules of hospitality, which apparently states that a guest should be resting comfortably somewhere other than on the street. Unfortunately with allergies flaring, I am not handling it too well.

I do manage a brief foray into the countryside to observe farmers at work shocking stacks of sorghum and millet and harvesting corn and young women herding cows and goats from the village to the farms for grazing. Walking alone on a small country lane provides interest and helps my disposition.

After two days, I tell Suresh I am ready to return to Pushkar. He had suggested I stay another day but I tell him that two is enough. Sonu and I catch an early bus back to Ajmer and another one on to Pushkar.

Briefly Nepal before a Month in India

It is always a marvel to see how many people and goods can be put on a bus. We make it back and I am glad to see Suresh again. Suresh arranges the use of a house of my own to stay for the rest of my time here. It is welcome news. I confess I look forward to having time and space to call my own.

A House of My Own in Pushkar
The house is on the outskirts of Pushkar near Gular's Temple on a sandy slope above the city near a palace and a school. The house belongs to "Big Mama's family," one of Suresh's aunts and uncles who owns the house but who prefer to stay in the family compound. Perhaps it is because to retain rights to the compound descendants have to reside there, but also I think because the aunt enjoys the sociability of the larger family, preferring not to be alone. By contrast, being alone really appeals to me. The house is fairly large with a large room and a big bed, opening onto a large patio with a kitchen, toilet and area for showering. Upstairs there is a large roof from which to view beautiful sunsets. I like it.

The water drum has been filled and Big Momma (the aunt) comes to clean the floors. The kitchen is not yet hooked up with gas and I continue to take major meals at Suresh's house anyway. Needless to say, it all suits me just fine and I am given keys for the locks. Suresh and Sonu come to spend the first night with me, so I am not exactly alone here. They bring pizza and cold drinks and we spread a mat on the roof upstairs, soon to be joined by another friend Papsa. It is wonderful eating under the stars, with a full moon arching across the night sky. Papsa stays to play music from his mobile phone, making the evening complete.

It is necessary for a foreigner to register with the police when staying in a private house. Most countries get nervous about foreigners staying apart from hotels. In the afternoon, Suresh arrives with a police agent in tow and we serve the obligatory chai while the policeman quizzes me about where I am from, my occupation, when and why I have come to India, when I am leaving and why would I want to stay in a house instead of a hotel. It seems that I will be approved, pending perhaps a little payment made on the side. When he leaves Suresh tells me how much he wants. It bothers me but Suresh has to live here and I don't want to make it difficult for him. Because of his connections he was able talk him down to 1000 rupees for the privilege of doing the job for which he is already being paid. I chafe but give Suresh the necessary money. At least now I am legal.

It is Sunday and I rise early to climb the sacred mountain Savrati, to the temple at the top to Lord Brahma's sweetheart. It is a steep climb especially the last part making me glad I had started before sunrise. The sun comes up as I near the top. A group from Israel is there watching monkeys scamper about. I do not actually go into the temple, but drink chai while I watch the monkeys. I also talk with an aspiring young lawyer from Tel Aviv.

As we make our way down, we meet faithful worshippers beginning their climb up. They include families with elderly grandmothers, obviously experiencing pain as they make the difficult climb. Most climb barefooted. I sit for a while at the top and take in the beauty of the surrounding landscape looking down on the city of Pushkar nestled serenely around the lake. As I engage in my Sunday meditation I pray for the people of Pushkar. The descent is dangerous at times and one grandmother slips and falls, but she is alright.

Trip to Gujarat
Suresh wants us to take a trip to the state of Gujarat located to the southwest, the home state of Mahatma Gandhi, bordering the sea and also nearby Pakistan. Our destination is the city of Mandvi, a shipbuilding port on the coast, where Suresh has a friendship with Manu, an astute business and community leader. They met at Pushkar when he came for prayers at the sacred lake. Suresh had made the trip once

Briefly Nepal before a Month in India

before and enjoyed the man's hospitality and wants me to visit also. His friend agrees to host us there.

We leave early for the challenging trip, dealing with India's traffic. Add to it, that neither Suresh nor the driver knows the way there. You can imagine how the day unfolds. Start-up, stop, swerve to avoid potholes and oncoming traffic barreling head-on in our lane. Mix in ox carts, cattle herds, goats, tractors, bicycles, buses and millions of heavy-duty trucks loaded with all kinds of merchandise. India's roads are filled 90% with heavy-duty trucks. The other 10% are cars, carts, motorcycles and who knows what else. Marked lanes serve only for the entertainment of the people who constructed them. Drivers straddle lanes, seizing the best opportunity to pass, and dodging traffic on either side or up and down the middle. Not knowing our way doesn't help progress either. We stop to ask people "Which way to Bujg?" That they don't know doesn't deter them from offering directions. At times, we meet ourselves going in circles, traveling well into the night, with a driver who has trouble with night vision. I begin to worry, but on we go, arriving at 2:00 a.m. Our host meets us some distance out, in order to lead us down a small lane toward the sea, where he has a vacation house for us to use the first night.

Our host Manu is in his sixties, quite successful and outgoing. He's the kind of person who scoops you up and gets you involved before you know what is happening. He joins us this morning for breakfast and then takes us to the shore and hires rides for us on horse and camel at the beach, after which he takes us into Mandvi to his office for tea. He has business meetings to attend to and arranges for us to tour Mandvi Palace just outside of town, with the help of his grandson, a handsome young man. The palace is a beautiful stone mansion of several stories, now a museum with adjacent guest cottages. In its day it was a thriving social and political center presided over by the Maharaja. From the roof one looks out to the sea. Glass cases are filled with trophy tigers and leopards, hunted on the property in an earlier era.

Distant Lands

Toward evening, Manu escorts us to the small village where he grew up. He owns land there, growing cotton and peanuts, which has made him a rich man. We drink chai with the locals who are delighted to see him and drive to a remote area beyond the town to a Hindu temple complex, where we are warmly greeted by the holy man who invites us to sit in his apartment, sharing snacks and drinks with us, along with lively conversation. We are about six people including Suresh, a local school language teacher, Manu, his business associate, a young man from the temple and me. The holy man is young man, with a full beard and a sharp intellect with an engaging social manner. After much talk and good natured banter he invites us to the dining area for dinner. Cots and pallets are arranged for us on a portico of the temp for sleep outside with ceiling fans overhead, listening to the sounds of birds filling the night air with song. It is a nice way to sleep.

It is the sounds of the birds, along with noises of temple preparations, that awaken us in the morning. Showers are taken and chai served. I accompany Suresh to the temple for his prayers. A young workman is busily decorating a large and rather realistic looking phallic image of the Lord Shiva, attaching flower petals to it.

The holy man accompanies us as we ride back to Mandvi, showing us the temple's fields of cotton and peanuts. The temple is prospering under his spiritual and business guidance. Back in town, we wait for a community meeting Manu is hosting to break up, so we can all have lunch together. Waiters busy themselves back and forth bringing all kinds of foods, sweets, and breads. We eat our fill.

The area is known for its ship-building on an estuary of the coast. Some 30 craft are in various stages of hand-made construction, some quite large. Pits are dug in the to serve as dry docks. All the lumber appears to be hand-crafted. It may take years to build some of the larger craft. We drive on to Bujg, with a friend of Manu's who guides us, stopping at another major temples, located in a quiet forested area, to sit with the holy man there who speaks some English and welcomes us with chai.

Suresh wants me to meet his new fiancé Deepika on our way back. She and her sister arrange to meet us for a late lunch at a restaurant on the highway a few kilometers from Nimaj. It is only their first meeting since getting engaged. She and her sister break convention by coming to meet us, with only her mother giving consent. They make me promise not to tell anyone of the meeting. I admire her for her daring. After a pleasant lunch, we take both of them by car back to their village, but let them out near a bus stop, so they can walk home without being observed with us.

Back in Pushkar, I unwind weary legs, cramped far too long in the car, making it hard to walk. My body is sore from every bump and bounce of traffic slow-down bumps placed on every road to control speed. I vow to take no more car trips. I'll go by train or bus next time.

It's My Birthday and All India Celebrates!
India's houses are festooned with lights, markets are loaded with ample supplies of sweets, sugar cane fronds, oil candles are filled and lighted, fireworks echo across Pushkar Lake, everyone sports new clothes, families gather, prayers are being offered and offerings are made. All India is celebrating. It is October 27, my 72nd birthday. In reality it is also Diwali, the major festival of the year, only coincidental to my birthday, but I choose to think of it my way! Diwali is a festival of lights, reminding me a lot of Christmas back home, with the lights, gifting and gathering of families. All work ceases and the people are in a joyous mood.

Friends gather at my house to celebrate my birthday. We put lights on the house, order pizza and snacks and enjoy friendly banter, as we shoot fireworks from the roof. A decorated cake is presented and I blow out the candles and make a wish. It is a nice time among dear friends and new acquaintances. One of Mohit's uncles shares my birthday, so we invite him to celebrate with us.

Days and Nights in Pushkar
I enjoy morning walks to the nearby countryside. The city borders both desert and mountainous terrain, but on one side is a lush farm-rich valley laced with small country lanes. I walk down a country lane, with a sign advertising "Whine Shop." Misspelling of English on signs and menus is common, making for some interesting interpretations. I imagine a shop where people go for grumbling and crying over their misfortunes. Another sign in town advertises "The Sixth Sense of the Seventh Heaven Restaurant." No doubt the food there is out of this world or maybe just incomprehensible to the other five senses. One item on a menu unknowingly advertises a body part that I dare not mention on this blog.

Continuing down narrow country lanes past fields of cabbages and other vegetables, I watch workers pluck blossoms from fields, the famous Pushkar Rose, for use in ceremonies at the temples. I pass huts with mounds of hay for the cattle. A sign points to the "Exotica Guest House." I wonder what a stay there might be like.

On the way back, I meet a procession of turbaned men carrying a litter with a corpse wrapped in gauze. An elder member of the family has died during the night. The body was washed, wrapped, and is now on its way to a funeral pyre for burning, one subtraction in the human population with little impact on the growing population, evidenced by surging crowds on the main street entering the city. India's youthful population is growing by the minute. Statisticians tell us that tomorrow, October 31, a child will be born in the Utter Pradesh state, India's most populous territory, marking the birth of boy or girl who will become the planet's seven-billionth living person. Celebrations are planned there to mark the milestone, along with notes of concern, that within twenty years, India is projected to become the most populous country on earth.

I search too for an English-language newspaper to read, and sit to chat with a young man from Denmark, Jonas by name, who is here learning Hindi. By 10:30, I report to Suresh's house for a breakfast of curd, rice, dahl and a vegetable mixture and chapatti. The family gathers to watch me eat. By 11 or noon, I am back at my place, ready to shower, taken from a bucket of cold water using a dipper. Suresh joins me for a nap during the midday. At night, we snack and walk the streets watching people at the side of the lake for quiet meditation. Last night I was joined by three young Indian Christian boys on mission to share their faith with tourists. We talk and pray together. I give them a small donation for their work.

At 9:00 p.m., I return to Suresh's house for the evening meal, after which I return home to prepare for bed. Either Suresh or his brother Kamal, and sometimes a cousin, comes to spend the night with me. The family would never consent to my sleeping there alone. The guys usually get up at 5:00 to shower and shiver from the cold water, as they prepare for their service to the faithful at the lake. I stay snuggled under the blanket in the cold morning air to wait for sunrise, a typical day for me. Life is good.

Pushkar Camel Fair
The desert springs to life almost overnight, with a city of Bedouin tents stretching to the horizon. Thin-legged nomads, wearing *dhotis* and bright turbans sit around campfires discussing trading deals for camels, horses and cattle. Next year's family weddings may well depend on the deals made in the barter of camels.

Camel Fair Encampment

The Camel Fair is a festival—a glorified state fair, if you please. Ferris wheels dominate midway entertainment and spring up overnight as well. Vendors come from near and far to sell their wares and cheap souvenirs. There are cooking pots, pans, scissors, rakes, camel saddles, bridles and blankets to sell as well. Everything is hawked.

This year's crop of tourists is up from last year, perhaps more than double. The largest contingents appear to be from Israel, European countries, as well as Australia, China and Korea. A few are American, yours truly included. Vendors call out to tourists, even following them down crowded streets or among the camps relentlessly seeking to sell something. Every form of deformity is represented by some beggar, some of whom I recognize from previous years, with no limbs or one limb. Holy men in scant garb carry metal buckets begging. Foliage is offered for sale to devotees for feeding the sacred cows crowding the streets.

Pushkar Lake is busy with ceremonial bathers. Suresh and his family work from 4:30 in the morning until night helping with the prayers, gaining income for their livelihood from it. Last night school groups competed in creating colorful mandalas of light and flowers on the steps of the temples bordering the lake. One man sits cross-legged before a tree, hands raised in prayer.

The noise level of the streets increases proportionate to the surge of humanity and animals. The fair goes for eight days, with cultural dances and scores of events to watch or to avoid. It is a phenomenon, in which I am now a vetted participant.

Looking for a Bride in Jaipur
We make a trip to Jaipur to look for a bride. Not for me or Suresh but for Prashant, his future brother-in-law. He is taking an opportunity to meet a girl's family, so both can size up the other for a prospective marriage. We hire a car and pick up Prashant in Ajmer, coming from Nimaj. They drop me off to spend a day with Navneet, while they go about the business of meeting the family. Navneet is in Jaipur studying for a criminal justice exam. With some searching on our part, we find where Navneet is staying, a nice roof-top room with a couple of students, one of whom is preparing for a test that very afternoon. Suresh and Prashant drop me there and go about their mission to gain a bride, telling me that the meeting will go for about an hour and half, but knowing India, I know it is more likely to take most of the day. Navneet and I enjoy time lounging around the room, catching up on his recent activities and recalling times we have traveled together.

As I suspected, the hour and half meeting turns into all day event. The roommate comes back, quite dejected that he failed the test with a grade of little over 50%, a bump in the road to his passing the difficult exam. Navneet and I spend time practicing English, using an English dictionary for time well-spent. A walk to a nearby park gives us a welcome break. It is nearly dark by the time Suresh and Prashant return

Distant Lands

to report that their mission has been a success. Prashant shows me a picture of the prospective bride, a beautiful girl.

We celebrate our day of marriage-making and English learning at a favorite restaurant in Jaipur, the Bombay Barbecue. Suresh and I had been there last year on my birthday. Bombay has since added live music and some of the patrons get up and dance to a combination of pop songs and blues from America, which is heaven-sent for me. We enjoy the evening and fairly well stuff ourselves. It is nearly 11 p.m. by the time we start back Pushkar, not arriving until 2:00 a.m. Prashant stays the night with us at "my" house.

Saying Good-bye to India

"Good-byes" are hard. Part of the angst of travel is meeting people, becoming close friends and then having to leave them to their part of the world as you go to yours, with a whole planet separating until such a day that you might come again, or perhaps never.

My last day is especially hard emotionally. My friends break down in tears at the prospect of my going. "We will miss you" and they ask "When will you come back? Please come back soon." I attend a birthday party for little Lucky, one of the young cousins who lives in the family house, before I leave. Cake and goodies are served to guests including a young couple from France. Dinner is served in an apartment at the nearby temple, heavy wheat cakes, spicy onion, potatoes and sweet rice for dessert.

We say good-bye to relatives in the distant villages by phone, all asking "When will you come back?" There are gifts to be given, too many in fact to fit into my already stuffed suitcase, so I must now carry an extra bag. It's hard for them to appreciate that I have yet a half a world to go. No matter. The gifts are given and cannot be refused. "Do you need money?" "Please take my mobile phone and use it so we can call you." They are generous to a fault, these dear Indian friends.

There are blessings to be given—a red smear on my forehead with garlands of Pushkar roses to drape around my neck with the smell of sweet fragrance to mix with the tears. The taxi comes to take me to Ajmer's train station for the 1:00 a.m. departure for Delhi. The taxi chugs and bounces up the hill to "my" house where I retrieve my bags and sacks of goods to take. Suresh's father and brother assist me in loading it up. Then Suresh and I make our way through the cold night air to Ajmer. "How can I live without you?" he pleads with eyes sincere and mournful, dripping with tears. At the station, quiet for once at this early morning hour, we sit to await my train. Suresh helps with my luggage and makes sure I am comfortable before we say our final good-byes.

In Delhi, the air is somewhat cool for a change. I have promised to meet another friend, before leaving India. He comes tonight, a young business man I met three and a half years ago on the train from Mumbai to Delhi, during my first trip to India. We have stayed in touch ever since and now finally we will have dinner together to meet once again.

My world continues to shrink. My heart hurts as I say good-bye, yet I am happy and blessed by these people, whose hearts never shrink and whose love remains boundless.

I board the flight to Kathmandu.

5

Thanksgiving in Nepal

Friday 18 November

From Nepal: Congratulations on a Fifty Year Reunion
I have returned to Nepal, whose weather is in sharp contrast to the hot days of India, to a point where it feels cold here. My body adjusts, especially as we head up into the Himalayas. I am making the jump from summer to winter and from low-altitude to the highest on earth!

Before I continue, I must make an acknowledgement. Back home this weekend I am missing the celebration of my fifty-year (1961) class reunion of Oklahoma Baptist University. I remember and wish my classmates the best and regret not being able to attend. Given the option of making this world trip and time spent in the Himalayas or being at the reunion for a single weekend—well, you know which one I chose.

Oklahoma Baptist is a quality university, well-ranked nationally, a good experience for me when I arrived in 1957, straight from a farm in western Oklahoma, green and naive. You could tell I was a green country kid when you saw me with my "high rider" jeans worn a bit too short but we had to wear them as long as we could. I arrived by bus and everything was new for me, giving me a sense of wonder, much like

Thanksgiving in Nepal

my travels today. I soon met friendly students who welcomed me into their circles. That first week, I met the girl I would marry, a city girl from Tulsa and we were married after graduation. She died in 1999, well short of this reunion and well short of our fiftieth wedding anniversary, both of which occur this year.

My best OBU story, from my travels, came on my first around-the-world trip when I crossed from Mongolia into China on the famed Trans-Siberian Railway. We backed the train into sheds, raised every car with us still in it, and replaced the undercarriage wheels for the standard-gauge rail track of China, as opposed to Russia's narrower gauge. Once we rolled into China, the first immigration official to board asked for my passport. When I handed it to him, he looked at it and asked "Oklahoma?" I said "Yes." "Do you know Shawnee, Oklahoma?" I said "Yes." "Do you know Oklahoma Baptist University?" I said again "Yes, I am a graduate from there." He then told me that he had been a transfer student there for a short time. How unexpected to find a fellow OBU student working Chinese immigration aboard a train at midnight on the Mongolia-China border. Small world indeed.

Now I'm in Nepal, planning to leave tomorrow by motorbikes to tour the country and trek the mountains. I hope I am up to the cold and the altitude. The airport terminal is filled with tourists, many from Germany here for the trekking season. I may have to borrow warm clothing or buy a coat to wear, along with gloves and a warm hat. My friend Manish promises a trip eventful and beautiful. I know it will be cold for sure but he assures me we will enjoy thermal springs up in the mountains.

Thanksgiving Week in the Himalayas
We pack gear and mount two motorbikes for the nine hour trip to Pokhara, west of Kathmandu. This is the week of Thanksgiving in America and I'm trekking the Himalayas. It will be my biggest challenge so far. The road out of Kathmandu crosses a mountain pass and

then descends along a river. The sides are steep. You drop off the road and there's only the river below. Fortunately there have been improvements to the busy highway since my last trip. Leaving on a Saturday helps too, for the traffic flow is down from "impossible" to "nearly impossible." It is cold but my thin wind-breaker jacket with several layers of long-sleeve shirts underneath helps. I wear the helmet I bought last time. There are four of us--Manish, his brother Sonu and their friend Raju, plus myself. We stop along the way for breakfast, then at a favorite fresh fish place.

In Pokhara, we obtain the necessary permits for mountain trekking by motorbike, a challenge to my 72-year-old bones and promising to be extremely cold for me at times. The others are more acclimated. I hope I'm up to it but look forward to the challenge. Manish promises "the most spectacular scenery ever." We plan to bike up as high as we can and hike from there.

Pokhara is full of tourists for this is the prime season for trekking. The skiers are a little better prepared with more appropriate clothing. I decide to buy warmer clothes before we leave.

Adventure to the Roof of the World: Part One Ascent
We pack our gear and head toward the mountains from our base in Pokhara. With my heavy yellow coat promising wind and water protection and water and wind-proof pants over jeans, I am as bright as the sun and as warm. We are on two bikes. Our plan is to ascend the mountains to reach the site of a sacred and remote temple called *Muktinath*.

The night air is cold as we depart. We fill our bikes with petrol and head out of Pokhara toward the mountains ascending along a small river valley for a time, after which we drop down on the other side, crossing a valley to make a new ascent, along the Kali Gandaki River, which I am told originates in Tibet. The river flows through a drier and

Thanksgiving in Nepal

remote part of Nepal, whose upper stretches remind me a lot of the terrain I found in Tibet during my visit there in 2001.

We stop occasionally for tea and breaks from the rough road. Much of the road is still being carved out of a previous trail and we encounter evidences of frequent washes and landslides, some of which are fairly recent. We wait for a tractor to fill a portion of the road, before we can cross. It is rough going with me bouncing on the back of Sonu's motorbike. Mud holes are especially challenging, one of which succeeds in claiming us. Our bike goes down into the muddy water. I am fortunate to have no cuts or scrapes, but my backpack goes into the water along with Sonu and me filling everything with muddy water. We look like two pigs wallowing in a favorite mud hole. When I come up out of the mud, Manish notices that I am without my glasses. Had they been thrown off when we went down? About that time a large bus comes along, squishing its way through the mud. We search in vain for my glasses, even to the point of trying heroically to drain the mud hole. A small girl watches our efforts with amusement, as we fish around in the mud but we do not find the glasses. I have only a faint recollection of taking them off to clean them, when we made our last stop for tea but could not be sure. Finally we give up on finding them and I resign myself to "feel" my way through the Himalayas without glasses. My sight isn't all that bad, but things do get be a bit blurry at times. I might as well get used to it.

We stop for the first night at a guest house in the small village of Dana which is adequate for our needs. A single toilet is located downstairs and across a small street some distance away from where we are staying. Unfortunately during the night, I have a most urgent need to go but have only my mobile to provide light. Once outside my mobile battery gives out. Not wanting to wake the others, I desperately, grope my way in the total darkness, thwarted by a gate that has been closed. I have no option but to take the gate apart. Once inside the yard, where the toilet is located, I grope my way in total darkness to locate it. I know this is indelicate, but I had to feel my way to locate the hole in the floor, not a pretty picture, believe me, but necessity was primary.

We continue our climb the next day encountering steeper slopes and muddy places. We get off the bikes to hike as the drivers roar forward up the steeper inclines. The sun is out and my excess clothing becomes too warm, which I begin shedding. It takes a while for me to acclimate to hiking in this altitude, requiring frequent stops. Manish gives me a large clove of garlic to insert between my teeth and cheek to suck on as I go, maintaining that the garlic will help me to avoid altitude sickness. Apparently it worked. Manish checks frequently to see if I or the others have headaches or other symptoms, but everyone is fine. Should any of us develop such symptoms, our only choice will be to make a descent, even if it occurs during in the middle of the night.

Higher up, we pass through the city of Jomsom where, surprisingly, there is an airport. It may be one of the highest in the world, but also one of the most dangerous. Small planes bring trekkers here and must arrive early in the morning before mountain winds gear up. The wind here gets squeezed between the surrounding mountains and grows quite fierce by mid-afternoon, making it dangerous for aircraft. Fortunately, we are going with the wind and not against it.

This area is extremely dry. Silt deposits leave a fine powder, which when stirred by every truck or bus that passes us, penetrates our clothing and gear. We wear protective cloths over our noses. We pass through a series of small villages, whose people subsist on farming small patches of land near the river. Water running down from the mountains provides the necessary irrigation. From Jomsom, the road follows the riverbed over rounded pebbles, hardly resembling a road. I hope Manish knows where we are going. By late in the afternoon the winds become much stronger. Shadows darken the river valley. I am thinking that this would be a desolate place to be stranded, but Manish seems to know the way. From the river bed, we again ascend until we come to the village of Kag Beni, where we find lodging for the night at the Asia Guest House. Temperatures plunge sharply as night descends. The hosts serve us in the kitchen before a small fire shared with the Nepali family who runs it. They bring heavy quilted comforters for us to sleep under; we huddle close together for warmth. It is a cold night.

We are served breakfasts of omelets and toast as we watch two mothers busy getting young children ready for their school day. Our next ascent is a sharp one, requiring a good bit of hiking on my part to reach the plateau that will lead us to the village near *Muktinath*. The road is quite steep and I have lost the hiking stick I had purchased for this trek. The arid terrain adds to the difficulty.

Young Men after run through Muktinath Temple's Icy Fountains

Eventually, we are able to reach the famed *Muktinath*, high in this remote area of Nepal at 3800 meters. The temple sets above the surrounding villages, occupying the base of the higher snow-capped peaks beyond. We climb the final steps to gain entrance through an arched gate. The temple is a small one, but notable for its feature of 108 flowing fountains of icy water cascading from the mountains above. The fountains form a semi-circle behind the temple itself. Pilgrims come to run the gauntlet through the icy water, where icicles and icy patches form where the cold waters fall. Once the pilgrim runs through the fountains, he makes successive dips into two cold water vats just below the temple. A few young men from Kathmandu have just made the run, and they urge me to do the same, though I at first say no. Then I begin to reason that I have come this far, so why shouldn't I? I would regret later not having made the attempt. Either I am game or just plain stupid. I strip to my underwear and head for the icy fountains as my friends capture the run on video. Icy waters hit my head and shoulders like daggers as I make it around, being careful of my footing because of the icy conditions. The fountains' spouts are too low for me to stand erect and I have to hunch over as I go. Completing the semi-circle of fountains, I head for the two vats of water and plunge in each with its brutally cold water, hollering loud enough to wake a Yeti, but feeling good once I've done it. There is no towel for drying, so I stand in the warm sunshine for a time. Fortunately, I have a dry pair in my pack to change into. The young men are pleased that I actually did it. Once dressed, we circumambulate the outer temple in a clockwise fashion, ringing the bells. Sonu and Raju prepare offerings to enter the inner temple, which is forbidden to non-Hindus, so I remain outside.

It is a great moment. I walk toward a nearby clearing, offering a magnificent view of the mountains beyond, to stand prayerfully for a moment of quiet meditation, rejoicing at the wonders of creation. These magnificent mountains formed millions of years ago, when the Indian tectonic plate began its slide under the Asian plate, which is still going on. Creation is an ongoing process!

Thanksgiving in Nepal

Thursday 24 November Thanksgiving Day

Adventure to the Roof of the World: Part Two Descent

After some time, we prepare for our descent. I buy Tibetan-style scarves from a young lady as gifts for my daughters back home. Descending goes much faster and easier than coming up. I am amazed by how steep the road looks when going down. Retracing our route provides new angles for viewing some of the most magnificent scenery imaginable. The road is rough but I am glad that we have made this trip. It is too soon to relax, and I pray that our bikes hold up in the rough terrain without mishap, especially along the more desolate stretches.

We make it to Jomson in time for lunch, after which we continue down along the cascading river to the village of Tokche, noted for its apple brandy, to stay the night at a small guest house. Magnificent mountain views shine brilliantly, highlighted by the sunset as the evening approaches, and the same when sunrise lights up opposite peaks the morning, making this a most enjoyable stop, not to mention the sweet taste of the brandy.

The long descent continues until we reach Tatopani with its thermal baths. We shut down travel by mid-afternoon, with plenty of time to enjoy leisurely soaks in the hot water. The hot water feels good to our bodies, helping work out soreness from the rough bike rides. Other tourists come to languish in the baths as well. For me, personally, it is the perfect ending for Thanksgiving Day. About this time most of my family and friends back home are putting the turkey on the table. While they enjoy eating turkey with all the trimmings, I am high in the Himalayas, soaking my sore muscles in the warm baths of Tatopani. Life indeed takes interesting turns.

On our final day, we face the challenge of roads made difficult by muddy and slick surfaces, with a single misstep easily land one in the raging river below. Moving through these areas is not easy. I prefer to get off and walk at the more difficult places, so as not to add weight to the bike as it sloshes through the mud. Once through that area, we make a most welcome stop for tea at the same place we had stopped when coming up. Imagine my surprise when the lady of the shop greets me, holding high my glasses! I am relieved to get them back. I had left them there instead of their being lost in the depths of a mud hole. My friends don't know whether to hug me or punch me in the nose. I will get a new pair when I get home. For now it is a relief to continue my journey, this time *in focus!*

Safely back to Pokhara, which is much colder than before, we express our gratitude to have made it back in one piece without major mishap. So much could have gone wrong, but as in life one goes for the goal and takes whatever comes. Better to reach for the stars than to sit cautiously by. Incidentally the stars in the dark nights of the Himalayas provided one of the most brilliant views anywhere on the planet. They are truly wonders to behold!

Travel Tip: Never Pee on Boot of a Soldier with a Loaded Gun
Sometimes learning comes about the hard way, the little lessons along the way to keep the traveler safe. I learned a valuable lesson in Pokhara our last night there. The lesson was "Never pee on the boot of a soldier with a loaded gun." Good advice let me tell you!

We had rowed our way across the beautiful lake called Fewa (pronounced Feva) late in the afternoon following our strenuous trip down from the high mountains. We enjoyed snacks and hot drinks at a restaurant overlooking the lake, relaxing until nearly sunset before starting back across the lake in our rowboat. It is completely dark by the time we reach the other shore, in fact it so dark that we practically grope our way up the hill.

Thanksgiving in Nepal

Rowing Lake Fewa at Sunset

I have to "go" really badly, and in the darkness I make out the dim outline of a high wall just ahead of us and head for it. It's not unusual in countries like Nepal to take care of nature outside, along the road or wherever you happen to be, so I think nothing of it.

Just as I unzip to do my business, a strong voice yells out in front of me, sounding quite serious as a warning. It is in Nepali and I don't know what was said, but I instinctively "retract" before relieving myself. My friend Raju yells at me "Keith, get away from there." It is then that I dimly make out the form of a soldier with a gun, standing in front of me in the darkness, less than two feet away. I had been about to pee on his boots! I didn't realize that the wall I sighted was part of a military compound and the soldier in front of me was stationed as a sentry on duty. What had been so urgent, the moment before, was now scared back in me, and I was able to make it all the way back to our hotel to use a proper toilet.

We laughed about what might have been, even if the sentry was not amused.

I thought of possible newspaper headlines for the next day: "American Tourist Shot While Peeing on a Nepali Soldier!" Talk about embarrassing, not to mention dangerous. It could have become an international incident. So be careful out there, travelers.

Fortunately our last day in Pokhara is otherwise without incident. We take a mountain of our dusty, dirty, mud-soaked clothing, including our coats to be laundered. They charge by weight and this laundry cost us more than the hotel room, but we again have clean clothes after our five days on motorbikes. I go for a shave and a massage at a local barbershop. The massage is thorough and my aching muscles feel much better afterwards.

I will be more careful with soldiers I encounter in the future. Lesson learned.

Sacrificing Goats at Mountain Temple
After a night in Bandipur, we again visit the mountain temple of Manakamana on the way back to Kathmandu, reached by cable car crossing the river and up the steep mountain, this time in the company

of goats, chickens and an occasional small buffalo to be sacrificed at the temple there.

We check into a guest house atop for the princely sum of $5 for four people and stroll about stopping for tea on a remote side street in a small garden out back where fresh produce is raised. Corn cribs are mounted on poles hold the crop already gathered. Marijuana plants grow tall on these slopes and in backyards quite commonly here. We drink chai as Raju harvests some for his use.

My friends prepare offerings to be given at the temple for a day of special sacrifice. By the time I join them, long queues have formed, snaking their way toward the small inner temple. Bells ring and chants fill the air. The temple is constructed in typical multi-roof fashion, with supporting beams on which are carved sexually explicit representations of fertility. People approach the square in front of temple pulling reluctant goats who bleat repeatedly. Sacrifices begin about 8:00 a.m. after special prayers and chants are made. A priest comes to the place of sacrifice and chants there for a moment. I am invited to enter the actual sacrifice area to observe close up, and I do mean "close up." The first offering is brought, which is a basket of eggs. Each egg is pierced by the priest and part of the egg is thrown on the altar. The first goat is brought, a black one. His head is pulled back and a sharp knife swiftly severs it. The head still flicking its ears rolls to one side to be quickly picked up and placed on the altar. Blood gushes from the goat's torso almost hitting me, but I quickly step aside. It is a gruesome sight even for this farm boy, who helped butcher animals on our farm growing up. The next goat is brought, a white one. By now I have had enough and make my way past the line of waiting goats back to the courtyard.

Good bye Nepal
The bikes are dirty and in need of repair, when we return to Kathmandu. Manish's bike is taken completely down, bearings replaced and a general tune-up, along with a thorough clean-up.

Distant Lands

For my last full day, I visit my friend Lokman at the Kathmandu Prince hotel, who has invited me to have lunch with his family. Getting there develops into a series of "let's see what else can happen?" Manish had gotten something in his eye at the bike repair shop, which suddenly gets worse so he turns around to return home unable to see well and calls his brother Sonu to pick me up and take me for my lunch appointment. Sonu gets caught in Kathmandu's impossible traffic and is nearly an hour late arriving. We start once again, when a large screw punctures his tire and we have to push the bike to a bike shop to repair the tube, which they say will take about five minutes but we are not so lucky. The tube is damaged too much to be repaired and we have to send for a new tube. Twenty minutes more goes by before we get the new tube in place and on our way again, only to encounter Kathmandu's traffic in a snarl! By the time we reach the hotel, I am two and half hours late. Lokman takes it in stride of course and we mount his bike to go to his house, where his lovely wife waits for us and warms lunch again. It is good to see this dear family.

The two girls, Luna and Lena are away in school, but return a little after four. They've grown a lot since I last saw them. Shy at first, they tell me about school and both are doing well. I give them chocolates as a gift and we relax awhile before Manish, who is feeling better by now, comes to get me, and takes me to a local outdoor place, specializing in a hot local drink of boiling hot water poured over millet seeds to drink through a filter for its sour and sweet taste.

My suitcase contents having grown steadily. Packing for departure, I succeed in getting most everything stuffed in, but leave my bike helmet for Manish to use with other guest trekkers. After bouncing up and down on the suitcase a few tunes, we get it zipped. If there is an explosion on the airlines, it will be my suitcase coming apart!

I will miss Manish and his family. They have been good to me. Nepal has been an adventure, every bit what I had hoped for. The Himalayas hold a special magic for those who trek its slopes. For a send-off gift, Manish gives me a recording by Bob Seger called "Going to Kathmandu."

Saturday 3 December
Briefly Bangladesh
The sun is setting when the plane touches down in the capital city Dacca by English spelling and Dhaka officially. Bangladesh is barely above sea level built among the marshes and inlets of water visible from the plane as we taxi to the large airport.

Twenty years ago in Berlin, I had befriended a Bangladeshi whose luggage had been delayed. He needed a ride to the Berlin airport to retrieve the luggage. I was on my first trip to Europe and had rented a car for a week's adventure driving around Germany without plan. It was shortly after the Berlin Wall had come down. I had driven through parts of East Germany on my way to Berlin and was staying in the same guest house that the guy from Bangladesh, a diplomat, was also booked. It became a comedy in our attempts to find the Berlin airport without the benefit of maps. When we would stop along a street, Mr. Bangli would jump out of the car to ask someone for directions who often did not understand well and then he would have trouble translating them for me but we eventually made it in spite of the comedy of errors. With gratitude he offered to buy our lunch if we could find an Indian restaurant. Have you ever tried to find an Indian restaurant in Berlin by chance? We gave up of course and I took him to a McDonald's which I knew about at least. It was a mistake. To this day, I can still see him spitting ice from his coke onto the table and I'm sure it was the most miserable meal he ever attempted to eat. I still wonder whatever became of the Bangladeshi man.

After a lay-over of six hours, we board another Bima Bangladesh aircraft for the flight to Kuala Lumpur. Malaysia filled with workers for Malaysia and the same three Westerners, including me, who had been on the flight from Kathmandu.

Sunday 4 December

Losing My Journal—Santa Claus comes to Kuala Lumpur
We arrive in Kuala Lumpur in the wee hours of the morning, to an airport that is new and modern. I gather my bag and head outside to find a taxi, but first stop at an ATM to get local currency, placing my travel journal on top of the machine while I operate the keys. The machine gives me difficulty. A taxi driver steps up to help, distracting me. When I leave the machine, I forget about the journal and fail to miss it until I am in the city, quite some distance away. I am sick about the loss of an important part of writing about my travels. The taxi driver drops me at my hostel and leaves before I discover that the gate is locked and the buzzer does not work. The phone numbers I have for the hostel are not correct. Here I am stranded in the middle of the night in a strange city, not exactly a new experience for me. I spot another guest house nearby with lights on and go there. They have a room available, which I book immediately, not worrying about losing my $5 deposit that I made for the other place. Mostly, I regret the loss of my journal.

Kuala Lumpur is a modern city on the rise, literally. Tall buildings are everywhere with new ones under construction. With its famous twin towers, it recently boasted the tallest building in the world, until Dubai topped it this year with its needle-like structure, which I had seen earlier on this trip. Business is booming. No recession here. Highways are modern and crowded with automobiles.

Malaysia is predominately Muslim, about 60% with maybe 20-some per cent Buddhist, 10% Hindu and 8% Christian. Sidewalk cafes are busy with customers. Kuala Lumpur boasts, along with New York City, being the "City that never sleeps." Clubs and bars do a hopping business all night long especially on Friday for the beginning of the weekend.

At a sidewalk café, I review a menu with such offerings as "Clay Pot Drunken Frog" and "Shark Fin Soup." I pass these in favor of prawns

Thanksgiving in Nepal

and green peppers on steamed rice, which is delicious. Southeast Asia is the delicatessen of the world. While I eat, a most strange phenomenon begins to occur, first as a drizzle, then a down-pour and finally a deluge. Rain! I had seen very little rain since the summer. Was it in June or maybe it had been in August. It is rain, loads of it. I fight the desire to run out and splash in it, like a child.

Baptist Church Kuala Lumpur

Distant Lands

Today being Sunday, I make my way to the Kuala Lumpur Baptist Church, near to my hostel. It is my first time to be in a church since starting this trip. I am welcomed at the door by a friendly couple, who greet people as they arrive, who introduce themselves as George and Wendy Liew. They tell me about a special Food Fair the church is sponsoring today to raise funds for an Old Age Home. I buy a ticket for the lunch which will follow the services. Friendly ushers direct me toward the 9:30 English service, where I find a choral group rehearsing. Soon we are joined by about 500 others, many of whom are young people. In all, some 2000 attend various services at this church, with services offered in English, Chinese, Filipino and other languages. It is the third-oldest Baptist church in Malaysia, 59 years old next week to be exact.

We sing "Joy to the World," led by an exuberant praise of young people. I choke up a bit as I join in the singing. After being with lovely Muslim, Hindu and Buddhist people all these months, I get a little emotional hearing familiar songs of joyous faith. Congregational music seems unique among Christians at worship, who have long taken popular songs of the street and other venues—rock, blue-grass, or bawdy sailor ballads and turned them into songs of faith. "Amazing Grace" is an example.

Vacation Bible School children come to sing, dance and to share the results of their week. The kids invite the pastor to join in and he soon is dancing with them. A choral group takes Louis Armstrong's "What a Wonderful World" for a finale to the service, reminding congregants that the world, with all its troubles, is a wonderful place to be celebrated.

The pastor leads the English and Chinese services. As part of his sermon, he sings three songs. Later when I meet him at the lunch, I joke with him about being a singing preacher. One of the members tells me that what he did today was unique, in that he both danced and sang, quite different for him. In his message I remembered him saying,

Thanksgiving in Nepal

"Mistakes are never final. God can use even our blunders to do wonderful things." A good reminder.

After services George and Wendy accompany me to the Food Fair which is held under a canopy outside the church. My ticket entitles me to a variety of home-made cuisine. I join a group at a table and am introduced to NG and his wife. English does not have an easily-sounded equivalent for NG, so he suggests that I call him by the initials N.G. He is a retired diplomat, having served as a diplomat and ambassador in several capitals of the world, from Ottawa to Moscow and finally Warsaw. He is an intelligent and delightful man. We discuss religious liberty issues that the Christian minority here faces.

After gorging on food, George and Wendy give me a tour of the city, including the famous twin towers, which houses a modern mall. George works with contractors and tells me that he had a part in the building of the twin towers. He proudly shows me the marble design in the entry he had put together. Surprisingly I see a Santa Claus inside the mall. Muslim families line up for photos with Santa. I can't resist, joining the line as well. I say to him "Santa Claus in Malaysia? I can't believe it!" He replies with a decidedly American accent "Santa has traveled a long way. Ho Ho Ho." Santa seems quite at home on the far side of the world.

We tour China Town with its kiosks lining the streets offering cheap goods. One young hawker, no doubt with tongue in cheek, calls out "Come get your *genuine-copy* Rolex Watch!" I resist the temptation. We stop at a food stall for a late afternoon snack. Wendy orders fish balls with noodles for me and George brings beer and fries. For a sweet, we enjoy ABC ice cream-cream over ice made with gelatin cubes, peanuts, beans, corn and other things in its base.

The joy of my travel has been meeting and making wonderful friends such as George and Wendy, who have graciously introduced me to Kuala Lumpur.

Distant Lands

Lazy in Malaysia

After biking and trekking last week, I decide this is a good time to be lazy in Malaysia. Maybe it's the heat and humidity, but my life needs to slow down a bit, though Kuala Lumpur is not exactly the slow-down city one might imagine. It bustles with energy and never sleeps, but it's also a good place to slow down too. I read in a newspaper about the below-freezing weather back home, and wipe the sweat from my brow.

I walk around most mornings visiting sites and local malls. They have some of the biggest malls I've ever seen and it is Christmas everywhere. Even street side shops play Christmas music. I hear "I'm Dreaming of a White Christmas," which is unlikely ever to occur in Malaysia.

People represent a rich variety of nationalities: Malays, Chinese, Indian, Nepalese, Vietnamese and Western tourists. I sat last night in a café, enjoying shisha from the Middle East and chatting with a Turk from Izmir, who was cooking lamb and chicken for donner sandwiches. Like me, he'd been all over the world. As in many big cities, prostitution is rampant, with girls hanging from doorways calling out "massage," or old women approaching with offers of a "young girl." Human trafficking is a growing problem worldwide. I see young ladies hanging on the arms of tourists of various ages. While I chat with the Turkish guy, a Vietnamese girl stops to ask the Turk to call her after work. He says to me "Why not?"

There are friendly people. A man talks with me as I walk along the street. He thinks I might be American. He's tells me he is a shop owner and that as a young person he had been taught English by a lady from Colorado, whom he had always appreciated. He complains that he is getting old at 52 and that his legs are giving out. It's a hard life. I tell him I have just come from the Himalayas at age 72.

It's fun to chat with the young men at the hostel, run by Pakistanis. One young man worries about his family back home in Karachi. "It's different there now," he says "and dangerous."

Thanksgiving in Nepal

Business is booming. Construction is everywhere, fueled by the market to supply cheap goods to the likes of Wal-Mart. I buy a few "summer-style" clothes to wear for here and when I am in Vietnam, my next stop. Amid the unabashed commercialism of Christmas in the malls with their Santa's and the requisite "Here Comes Santa Claus," I stop to listen to a beautiful Italian baritone rendition of "O Holy Night," playing on the speaker for an audience mostly Muslim.

Christmas is on the way.

Stuck Two Days in the Low Cost Carrier Terminal (LCCT) at Kuala Lumpur Airport

I should have guessed my day might go downhill. To start with I am misdirected for my international flight to Vietnam to the KL International Airport, only to discover that it leaves from the domestic terminal, requiring a bus ride to the LCCT terminal for domestic flights. At check-in, I am informed by the agent that "no-way, Jose" can I fly to Vietnam without a pre-approved visa. She directs me to check a web site where I supposedly can obtain the needed documentation in "three or four hours." The last flight out is at 6:50 p.m. so I think maybe I should be able to make it.

But no!

The website promises the necessary documents by 6:00 p.m. but that turns out to be Vietnam time, which is one hour later for some unaccountable reason, given that Vietnam is east of here. Go figure. Anyway, I hope against hope that it might still come through before the deadline when my flight takes off.

I wait and wait but nothing happens! My emails go unanswered. My flight by now has gone and I arrange a costly (for me) room in the only available hotel near the airport, which I'm told is a "seven-minute walk" away. I call the visa service to speak to the owner, a Mr. Than who answers and says he will check into it. Nothing happens. Finally word comes through at 11:00 p.m. concerning my "rush" visa. Apparently he forgot to send it as promised. When I complain about paying premium prices for the "rush" work, he gets offended and blanks me totally, abruptly cancelling my visa request!

I have to start all over again with another service, which by now is Day Two. Like before, approval is promised about the time the last flight leaves. I hang around waiting, hoping it might come a few minutes early. I have my doubts. Perhaps I should change destinations and by-pass Vietnam, but two of my flights depend on the flight I've booked out of Vietnam. I'd have to eat a lot of airplane fare to make the change, plus the penalties. Catch22.

So, what to do? Nothing, absolutely nothing! Hang out. Wait. Drink coffee at Coffee Bean, which is expensive like Starbucks, which is also available. Eat at McDonald's. Ugh! Watch the throngs come and go. The terminal is like a zoo!

It is life in the slow lane, a "nowhere" lane to be more precise. It is the "joy" of unplanned don't-work-out-everything-before-you-launch-into-the-unknown kind of travel that I do. Sometimes I pay the penalty. Despite such unforeseen down times, for the most part, my travel has always been an adventure. So what's another day spent at an overcrowded domestic terminal in a far-off Asian land, just being myself—ever the wanderer. Yep, finally tonight, too late to fly of course, my visa letter of invitation arrives. Now the airline must accept me as a passenger. I will try again tomorrow.

Friday 9 December

Good Morning Vietnam!
Where is Robin Williams when I need him?

It is early morning when I arrive in Ho Chi Minh City. Locals still call it Saigon. I am two days late getting here, but entry is not a problem

Thanksgiving in Nepal

since I now have the proper credentials. It is hot and humid and I must have looked a little strange leaving the Kuala Lumpur airport wearing my heavy Himalaya coat and two pair of pants. Before I could board the flight they told me that my suitcase was overweight and would charge an additional $70 for it, so desperately I pull stuff out to wear or carry no matter how ridiculous I look. I throw away some t-shirts and toss some of the heavier stuff that I don't need for these tropical climates, but wearing a coat in Southeast Asia? Really!

Entering a new country requires the usual trip to the ATM to get local currency. The exchange rate in Vietnam is 20,000 to 1. I key in 400,000 to the amount column thinking that it should set me up in good stead, but I am not thinking clearly and I am shy by one zero. My taxi to the guest house quickly eats up 200,000 of that. I had gotten only $20 from the ATM, making greedy bankers quite happy in gouging me half the amount for using their ATMs. I should have entered 4,000,000!

My guest house is stuck away in an alley and reservation cancelled since I was two days late, but the owner is accommodating and arranges a nice room nearby at his sister's guest house, with the promise of full use of his house computers when I need them. I stop at a street side cafe for a cold drink and am immediately approached by eager young university students, with an assignment to interview a foreigner, and I look like a gullible candidate. They tell me they are math and business students and quiz me about my travels, my impressions of Vietnam (of less than two hours), and what I did before coming to Vietnam. They kindly invite me to share a pizza with them. They are quite charming students and I wish them well.

I need a barber shop for a haircut which ends up costing 50,000! Hold on, that translates to about $2.50. I am thinking I like these odds. Tonight, I promise myself some *Pho Ga*, Vietnamese for chicken noodle soup, one of my favorites.

Distant Lands

Boating the Mekong River

The Mekong River Delta, about 110 kilometers from Saigon, is the destination of a bus trip for about twenty of us on a tour I booked through the hotel. I get acquainted with a young couple from Scotland, taking a year off from jobs to tour Southeast Asia, Australia and New Zealand, with a possible trip to South America.

We cross the wide delta's fertile rice fields. Vietnam is now Number Two in rice exports (behind Thailand), and surprisingly also Number Two in coffee exports (behind Brazil). We see fields being inundated with water, while others are being harvested. Rice requires a 90-day growing period from planting to harvest, so multiple crops grow each year. The soil is deep and spongey from years of silt deposits brought down from the Himalaya Mountains. I first encountered the Mekong River while in Tibet ten years ago, a very different river there of course. The river flows through or borders six countries on its way to the sea. It is about three times wider than the Mississippi and millions of people depend on it for a living.

Mekong River, Vietnam

Thanksgiving in Nepal

We transfer to a motorboat and come alongside the famed "floating markets" of the Mekong. Each boat offers a particular fruit or vegetable. People come by boat to buy, and when the supply is gone, the boats return to load up again. Houses line the dirty river. People get all their water from here—for drinking (boiled first of course) and for bathing, washing or toilet.

Rice is being processed into its many forms of food and drink, from puffed rice to rice paper and rice wine. Each process is demonstrated for us with samples given the group. We enjoy good candies, made from coconut, which is also demonstrated.

Crossing the wide Mekong to a small, muddy estuary, quite shallow as the tide goes out, we transfer to rowboats to complete our journey to have lunch on an island. The row is worth the effort. We are served "elephant-ear" fish, perched on small table stands, cooked crispy. The server demonstrates how to make spring rolls with the rice paper, fish and fresh vegetables. Delicious! We feast, ride bikes and rest briefly in hammocks before our return.

Fish at the Mekong

It is a three-hour bus ride back to Saigon, but the day has been worth the time and effort. Tomorrow, I will explore Saigon for its history and future.

Saigon: City of Motorbikes
Saigon, or more correctly Sai Gon, is a city of motorbikes. The population of the city is nine million with six million motorbikes and almost a million taxis. There is a constant "hum" from the sound of the bikes. Most are the small, lighter versions, since cars are horribly expensive because of import duties, so motorbikes are the only feasible means of transportation. Motorbike traffic involves the art of choreographing. I watch at one four-way intersection which is without traffic lights, as several lanes of traffic converging each way. No one stops. The traffic dances its way through the intersection from four directions, without mishap, only slowing slightly. When you cross a street you just insert yourself into the traffic, being careful to be predictable in your movements so that bikers can weave their way around you. It's scary but doable.

I visit a very fine museum of the history of Saigon dating from its earliest times. Young couples outside are using the classic old structure as a backdrop for wedding photos. Being a Sunday, it is in full use. One of the favorite poses is beside an old classic car, parked outside for an interesting prop. The museum includes the artifacts of war—American helicopters, tanks and downed fighter jets.

Since it is Sunday, I attend services at the central and magnificent Notre Dame Cathedral. The place is packed. Acoustics are phenomenal and the choir is superb. Unfortunately I arrive after much of the music is completed, but I do hear a fine sermon delivered by the retired former chaplain of the University of California Irvine who is now serving sabbatical in Vietnam. He tells a great story at the end of this homily about a blind boy who sells apples on the street to help his family. A motorcycle hits the apple basket and the apples scatter into the street.

Thanksgiving in Nepal

Vainly the boy tries to retrieve them. A man sees what has happened and gathers the apples for the boy. The boy in gratitude raises his hand to feel the face of his benefactor. The boy asks "Are you Jesus?"

The Presidential Palace of the former South Vietnamese president is an interesting place to visit. They still have the helicopter in which he flew, fleeing the country after the 1975 capitulation. The palace is now called "The Reunification Palace."

Next I visit a "War Remnants" Museum, containing many of the machines of war left by the U.S. military, millions of dollars' worth of equipment. Inside photos are displayed of the savagery of the war, including pictures of the use of defoliants from "agents pink to orange." Photos of maimed civilians and of deformed children are on display. I also have seen several such children. Another section details "War Crimes." I am taken aback by a display showing the captain of a Navy Seals team, who entered a village one night and disemboweled all the residents, men, women and children. Only one girl survived to tell what happened. The Navy Seals Captain's photograph is identified. It is a man, later to become a U. S. Senator, no doubt elected for his "heroics" in Vietnam. War is savagery unleashed. Of the three million Vietnamese killed in the war, two million were civilians. The displays are one-sided for sure. There were plenty of atrocities all around. Vietnam later went to war with Cambodia, infamous for the "killing fields." I feel sick by the end of this visit. My camera gets stuck and I cannot record more photos, which is probably for the best. Those who support war should witness first-hand the savagery of what they so quickly advocate. Walking the streets of Saigon later, I see men of about 40 years of age, without limbs and begging. The people I've met have been most gracious to me and I've felt no animosity toward me as American. Perhaps those horrible days have receded in memory. More likely, it is a new generation which has come on the scene without that memory. Vietnam is a young country.

Distant Lands

The motorcycles keep humming by.

I check out of my guest house, paying the princely sum of Two Million Two Hundred Thousand! Don't worry. That translates to about $110 USD for four nights, including the tour package to the Mekong Delta. My newspaper today cost Ten Thousand.

Friday 16 December
Hong Kong, Hong Kong

Hong Kong: Ultimate Urban Environment

Hong Kong is urbanity in its ultimate form. Everything is vertical. Tall commercial buildings define the skyline, thousands and thousands of skyscraper apartment buildings and millions of people crowd into a small space at the edge of Hong Kong Island and across on Kowloon Peninsula where I am staying. Hostels of the budget variety are located in "mansions." Don't be put off by that word. It simply means building. A single building like "Chung King Mansion" where I am staying is home to dozens of hostels, sandwiched between various floors offering rabbit-warren-size rooms at reasonable prices, reasonable for a large modern city like Hong Kong that is. Mine is clean but I have to be careful when I turn around in it. The bath is "ensuite" which is fortunate. A shower hose is located above the toilet, a common arrangement in these parts of the world.

Hong Kong is easy to navigate actually. Its infrastructure is modern and one of the best in the world. You can buy a card to use for the metro trains and buses to take you to all parts of the city. Everything is up and down, but there are hundreds of escalators in the city, and moving sidewalks outside that take pedestrians up the steeper slopes. Abundant and well-attended city parks provide a necessary escape for this country boy from the steel, glass, glitter and crowds of the city.

Hong Kong is a shopper's delight and at this season is sold out. I have real trouble finding places to stay, especially this weekend, requiring me to move to a different hostel where I pay New York prices and it doesn't look as clean as the one I left, but it beats being on the street. The stores are modern and actually spacious, filled with people shopping in droves. It is the Christmas season, so everything is decked out for Christmas.

I connect with a friend I had met two years ago, meeting him quite by accident at a pub where I went for a sandwich and he still remembered me. He has two days off this week to show me around Hong Kong.

Hong Kong Harbor

Louis takes me to the city of Stanley. Stanley is the original British settlement on the far side of the island on an inlet, a quaint little town of slow pace except on week-ends, when shoppers come from the city to shop in the street bazaar. It is quiet on this Thursday and the sun is out. We walk around and shop a little before enjoying a lunch by the bay. The wealthy have houses here. Mercedes are the common car on the streets. Stanly is also where British administrators were imprisoned during the Japanese occupation of WWII.

My hostel on Nathan Road in Kowloon is a multi-cultural maze of Chinese, Middle Eastern and African peoples. Tailor shops are everywhere. Cheap copies of watches are hawked loudly each time I walk along. McDonald's, Burger King and KFC have multiple outlets. In fact the nearby McDonald's is spacious, clean and busy, becoming one of my restaurants of choice. There are many Chinese offerings in the area, so I mix it up. My won ton soup last night was good.

Last Day in Hong Kong
I awake Sunday morning to a clear day in Hong Kong and my last day here, the finale of my third around-the-world adventure. I head home tomorrow, after three months and two days of travel. I am ready to go home, though I will stay only four short days, before hopping on a plane for Pittsburgh to be with my oldest daughter and her family for Christmas and New Year's.

The Tsam Tsha Tsui Baptist Church is located nearby on Kowloon Peninsula. Their English services start at 8:30, which I enter while the services are in progress. At a fellowship over tea and coffee after the services, I visit with a businessman, a banker by the name of Alex, who divides time between Toronto and Hong Kong working for the Canadian Nova Scotia bank. He calls Hong Kong his home.

After church, I enjoy a Sunday afternoon stroll in Kowloon Park, take a ferry ride across the bay to Hong Kong proper, among people out for strolls, doing martial arts, painting or relaxing in the sunshine. The weather has been cool and a jacket is required. I enjoy the ferry ride across the bay and have lunch at a French restaurant.

It's time to return. I repack my suitcase, hoping the airlines don't hassle me about the weight. I make one final move, returning to the original hostel for another postage-stamp sized room. Hong Kong has been booked full, making this the fourth time I've had to move in order to obtain a room. That's what I get for not booking ahead. Who'd thought December was such a prime travel season here!

Of the world's large cities, I have to hand it to Hong Kong for how it has managed its growth and development. It has the best infrastructure around, making the dense city fairly easy to get around on the Metro Transit system, ferries and buses, all crowded of course. Were it not for the nice parks I'd go nuts.

Heading Home
My course takes me north over China, just to the west of North Korea. About the time I am flying over, North Korea below is announcing the death of Kim Il Jong, North Korea's volatile dictator. I recall the time when I passed over Pakistan at the time Osama Bin Laden was meeting his reward, making this my second momentous fly-over. We continue over Siberia, Alaska and down over Canada into Chicago, arriving precisely at 8:30 a.m on May 19, having left Hong Kong precisely at 8:30 a.m on May 19. Fast flight, huh? A blizzard is howling in the western part of our state. Something about my returns seems to trigger the weirdest of weather.

The immigration official in Chicago looks at my passport, with its many stamps and says "Welcome home." It is a nice touch.

Part Three
2012 Multiple Deserts, Weddings and the White House

"The traveler was active; he went strenuously in search of people, of adventure, of experience. The tourist is passive; he expects interesting things to happen to him. He goes sight-seeing."
–Daniel J. Boorstin

Except for a trip to Egypt, my travels in 2012 were prompted by the weddings of several dear friends in India. I go first to Egypt, however, still in the midst of its "Arab Spring." I want to reconnect with friends there. The weddings later in India turn into a marathon of six consecutive events, testing the physical and emotional endurance of this 72-year-old traveler.

1

The Deserts of Egypt

Tuesday 10 April 2012
Edmond Oklahoma, **USA**

Off to Egypt
A visit to Egypt at this time could be problematic, for they are still in the throes of the Arab Spring. Perhaps things will remain calm enough for me to make it through. Numerous Arab Spring demonstrations of late have transpired throughout the Middle East.

First Night in a Tent!
It is late afternoon by the time I arrive at the Bedouin Hostel in Old Cairo. The shops are filled with local Egyptians. Posters line the surrounding walls celebrating the revolution in Egypt that so recently overthrew Hosni Mubarak. Conversations at the tables concern these recent events; mostly there is a feeling of triumph. I enjoy a late lunch at the hostel Egyptian-style with the young staff. My friend Karim sends word for me to come to Giza tonight. Giza is located on the west side of the Nile where his brothers operate a stable of camels and horses for tourist safaris to the nearby pyramids. Young Hamid is assigned to accompany me by taxi to Giza. Navigating Cairo traffic is an experience in itself. Reaching Giza, we turn from the main road onto a familiar alley leading to the stables where Karim is waiting to receive me, seated inside a Bedouin

tent on the stable grounds. It is a new addition. Karim motions me to sit with him one of the cushions, while he introduces me to friends gathered in the tent and orders a feast for a late night dinner—Egyptian flat bread, various vegetables, and cheeses and chicken, all eaten by hand or scooped with the flat bread. We banter back and forth, catching up on each other's lives. Karim suddenly announces that I am to stay the night in the tent to be ready for a camel ride to the pyramids in the morning. It is his way, not to ask, just to assume and insist. Hamid is assigned to stay the night with me in the tent and prepares two pallets with blankets to keep us warm on this my first night in Egypt. From past experience, I know I am not likely to see the hostel again, or my luggage, for the next several days. I learned the hard way to pack a small bag of toiletries, medicines and a change of clothes anytime I come to these stables for I never know what's going to happen next, or when I might return. Sleep comes fairly easily, as I am tired from the flights, disturbed only by the sounds of barking dogs and horses kicking against stalls, sometimes waking both Hamid and me. Welcome to Egypt!

Giza, Egypt

Pyramids and Oasis in the Desert
Hamid and a friend Adam accompany me to the pyramids the next morning. Hamid joins me on the camel, while Adam rides on a horse alongside as we make our way down back alleys toward the security gate, which leads into the desert toward the pyramids. Security must be cleared and fees paid before entering. The security officer takes a fancy to my pen and asks for it. It is common in Egypt for someone to express interest in one's possessions, and then to expect them to be given as gifts.

The three of us ride forward into the desert. The pyramids are not that far from the encroaching city. Camels are not the smoothest transportation available and can be a bit of a challenge. No doubt you have heard the joke in business and professional circles describing the camel as a horse put together by a committee. The real joke is that camels are one of the most efficient animals around, perfectly adapted to the desert environment. Score that one for the committee!

The Deserts of Egypt

We climb nearby hills to a location especially suited for photographic views of the pyramids beyond. Hamid and Adam shoot photos with me jumping and holding my hands and fingers just so, for different effects pyramid photos, making me feel like a tourist doing it, but it is fun. I have been to the pyramids before, but always in a hurry before and this time I hope to spend a little more time to really see them. We approach one of "Great Wonders" of the world with awe. A lot of time, skill and back-breaking labor went into their construction. There are nine pyramids in all; the earlier ones are smaller and more primitive. A long Nile boat was uncovered recently at the base of one of the three "Great Pyramids." Archaeologists continue to unearth new wonders.

Adam and I climb part way up the Great Pyramid on stones that are huge and not easy for someone my age. I try to be careful not to fall and injure myself right off the bat. We make it up a couple of levels, high enough to see other tourists meandering about on camels beneath us. The Sphinx is a short distance away, the head of a man or god with a body of a lion, standing guard to the east facing the rising sun. It requires another fee to enter there. Again we take photos for strange effects, such as kissing the Sphinx.

After some time, we return to the stables to find Karim preparing for our trip to el Fayoum, an oasis in the desert to the southwest of Cairo which is also his home village. I had been there before without prior warning or preparation. He tells me that this time we will stay in a resort guest house on the lake, owned by the parents of Semo, one of the clerks at the Bedouin. We soon take off in a van across the desert, from time to time being stopped and inspected by security forces along the way. There is a large lake there, making Fayoum one of the largest oases anywhere. Karim's father-in-law welcomes us with a feast for a late lunch, after which we move on to the guest house located at a resort on the lake not too far away. The house had obviously not been opened prior to the season, for the floors were not swept and the bathroom is grungy dirty. Only the bedroom where I am to stay is properly prepared. There are a couple of couches in a living room, and everyone gathers there for tea and the usual banter among Egyptian men. Toward dusk we another great feast and drinks, with obligatory smokes of the ever present *hashish* quite commonly used in Egypt, putting everyone in an expansive mood with much welcoming words and gestures for me, as if I am visiting royalty, or better yet a long-lost family member. It makes for an interesting evening.

Karim and I break away from the others for a walk down by the lake to enjoy a beautiful sunset. We had come here on my first trip and had eaten fish by the seashore. It was a great memory to recall. When it was time to sleep, he and the others claim the couches and pallets on the floor, while I have the bedroom to myself. At least my second night in Egypt is with a roof over my head, not likely to be the case over the next few days.

Badry Safari Camp somewhere in the Sahara

We buy fish freshly caught from the lake on our way out of town, taking first the road toward Giza, after which we turn west into the deep Sahara Desert. Our ultimate goal is the "white" and "black" deserts though Karim seldom is forthcoming on specific details. It seems as if we drive forever with nothing but desert to look at. I ask "How far?" He doesn't give an answer. This leg of the trip could be several hundred kilometers or maybe as much as 200 miles! He says we will be a couple of hours short of Libya in Egypt's Western Desert. We will make it a two-day journey to reach the White Desert.

After endless sand and rocks, we finally drop down into a valley lush with palm trees and obviously an oasis. After traveling through the endless desert, an oasis is a sight nothing short of paradise! Lush gardens and fields are surrounded by trees with a thriving town in the middle of nowhere. The Badry Safari Camp is located at the edge of the town where I am shown to a thatched hut which will be my room. It even has air-conditioning! Better yet a real shower in a common bathroom a few steps away. Obviously it is a set up for tourist groups. I claim the shower to wash off the desert dust. Karim tells me that we originally were to have joined a safari to the two-colored deserts, but being late we will spend the night and go tomorrow, which gives us time to relax in a large dining area with a gentle breeze to cool us. There are pads for seating at low tables and we are served a late lunch and just hang out until night, when we have our usual late-night dinner. There are only three other tourists present for that meal, a guy and girl from New York and a girl from New Jersey. After dinner we all join together around a campfire. The guy from New York is a musician, who plays in the subways in New York City, if you've ever been there to experience such concerts, which are often quite good. With a little coaxing, he serenades us around the campfire with his violin that he has brought with him. Karim borrows some drums and joins for some lively Egyptian-style music. At midnight I leave the group to get some rest. The desert air is cool enough by now that there is no need for the A/C. Mosquito netting is available to keep me away voracious desert mosquitos, which have already taken a toll on my face. They and the flies are desert annoyances one has to put up with.

Camping in the White Desert
It is hard to pinpoint locations although I know we are traveling mostly west and some south. All we see is sand, rocks and hills as far as the eye can see. Each time we crest a high point in the road the horizon stretches ever more endlessly before us and once that is reached there is yet another and another *ad infinitum* beyond that. I marvel that camel caravans were able to cross the endless Sahara. We are lucky to have a paved road to follow, allowing four-wheeled vehicles access to these nether reaches. On we drive relentlessly—how far I do not know. We pass through the Black Desert, made black by volcanism in this part of Egypt, dating from many millions of years ago. Volcanic cones dot the horizon and beds of black lava spread across the desert sands which are now crumbling and blown about as sand, making it the Black Desert. We plan to explore it further tomorrow morning, so we just pass through today. The White Desert is made white by chalk formations, remnant of an ancient sea which covered this part of Egypt. Leaving the paved road, we head into the sand on a slightly

down-hill slope, threading our way through the eerie sentinels of chalky rock, which gives the whole area an other-worldly appearance. The sand makes for tough going, even for our four-wheel drive vehicle. Our driver keeps up speed for momentum, zig-zaging through the surreal landscape, stopping at a sharp slope for photos, looking over an expanse of white monuments below. We keep moving. The formations include various shapes such as birds, donkeys, and even one like the Sphinx. I insist we stop for more photos only to be disappointed because my camera battery gives out. A young man and his girlfriend from Medellin, Colombia, traveling with us, promises to share their photos with me.

Egypt's White Desert

The Deserts of Egypt

Eventually we stop a spot of sand, surrounded by large columns of white chalk like sentinels, as a suitable site for our camp-site. The driver rolls out carpets, pads and sleeping bags from the vehicle. Wood, which had been latched to the roof, has been brought for building our campfire. Our driver proceeds to prepare our dinner with vegetables cooked in boiling water, rice and chicken grilled over the open fire. While the preparations for dinner are made, the rest of us explore the area by foot. The winds die down, making a spooky stillness as the sun sets behind the columned white pillars standing guard over us. I continue to walk away from the campsite and imagine being alone in this desert, with no one near for hundreds and hundreds of miles. It is an eerie loneliness. The desert now is almost without any sound.

Once the sun sets, it is total darkness, except for the stars which come to dot the sky by the billions. They are visible as I've never seen them before. The night is clear and moonless, leaving me totally fascinated, wishing my Astronomy Club friends could be here to see it with me. No wonder the great religions of the world come from desert backgrounds. One can hardly be under such stars, without contemplating the whole of the universe. I watch way into the night, transfixed by these numerous shooting stars and the wonder of it all.

Back at the camp, the dinner is ready and we enjoy a delicious meal, sitting on the small carpet. An Egyptian fox appears out of the darkness, having smelled our food. Its ears are quite large and the body is small, but it has a fox's tail. We drop leftovers on the sand and it shyly eats, before disappearing back into the darkness.

After viewing the stars for some time, I have no trouble sleeping.

Sahara Desert Storm

A light breeze from the east gives our camping experience a nice temperature for sleeping, not too hot and not too cold. That is about to change as we break camp and start back to the main road. The sky turns a pale yellow and darkens. A desert storm hits in all its fury as a cold front sweeps through. Winds turn to gusts, picking up the desert sands, flailing grains of sand hard against our vehicle, sounding like flying shards of glass as they hit. The sand bites as it hits the skin. We are barely able to see. The vehicle is whipped about. Reaching the paved road, we pass a truck carrying potatoes, broken down on the road. The wind is so strong that it picks up loose potatoes from inside the trailer to hurl though the air like missiles. Potatoes pop about as we pass cautiously. The poor trucker tries unsuccessfully for damage-control. An oncoming truck squishes through the fallen spuds, mashing potatoes with its wheels. The winds are fierce.

When we stop later at the "Crystal Mountain," only we three tourists are brave enough to get out of the vehicle for a quick look. Everyone else stays inside. As we return to the vehicle, drops of rain pelt us, along with the biting sand. It is raining in the desert, but not much and for not long. It may be all the rain for a year, but it is rain nevertheless, insufficient to stop the blowing sand.

At the "Black Mountain" of the Black Desert, we stop again, but do not stay long. We fight the wind and blowing sand all the way back on pavement almost covered by sand, picking up Karim's small car when we reach the first oasis, who then drives fast, worrying me because of the wind and sand, especially each time we meet a truck, with the resulting whip-lash almost hurling us from the road.

My legs are stiff and quite sore from being in the cramped car when we reach Cairo late in the afternoon. I had checked into the Bedouin Hostel five days ago and tonight is to be my first night to actually spend there.

What next? I am not sure. I focus on getting rest tonight, turning down Karim's request to return to the Giza stables for an evening. Enough is enough.

The Deserts of Egypt

Cairo Mosques and Boat Ride on the Nile
I hang out in Cairo for the remainder of my time in Egypt, enough for car rides for a while. I join with two new Australian friends Steve and Jodanna for a trip to Cairo's notable mosques, along with a visit to the ancient Citadel. We have difficulty finding a taxi driver who knows what the English word "Citadel" means. Finally someone is able to translate it as Al Hazra, and we take off to tour two mosques which are both quite ancient and impressive, with columns surrounding an open courtyard; the other is huge, almost to the scale of the Blue Mosque I had visited in Istanbul. We are rebuffed when we try to enter the Citadel, even though we had bought tickets for it, being told that it closes at 5 p.m. and accepts no visitors past four. It is typical Egypt that no one bothered to advise us of this rule when we purchased our tickets.

The Australians go on to other sites while I hire a taxi back to the Bedouin Hostel to join my two young friends, Hamid and Ibrahim, who have promised to take me for a boat ride on the Nile. We hire an entire tour boat, big enough to handle about 20 people and have it all for ourselves. Tourism is off, due to the political instability, and we are able to make a good deal. It is almost dark as we launch out into the Nile for a beautiful cruise up and down the famous river, past large hotels lining the river, listening to the sounds of the river and then Egyptian music, our own party on the Nile. No large tour groups for us!

Wild Wedding in Fayoum
We return to Fayoum, the oasis village to the southwest of Cairo, for a wedding party. Hamid, Ibrahim and I catch a ride on a van to the village, where we move from relative to relative, to be greeted by the men with a double-cheek kiss. At the groom's house we have lunch and then to other houses we are served tea. I think I drank four cups in about an hour at the different houses. The groom's group then loads up into cars, taking us to the next village, where the bride's house is

located. After some ceremonies there, we return as a caravan of cars, with honking horns and driving like maniacs. It is indeed a wild ride! The drivers wobble their vehicles wildly in a zig-zag pattern on the road, with horns honking, racing each other, taking up the whole road, forcing drivers of oncoming traffic off to one side, everybody wildly cheering and honking. It's their tradition. I gasp as a car pulls alongside another and a child is passed from one to another. I hold my breath, not believing it!

Demonstration in Tahrir Square
After a meal and preparations for dancing, Karim arranges a driver to take us back to Cairo, in order for me to catch my morning flight for India. Another demonstration is developing in Tahrir Square on a Thursday night. As we enter the area, our taxi gets stuck in the crowds clogging the streets in a hopeless gridlock. The driver announces that we can go no farther and asks us to get out and walk. The only way ahead is through the middle of the demonstrators. There is no other way to reach our hostel. The crowds are building by the minute, though at this point they are still relatively peaceful, but with time it turns to violence with time with people venting their frustrations. I walk with Hamid and Ibrahim straight through the gathering crowd, trying to be as inconspicuous as possible, though I snap a couple of photos as we walk through. The crowds are chanting slogans and loud speakers are blaring. It is no time to be hanging around, so we hurry through, hoping for the best. Fortunately we make it to the other side without incident.

Given the nature of the wedding caravan and the political demonstration in Tahrir Square, I am happy to be leaving Egypt, while body and soul are still intact.

2

India—Wedding Negotiations

Monday 23 April

Pushkar and Wedding Negotiation

My smiling friend Suresh has come to Delhi from Pushkar by bus to greet me at the early morning hour of 1:00 a.m. We stay at Suresh's friend's house in the sprawl of Delhi giving the driver of the taxi some difficulty to locate. Eventually we find the house and claim a few hours' sleep. The next day, Suresh sets out to buy clothes for family members and later in the afternoon we transfer to a hotel to be near the train station to catch an early morning train to Ajmer near Pushkar. The hotel is nice with air conditioning which helps us cope with the heat. Delhi is already quite warm. Suresh had arranged the train ticket ahead by first class at my insistence. I have traveled general boarding before, which would be more than challenging in warm weather. Trains in India, and for that matter buses, are a contest to see how many people can be crammed into one space. With the heat, I knew it would be too much for me, so we enjoy the good service that goes with first class, eating multiple breakfasts and drinking plenty of chai (tea) before arriving at the sweltering and noisy Ajmer station in the afternoon, where traffic is always pandemonium. Welcome to India!

Distant Lands

This is my fifth visit to Pushkar and sixth visit to India, almost like returning home. Suresh's family gives me a warm and enthusiastic greeting. This is time for serious marriage negotiations for Suresh and his sister Bebu for upcoming weddings. Wedding negotiation requires the skills of seasoned diplomat and Indian families exercise these skills to the fullest. I am asked to sit in on the discussion, though I understand little of what is being discussed. Suresh's maternal uncle and a family friend along with Suresh's mother and Suresh's future father-in-law are the principal negotiators, with conversations taking place primarily between the uncle and the future father-in-law, with Suresh's mother, sitting at her brother's side whispering comments to him, who then conveys them to the father-in-law to be. She is careful to veil her face when talking, and never speaks directly. Finally, the dates are confirmed and arrangements agreed on. There is to be multiple weddings in December. Suresh's sister will marry December 5 followed by Suresh on December 7, and followed by Prashant, Suresh's future brother-in-law, on December 9. Because Indian weddings are elaborate and quite expensive, families carefully find ways to economize without cutting back, and grouping the weddings makes for more efficiency. As a family member, I am expected to attend all of them as well.

My purpose in coming this time is to attend the wedding of Suresh's best friend Mohit, who is marrying within a few days. I spend a day with Mohit, who is recovering from sinus infections but doing better. His wedding plan got complicated when his grandmother of 87 died suddenly on April 4, requiring a period of mourning for the family. They debate whether the wedding should take place, as all for the men shave their heads for mourning, and usually do not participate in party events, but family members decide to go ahead and exempt Mohit from shaving his head. His grandmother was dear to me as well, and I grieve her death.

India—Wedding Negotiations

Mohit's Wedding

It is the wedding season, with the noise daily of bands at wedding processions. We plan to go to Jaipur the day after tomorrow to buy wedding attire, even though I came somewhat prepared, bringing two Indian-style outfits with me, but I will still need proper attire to cover four or five events. Such are Indian weddings.

Housewarmings and Engagement Parties

I go to a housewarming reception for the new home of Navneet's family recently built on the east side of Pushkar. It is a multistory house and is quite impressive. The family has invited a few family and friends, numbering about 300, for what they call a small party. Guests arrive and are shown around preceding the dinner to be served on a rooftop floor. Bread is baked in makeshift ovens, fueled by cow patties, which makes a proper fire for baking. There is also an engagement party for friend Papsa and his buddies, an all-guy thing, at a Krishna temple on the mountainside, where we sit chanting and sing in front of the temple, with everyone in a celebrative mood as the singing grows quite loud at times. A disturbed bee's nest had startled some of the early attenders, sending them running for their lives. Other than that, all goes well and we eat Indian style on the floor of a nearby building, before heading to Mohit's house, whose wedding was set to start the next day. We go there to greet two guests from Germany who have arrived, enjoying a time with these friends we had met previously at Mohit's brother's wedding. I stayed with Hank and Honjoerg last year during my trip to Germany.

Indian Wedding
Dressed Indian-style in white, I arrive at Mohit's room, as he completes dressing for the ceremony. He wears a pink traditional wedding suit with stylish dhoti. His brothers are smartly attired in suits with high collars, personally designed by the youngest brother Summit. We go by car to the wedding site, held in a large yard in front of a palace, decorated all around with cloth and a stage accented in pink, for a backdrop for wedding photos. Large cushions at the other end await the arrival of the bride and groom, who then sit for the actual ceremony. The area is carpeted and already filled with family members from both families, sitting in the usual cross-legged position. With fanfare, the bride and groom appear, looking quite smart and lovely. An elder Brahmin conducts the ceremonies, involving prayers and blessings. The elder family members participate, making blessings and commitments to uncles of the opposite family and so on with sisters, brothers, cousins and others. The two families thus become united. A special snack is served during this time.

The park is lined with tables of food served buffet style, with attendants cooking various dishes on the spot. Fruits and desserts are available as well. After the marriage ceremony, a brief break allows the wedding party to leave to changes clothes. I rush back to my place to change from the afternoon white to a traditional gold kurta with turban and

India—Wedding Negotiations

join Mohit and his bride and other family members to make the grand entrance to the grounds, once more making our way to the stage area. As a close friend, I am included with the family. Mohit has changed to a stylish Western suit with pink tie and handkerchief. Interestingly, I the Westerner wear traditional Indian attire, while Mohit and his brothers wear stylish Western clothes!

The bride and groom spend the rest of the evening posing for photographs with family, extended family and close friends, involving a lot of time to be looking into bright lights. I am included in at least four of the photographic sessions. Meanwhile guests enjoy a sumptuous feast and dance to music on a wooden platform, led off by Mohit's brothers. Little kids get involved, and certainly I and Honjoerg and Sandra, their guests from Germany, are expected to dance the night away! The festivities last until past eleven, at the end of which, the bride and groom are fed dinner, with about fifteen waiters on hand to bring anything desired. Various family members dip food and feed the couple with spoons as a gesture of caring for them. Once it is over, the brothers and Suresh help to clear the area for yet another wedding to be held there tomorrow. Graciously, I am allowed to return home to rest up for tomorrow when the groom takes to a white horse, and we dance through the streets of Pushkar.

Mohit's wedding concludes after five days with a dinner party for select friends and family on the evening of May 2. We had started April 28 with ceremonies and the groom's dinner followed on April 29 with the groom's wedding procession through the streets of Pushkar with much dancing before the groom on a white horse. On April 30, the wedding is transferred to the bride's village of Jayal, some four hours distant from Pushkar.

There is nothing quite like an Indian wedding.

3

North India—Himalaya Highs, Trance and Dalai Lama

Trip to Manali, North India

Suresh and I are ready to escape the grueling heat of Rajasthan, each day becoming harder to bear. For my final day, I visit to the village of Nimaj with Suresh's brother Kamal, at the invitation of Suresh's fiancée's family, who show me around the ancient village, its palace and the remains of an old temple. The old temple had been desecrated by Moghul conquerors who took offense at its display of images. Scattered remnants remain suggesting an artfully designed temple of great age. Two-thirds of the structure remains and is being preserved.

We tour Nimaj Palace, itself quite old and available today for guests who want to pay the price. We are shown around and allowed to visit some of the luxurious rooms. I promise a stay there the next time I visit.

After my visit to Nimaj, Suresh and I catch a late night sleeper train from Ajmer to Chandigarh in North India. There is nothing quite like sleeping on a rocking train! We arrive in Chandigarh, the capital of the Punjab at 6:30 a.m., with a day to spare before catching our bus to Manali, not scheduled to leave until 11:30 p.m. We make the best

North India—Himalaya Highs, Trance and Dalai Lama

of the day, renting a nice room in a hotel for the day and hiring an auto-rickshaw driver to visit the sights of Chandigarh. Chandigarh is a model city by India standards. Streets are well-planned and relatively clean, with dust bins available for trash, which help keep their city litter free.

We visit the famous Rose Garden, with its nice fountains and shaded areas and take in a couple of museums of art and natural history. After a rest, we launch out again to visit Chandigarh's famous Rock Garden, the work of a creative and eccentric man who collected rocks of all kinds to fashion into unique rock sculptures. There are surprises at every turn, waterfalls, grottos, creative sculptures, surreal figures, definitely a "must-see" for any world traveler coming to Chandigarh.

The bus ride from Chandigarh to Manali proves quite harrowing. The Volvo bus negotiates the narrow, winding road up the high mountains, narrowly averting being side-swiped by trucks and other buses. Around and around we go, some of the passengers getting sick and throwing up. Luggage is thrown from overhead bins. It is an all-night ride. I peer out at a beautiful mountain valley in dim light to see lakes and gorges. Manali is wonderfully and refreshingly cool after the stifling heat of Rajasthan. As we unload from the bus, Suresh's wallet is dropped or stolen and never recovered, in spite of vigorous efforts to determine what happened.

We spend a couple of days here before joining a couple of friends in Kasol, high up another mountain, before we go on to Dharamsala to see the Dalai Lama. At least that is our hope, whether we see him or not. Manali is a refreshing to escape the heat, one of the "hill stations" of the Himalayas, with their snow-covered peaks towering beyond. It snowed here last week in fact.

Mind Altering Visit to Kasol

After a couple of days in Manali in the crisp air, we hire a car to make our way downriver to Bundihar, then ascend another river valley toward the mountain village of Kasol to meet Honjoerg, the guy from Germany who also attended Mohit's wedding. The road is also quite narrow, dangling precipitously from the cliffs high above the river, as we negotiate turns with other vehicles, requiring some to back up for other traffic to proceed. Nothing stands between us and a sheer drop thousands of feet below. Our driver is not intimidated by any of it, hurling our small car around curves at other traffic, as I hang on for dear life. We arrive in the upper valley with snow-capped peaks towering over us. Traffic in the Kasol is in gridlock as thousands have come for a weekend of cool mountain air and especially to attend "trance" parties known far and wide. Kasol is a hippie's paradise. Young people with dreadlocks and flowing clothing gather in the town, looking more like something out the "seventies," as if a time warp has reversed us to another era. Stores sell psychedelic paintings and t-shirts. In fact, a friend from Pushkar has two such stores here. We visit with Honjoerg who allows Suresh and me the use of his hotel room to stay and plans to spend a portion of the night sleeping in one of the shops. He is here to attend a "Trance Party," something he has helped organize in other places and tells us the party is already in progress, down the river some distance, to continue unabated for three days. He tells me he has attended others in Goa and elsewhere and is quite keen that I go with him to see what it is like. He wants me to join him later tonight to check this one out. It will be a new and quite different experience for me.

There are others from Pushkar who have come to work here and we are soon recognized on the street by several.

North India—Himalaya Highs, Trance and Dalai Lama

Walking Bridge to Trance Party at Kasol

It is late afternoon when we hook up with Honjoerg again. We enjoy an early evening meal together at a nearby restaurant. At about 9:00 p.m., Honjoerg and I set off by flashlight down a dark, rocky trail, cross a suspension bridge over a fast-rushing stream and continue along a rocky trail skirting the raging river which leads toward the party site, hopefully without falling into the river. I admit that I'm a little apprehensive about how to react to all this, but curiosity kicks in, and we proceed. The entrance fee is fairly steep, but Honjoerg talks with the organizer about me. And they let me in free. Everyone is solicitous of me, treating me like some elderly celebrity come to hang out with young hippies at a trance party, high in this remote mountain area. The rocky ground is crowded already and everyone is in high spirits, literally. Small kiosks scattered over a hillside offer food and drinks. Music blares acid rock, loud and thumping, from a hillside of loud speakers. These parties are quite popular among young Israeli tourists. A girl dances while holding an Israeli flag. Hundreds dance in a cleared area under strobe lights, which blind us as we make our way through the crowd to a spot at the periphery where we sit on a rock and observe the crowd. Honjoerg narrates for me the dynamics of the action. Drugs flow freely, with police awareness. They check often, but by tacit agreement they do not bother, allowing drugs to be used inside and arresting only those who attempt to bring them in from outside. We later learn that some of the young men from Pushkar were indeed arrested for doing just that.

Honjoerg dislikes the style of music being played, preferring a softer more lyrical style of the trance genre. He tells me about his experiences over the years with cannabis, explaining how it clarifies the mind, enabling a vivid sense of reality. If friends back home could only see me now, sitting in the wilds of the Himalayas, steeped in the world of the psychedelic, they would be shocked or envious depending. It is an interesting experience I have to say. Honjoerg takes time and prepares his smokes. We sit for a while, and when my curiosity is fully satisfied, we head back, stopping to chat with the guys guarding the gate, who again treat me like some kind of celebrity. Don't worry. One trance party did not turn me into a hippie. At least, I didn't think so.

By contrast, I spend the next morning on a rock above the raging river, reading from scriptures for my Sunday meditation, reflecting on the soul-altering aspects of faith itself. Yet I was grateful that Honjoerg gave me the opportunity to experience something I had not seen before.

Now, we are ready to meet the Dalai Lama, if by chance, he is in residence.

Dalai Lama in Exile
It is a long, long bus ride through the night up and down high mountain roads to reach Dharamsala, in the Indian Himalayas. The Dalai Lama, spiritual leader of Tibetan Buddhism, fled from his native Tibet

North India—Himalaya Highs, Trance and Dalai Lama

in 1959 after the Chinese took over. They proceeded to kill millions of Tibetans, destroying thousands of Buddhist monasteries in an attempt to stamp out Tibetan Buddhism. The Dalai Lama became their principle target, while still a young man, hardly past his teen years, and he had to flee Tibet for India. Through the years since, he established himself in the world community as a man of peace and spiritual insight, though the Chinese still consider him very much a threat.

I had visited Lhasa, Tibet in 2001 with some of my family. We went to visit my niece Dierdre working there for two years as a nurse at a volunteer clinic, some distance out from Lhasa. Her family wanted to visit and had asked me to accompany them. I remember visiting the Potala in Lhasa, the palace of the Dalai Lamas. We ascended breathlessly the many stairs of the Potala at high altitudes and thin oxygen. Rooms housed burial stupas of the previous Dalai Lamas. One of the lamas who knew Dierdre, gave us a personally-guided tour of the Dalai Lama's living quarters, allowing us to see his throne. It is odd that we were allowed to go there, but the Dalai Lama is no longer permitted.

This Tibetan temple and educational complex where his residence in exile is located is in McLeod Ganj, up the mountain above Dharamsala. Suresh and I stay at a hotel nearby and walk to the temple itself. The narrow streets offer Tibetan goods similar to items that I have in my house which I bought in my previous trip to Tibet. The temple is modest, but interesting. We circumambulate clock-wise around the temple, spinning prayer wheels as we go. The Dalai Lama gives public lectures here. However, he is away at the time of our visit. We are not fortunate enough to hear one.

The village is relaxing with its majestic views of snow-capped peaks. I wouldn't mind spending a few days here but time is marching on. Tomorrow, we must catch a flight to Delhi, so I can connect with my flight back to the USA.

Distant Lands

Thursday 17 May
London, **United Kingdom**

London as the Olympic Torch Arrives

It is time to say good-bye to India as Suresh and I fly back to Delhi from Dharamsala, his first flight ever. In Delhi, we stay again in the home of Manu, Mohit's elder brother, who greets us warmly and we spend a nice evening with his friends. I say good-bye to Suresh at the airport, always a sad occasion.

I stop overnight in London, arranging stay at a bed and breakfast at the Wellington, an aging but somewhat classy hotel near Victoria Station. London weather is unseasonably cool, everyone wearing coats, with me not as much as a jacket to put on. The next morning, I walk to the House of Parliament, not far away and join a tour of Westminster Abbey. It had been some years since I had been inside. So much history has happened since then. Visiting Westminster Abbey gives visitors a full course in British history. No less than 38 sovereigns were crowned here. It is also the burial site of Britain's outstanding scientists such as Isaac Newton and Charles Darwin, as well as England's most noted writers like Browning and Charles Dickens. Services are held in the Abbey on a continuous basis. In fact, one is taking place while I visit. It is still an active church.

The Olympics are coming to London. In fact, the Olympic Torch is due to arrive in England within a few hours. I reflect on being present in Hong Kong when the 2008 Olympic Torch arrived there for its journey to Beijing just four years ago. British television happens to be broadcasting footage of a riot which broke out in Hong Kong four years ago when the torch passed there. It was next to where I happened to be standing at the time, and had it not been for an umbrella blocking the view, I might have appeared in the British news footage. How neat for me, now four years later, to be present when the torch arrives!

Suresh calls to tell me that his family has gathered at the home of his

North India—Himalaya Highs, Trance and Dalai Lama

dying grandfather. My prayers are with them as they prepare to face the loss of a family member.

At Heathrow, I board the American Airlines flight to Dallas/Ft. Worth.

Home
Flying west follows the course of the sun, making my flight from London's Heathrow airport an all-day affair. The plane is clean and service is good. My seatmate is a guy from Pakistan on his way to Plano, Texas to visit friends, his first trip to the USA for which he is quite excited. In the course of the trip, he shares contact information and invites me to visit him sometime. He operates a business in Ludhiana, India but his family lives in Lahore, Pakistan.

It is a little after midnight, in the early hours of May 18, when I get to my house. It is also my sister Gerry's 80th birthday in Colorado. Her children have planned a party and unfortunately I am not able to attend.

Before entering my house, my phone chimes with a message from Suresh. His grandfather has just died. According to Indian custom, the family will prepare the body for cremation and the funeral ceremonies will be concluded within 24 hours, followed by a period of mourning and ending with a special dinner of celebration. Male members of the family will shave their heads. Suresh is sad to lose his grandfather and so am I. He still recognized me when we visited him a few weeks ago.

Travel is a great instructor. I am reading a book by the Dalai Lama I purchased in Dharamsala, offering profound insights into what it means to be human.

Welcome home!

4

Marathon of Weddings

Though I have shared what it's like to participate in one Indian wedding, this trip's narrative tells about participating in a virtual marathon of weddings—six of them in a row. If you are thoroughly rested, join me for this part of my adventure in travel.

Wednesday 14 November 2012
Edmond Oklahoma, USA

Bags Packed
Bags packed. Holiday cards addressed. The planet beckons. The wanderer wanders. Thus I post on Facebook, ready for a new adventure. The sun rises somewhere between Oklahoma City and Chicago, on my way to Pittsburgh to share an early Thanksgiving with my eldest daughter and her family, before returning to Delhi via New York and Paris.

My grandsons Misael and Emiliano are a delight to see. Misael is turning into the typical American teen-ager, voice deepening and wits sharpening. He's fifteen. Emiliano at nine is still the affectionate and curious boy who delights in quizzes and such, offering me a set of trivia-style questions to shoot at him and he answers most of them. Why are kids today so smart?

Marathon of Weddings

We plan our Thanksgiving meal of turkey and all the trimmings, my first Thanksgiving to spend in America in the last four years.

Pittsburgh Pennsylvania, USA

Thanksgiving with family
Thanksgiving is the most American of all the holidays. It is a time for family, thankfully remaining largely free of commercialism. Ours is a traditional Thanksgiving dinner of turkey, potatoes, cranberry sauce and pumpkin pie.

After attending church on Sunday where my daughter serves, we enjoy a quick lunch on the way to the airport to begin my journey. I touch down briefly in New York City and Paris before flying on to Delhi, making this my eighth trip to India, surprising given that I found India the most challenging of all the countries I visited on my first trip around the world. India fascinates and draws me into its spell, like a swaying cobra mesmerized by the flute of a snake charmer. With dear friends living there I am becoming more intertwined than ever. The purpose of this trip is to attend the weddings of my friend Suresh, his sister and his bride's brother. What I don't know at this point is that there will be a total of six Indian weddings to attend in succession! Had I known, I would have doubled up on vitamins!

Namaste dear India.

New York New York, USA

JFK and Paree!
It is a beautiful fall day for flying! JFK's terminal is looking old and worn. What tales it could tell. I meet a couple of guys from Bangalore waiting with me at the gate. These guys are computer experts. One tells me he is an assistant professor of computer science.

In my travels, I had never been to Paris and now all I get to see is from inside the Charles de Gaule Airport, not that I haven't wanted to visit Paris, even on this trip, but unfortunately if I added it as a stop, it would have more than doubled the price of my ticket. So Paris must wait for another time.

The terminal for my departure is new and modern, state of the art in fact. It is early morning and not overly crowded. Outside, the air is foggy and the sky overcast on this cool fall morning. The flight to Delhi is packed with returning Indians. Unfortunately I get an interior seat seriously cramping my style and need to walk around. I'm already butt-sore from my time on planes. This will be a long flight, for Paris is only half-way to Delhi.

Bonjour!

Tuesday 20 November
Days in Delhi
My friend Neeraj has made a trip all the way from Jaipur to greet me at midnight, welcoming me to India, then catching a 6:00 a.m. bus back to Jaipur where I will meet him again in a few days. The days I spend in Delhi gives me time to adjust from travel. I enjoy a wonderful Indian dinner on my first night at a nearby restaurant, where I strike up a conversation with a young man named Anand. We talk well into the night, after which he invites me to walk with him to his house to meet his father. It is so easy to make friends here and find oneself involved with their families; such is the spirit of India. Never mind that I end up in the wee hours of the morning walking the streets of Delhi back to my hotel alone.

For dinner my second night, I meet my niece's mother and sister at a nice restaurant. I have brought gifts from my niece and nephew in northwest Arkansas to give them. Her mother teaches music at a Christian academy in Delhi.

Before leaving for Jaipur, I stop at a clothing shop nearby to select material for a custom-made suit that I have made for me for the upcoming weddings. It is 1:30 in the afternoon when I make the purchase and the measurements are taken. The suit is ready for me and delivered to my hotel before 8:00 p.m. Amazing!

Welcome to historic, intriguing, and lovely India!

Thursday 22 November

Jaipur—The Pink City
An auto-rickshaw delivers me to the train station about a half mile away. It is 5:00 a.m. Once the train starts moving, I worry that I have left my passport in my hotel room and begin a frantic search through my carry-on bag, unable to find it. Panic! Have I left it back in my hotel? Perhaps it is safely in my suitcase, but I have no practical way of checking it while on the train and would it matter anyway, because the train is already moving. I calm down and chill out and hope for the best. The problem is that without a passport, one can't check into a hotel or do much of anything. Sometimes there is nothing to do but just go with the flow. When I get to Jaipur I can thoroughly check my luggage, but for now I tell myself to relax and enjoy the train ride. The first class ride is without the adventure and drama that most Indian trains provide. Believe me I've been there.

The train arrives in Jaipur five hours later. A smiling Neeraj is on hand to greet me. We take an auto-rickshaw to a nearby hotel where I explain my passport dilemma. They allow me to check in provisionally for at least two hours. In the room, I unload my suitcase of everything but still no passport! Panic again! I decide to actually unload all the items from my carry-on pack that I had previously searched on the train. Nestled at the very bottom, I find my passport. Relief! All is well. Traveler's nightmare is over. There will be other times.

Neeraj proves to be an exciting and fun guide as he takes me around Jaipur on his motorcycle. We visit the City Palace created and built by the Maharajah who founded Jaipur. It is an architectural wonder in its own right. We visit the Observatory, a cosmological wonder of the first order, considered among the top ten sites to visit in the world. No wonder. Structures built into the ground and above ground were designed to chart the course of the stars through the heavens. It was built in 1732 quite advanced for its time and still a wonder to behold.

Our visits are without charge since Neeraj's uncle is an official here. Later Neeraj takes me to meet his family. His brother is about to get married and the family issues a special invitation for me to attend his brother's wedding. I will have time enough to return to Jaipur for a few days, so it will be the first of four weddings to attend while in India. There will be more.

Pushkar Camel Fair and Ceremonies
Arriving in Pushkar on the 23rd I am greeted at the Ajmer train station by the ever-exuberant and smiling Suresh my dear friend from the time of my first visit to Pushkar in 2009. This is my seventh time in Pushkar and will be my fourth visit to the famous Pushkar Camel Fair. We make our way over the mountain to Pushkar to deposit my luggage in a room before we go to be greeted by his family. The Camel Fair is just beginning. A colorful parade winds its way through the narrow streets littered with flower petals and lined with spectators who cheer as the bands, floats and camels parade by. Camels are brought to the fair from far and wide for sale and trade along with sleek horses and sturdy cattle. Events in the Mela Arena take place each day with cultural dances and music at night. A midway fair of rides brightens the night sky. Crowds grow exponentially each day of the fair. I enjoy making the rounds and find myself greeted quite often by the name "Keith Parashar," my name in India. I am considered part of the extended Parashar clan and have come to attend three of their weddings.

Marathon of Weddings

Brahmin Ceremony

The first is a wedding-related ceremony to attend, a pre-wedding ceremony for Suresh and his younger brother being inducted fully into adult Brahmin status, taking place in their home with rituals, chants, offerings and other significant symbolic actions lasting over two hours. Smoke fills the outer chamber of the multifamily dwelling on its way up to the rooftop. I watch with fascination as the brothers dressed traditionally in white Brahmin *dhotis* begin the rituals. Gifts are brought by family members and presented. Friends crowd around to look on. The women of the household sing before and after the ceremony, taking place around a small fire built on the concrete floor in the center. In one part of the ceremony, the brothers take up beggar's scarves tied to sticks to go out onto the street and beg for money to symbolize their spiritual wanderings. Prayers and offerings are made. It is my understanding that this ceremony is required before marriage.

We travel to nearby Ajmer to buy appropriate shoes to wear with my wedding attire. On the last night before I leave for the wedding in

Jaipur, Suresh and I join with friend Yuvraj for a walk around the town, visiting the fair in progress. We agree that it would be a good idea for me to spend the night with Yuvraj in Ajmer so I can catch the early morning bus to Jaipur for the first of the four weddings. I return with Yuvraj to Ajmer to his parents' home, who are asleep when we arrive at the late hour but get up to greet me. Yuvraj and I sleep on pallets upstairs.

The Marathon Begins in Jaipur
It was last year at the Pushkar Camel Fair that I first met Neeraj and we became instant friends. He told me then of his brother's upcoming wedding and hoped that I could attend. Since this wedding was to be in close proximity with the dates of the other weddings, it has worked out. The wedding actually began yesterday, the 27th of November with the traditional ceremony, but I missed that part. Neeraj seeks my assistance in shopping for a appropriate suit for tonight's ceremony. We visit a shop where he tries on several and we pick a nice suit for him. He is quite handsome in it. Tonight is to be the groom's reception, held in a gaily decorated wedding courtyard with a flowing fountain and a dance floor and stage for taking countless photographs with each visiting family units and sets of dignitaries, including the Minister of Education for the State of Rajasthan, who no doubt has attended many such functions before. When the music starts, the ever-enthusiastic Neeraj pulls me onto the dance floor to join the young set in dancing. I am usually one of the oldest dancers to participate in these weddings, but the youth seem to love my joining them on the dance floor. All is good. I am ready for the weddings to begin and hope I can keep up the pace of events. Perhaps dancing will add life to the limbs and soul to the heart. Anybody who knows me knows that I am not much of a dancer. I just move and jump around feeling quite awkward, but everyone seems little to mind and seem openly delighted by my participation. By the second night, I loosen up a bit as we do more dancing, thoroughly enjoy the occasion. The first night provides a food extravaganza with caterers offering every form of Indian fare and sweets. As

Marathon of Weddings

the night wears on and the dancing becomes more vigorous, Neeraj becomes so active that the inseam of his suit pants splits wide open. He runs home for another pair and returns, but it isn't long before the zipper of that pair rips open too. We're unable to make a repair on the spot so he runs home once again. This time he gets a pair of sturdy jeans. The jeans look smart enough with his jacket and he continues to enjoy the dancing. It is somewhat cold at night this time of year in Rajasthan with only a scarf to add to my outfit, when I really need a jacket. Early in the morning hours two of Neeraj's cousins mercifully take me back to my hotel on their motorcycle. The night air is cold, yet we have had a grand time. Later Neeraj and another friend join me at the hotel to spend the night.

The second night of dancing is hosted only for the groom's relatives and friends as the bride and her entourage relocates to her village to make preparations for their part of the wedding. This time Neeraj's older uncles and others join in, making me not the only over-the-hill participant. Actually the older set is quite good at it. Meanwhile in Pushkar the Camel Fair has come to a close. I can only imagine how hectic that last day was as hundreds of thousands show up for the final ceremonies at the fair and for one of the year's most religious events at the lake. It's a good time for me to have been elsewhere.

Our wedding moves to Niwad, the bride's village on the 29th. Suresh has come from Pushkar to join us for this part of the ceremonies and Neeraj arranges a car for all of us and a few others to make the trip of about sixty miles. Included in the group is a young man by the name of Nimaj who is quite a singer, who once was a contestant in India's equivalent of American Idol, placing 16th in the contest, quite an accomplishment given the population of India. His forte is voice impersonations, which he regales us with various impersonations as we go. The guys stop for some Royal Stag to imbibe on the way, sloshing it on us as they drink from plastic cups on the rough roads. We reach the village of Niwad and stop at a large Indian-style guest house reserved for the groom's family. It consists of rooms and courtyards absent of furnishings, where we gather to dress for the evening, if you can imagine a hundred people vying for the same space and facility, having only one or two bathrooms available. You get the idea. Everyone will sleep on pallets, which are now strewn with the clothes of those trying to get dressed, including the groom who is being outfitted in his regalia. There is to be dancing through the streets accompanying the groom riding on a white horse. Before it starts however, Suresh and I break away long enough to visit the family of his future brother-in-law, whose daughter will be given in marriage and who happens to live in this same village. They receive us at their small house, serving us tea and snacks. I am introduced around.

Upon return to the groom's party, the band strikes up and we set off with the groom and his horse through the streets of Niwad, our way lighted by strings of lanterns held by boys and girls. The dancing is frenzied, especially as we pause at certain points to allow everyone to join in. Yours truly is wishing he had taken more vitamins! This goes on until we reach the bride's venue with kiosks of food set up in a large open area. Again the night is cold but we endure. At 10:30, we return to Jaipur while adding two more passengers to be stuffed in like sardines.

Two-Elephant Wedding in Jaipur
Having finished the third day of the wedding of Neeraj's brother, we attend two weddings of friends of Yuvraj, who has now arrived in Jaipur from Ajmer. The first is a fairly modest affair, dancing once more in the streets of Jaipur with the groom on his horse. Wedding processions create major traffic gridlocks, especially in this city, already known for major traffic snarls, but no one seems to mind. It is just the way it is. In one of the snarls of traffic, I take a moment to meet the groom sitting on his horse as he waits for the way to clear. He seems happy by my presence.

Marathon of Weddings

We break away from this wedding to drive across the city to join the other one in progress, which is quite an elaborate affair, fit for a prince and his bride. Obviously this family is quite wealthy.

We get there just as the groom's entourage arrives riding two gaily-decorated elephants. After finding a place to park our car, we join the groom's entourage entering the soccer-field size courtyard, richly decorated from stem to stern with great fanfare. The groom spots Yuvraj and me and motions for us to join him to be introduced. When the advancing dancers spot me, they grab me by the arm, pulling me into the group to dance in the procession. Movie-style cameras on booms set up to record the groom's grand entrance zoom in on me while I am dancing. When I happen to look up, I see myself displayed larger than life on huge screens set up for the two thousand guests to see. Photographers crowd around to snap photos. As far as I can tell, I'm the only foreign guest present. The groom seems pleased and gives me a big smile as I make the best of my accidental celebrity status.

The bride arrives borne on a palanquin chair by six male attendants, reminiscent of Elizabeth Taylor's grand entrance to Rome in the movie Cleopatra. The groom joins the bride once she is let down to the ground and the two proceed up steps to a columned portico, built somewhat like the top of a wedding cake. I stand nearby taking videos as the whole platform rises hydraulically some twenty feet into the air, while fireworks explode into the night air. The nearby opening salvo nearly deafens me. As the fireworks display continues, the platform revolves slowly allowing the guests to see the couple from every angle. Once the fireworks subside and the couple has exchanged garlands of flowers, the platform descends back to the ground and they advance to the stage where throne chairs are set up for the purpose of taking photos. The wedding is both a reception and a dinner. Three of the four sides of the field are filled with kiosks offering every conceivable food, vegetarian of course. There are barbecued vegetables, South India fare, sweet corn and every kind of conceivable bread, Punjabi food, Chinese

Distant Lands

food, Rajasthani food, nearly every region of India is represented with its unique foods. Jodhpur-clad waiters bring sweet lassies to drink. We feast as we walk from table to table.

It is quite a wedding, costing multiple-thousands of dollars, no doubt. Yuvraj tells me that the father is an internal revenue commissioner, which may account for the wealth. Everyone is gracious and it is a class act from start to finish. By the end of this evening, I have racked up three weddings in Jaipur. It is time to move on to Pushkar for three more.

5

The Pushkar/Nimaj Weddings

Monday 3 December

Pushkar Weddings Begin!
I'm in Pushkar once again to attend three weddings in succession, one each for my friend Suresh's sister Bebu, for Suresh and for his future brother-in-law Prashant. I will give a daily account of the activities of these interconnected weddings as we go. Hindu weddings are filled with ceremonies both private and public, each wedding involves about five days' worth of activities. By clustering family weddings together, the families are able to make some economies of time and money. Little expense is spared in these weddings, which often require a lifetime of saving to pull off.

Day 1: We begin with the immediate family, which includes aunts and uncles and all who live in the same household. With drums beating, we make our way through the streets of Pushkar visiting each relative's house, to serenade and dance for them. The hosts provide chai or cold drinks to reward our efforts. This procession goes on for two hours as we make our way noisily through the narrow, winding streets. Traffic has no alternative but to deal with these frequent processions during wedding season.

Distant Lands

Day 2: We gather in front of Suresh's house to load seven carts' worth of gifts for Bebu's groom's family, everything from sweets to clothing, washing machine to refrigerator, television to water cooler. It is a gift extravaganza. We proceed by pushing the loaded carts, led by beating drums through the snarl of traffic, making a procession toward the wedding grounds, where the first ceremony is held in the early afternoon. Our arrival is heralded by an ever increasing volume of drum-beating announcing our triumphal entry to the grounds, bearing our carts loaded with gifts. Eager hands promptly remove the gifts and place them for display under an awning, where both families gather for the initial ceremony. Did I mention that the gifts included a motorcycle for the groom? Sweets and snacks are served by the groom's family.

A family priest guides the ceremony with the giving of food offerings and various ministrations of blessings. The bride and groom sit on pillows facing the family. The scene is a bit chaotic as people move about and talk among themselves. Photographers move among the seated guests, sometimes stepping on hands and toes. No one seems to be paying attention to what is being said during the ceremony, except of course the bride and groom. Part of the ritual includes the sharing of blessings between various family counterparts—father of the groom with father of the bride, bride's uncle with groom's uncle, bride's brother with groom's brother and so on. I discover that I am not the only foreign guest attending. A young man from New York, a friend of the groom, is also present. It is determined that the two of us should exchange blessings as well. I duly dip my fourth finger into the red paste mixture and apply the *tikka* mark to the forehead of Drew, a PhD student from New York, here to write a book about Pushkar for a doctoral dissertation on Hinduism. In turn he applies the blessing to me.

Once the ceremony concludes and further refreshments are offered, we adjourn until the evening to prepare for the main dinner reception. A compound is reserved for us to put on new clothes for the evening. It is dark by the time we return. A band is already playing loud dance

The Pushkar/Nimaj Weddings

music and a dance floor has been set up. The bride and groom endure hours of photography as each family unit comes to be photographed with them. Bebu appears quite shy and nervous. I catch her eye, giving her a big smile and she smiles in return. Generally brides show little emotion during these sessions.

Dinner is served on the ground on lines of cloth spread for seating, served by young boys with buckets to dip dahl and other foods into plates and hand out chapattis (bread) or sweets. Hundreds are fed in this manner in a relatively short time. We take to the dance floor for a few minutes, much to the delight of the young people. Drew shows up and joins in the dance.

When all the guests have been fed, all the photographs have been taken and all the dances danced, the bride and groom are seated to be fed by the hands of close family members, whether or not they want to eat a particular item. It's all in good fun. We adjourn for the night to the family compound to the rooms reserved for us, to sleep in groups on pallets spread on concrete floors.

Tomorrow, the scene shifts from the groom's family to the bride's family.

Tuesday 4 December

Gifts and Dancing on Day 3

The scene shifts to the bride's family (that's us!) at the place we are all housed in a compound of rooms opening onto a courtyard which is part of a temple complex. A large number of the bride's extended family has already come from Jethana the farming village of the mother's family. Today involves receiving gifts from the groom's family which have arrived in a sealed trunk weighing several pounds. We sit on mats and listen for our names to be called, whereupon we advance to the center of the room and sit on a small platform. A *tikka* blessing is applied to our foreheads and the gift is received. In my case, it is money

Distant Lands

but for most it is a combination of money and clothing. There are also gifts of gold and jewelry for the bride, all duly recorded by two elder uncles of the family. The process of gift giving has gone on between the two families since the engagement ceremony held some months earlier.

Family and friends continue to gather for tonight's venue, a dance competition of the bride's family, involving mostly the young children and teenagers more than the adults. Occasionally an adult performs a stylistic dance for the group. Some of the kids are quite good, showing the influence of Michael Jackson on some of the dance routines.

Today happens to be Suresh's birthday and we have arranged a birthday cake to be brought from Ajmer. Toward the end of the dance program, we beckon Suresh to a table, where the cake is presented and the candles are lighted as we sing "Happy Birthday." He cuts the cake and feeds the first pieces to his parents, his sister and then to me. At that point I take a piece of cake with lots of icing and smear it on his face, opening the door for the others to come and smear him with birthday cake. It is a tradition that I had discovered by experience in my own birthdays and is all in good fun. Later, I help Suresh wash the cake and frosting messing up his resplendent wedding attire.

Toward the end of the dance time, they call me forward and demand that I sing a song in Hindi. Those who know how badly I sing will wonder why, but I am game and sing the first bars of "Tere mast mast donain..." which seems to thrill them. They insist that I do a solo dance, but again that is not my forte, and I get Suresh to join me while they joyously twirl cash above our heads for the musicians grab, also a custom.

Tomorrow is the big day for the groom's procession by horse, as well as a sad day as the bride leaves her family to move into the groom's household.

The Pushkar/Nimaj Weddings

Wednesday 5 December

The Two Weddings Merge

Day 4 of Pushkar Weddings: Just when I think I have things figured out, they take an unexpected turn for me. I was so caught up in the sister's wedding that I forgot that my friend Suresh's wedding starts this afternoon with a ceremony of the couples involving the two families exchanging blessings and vows. This occurs while his sister Bebu's wedding enters its final day, which by now becomes the merging of the two weddings, like two streams converging. It all begins again with great fanfare as Deepika the bride and her family arrives to fill the wedding venue courtyard with a new set of people. Gifts are brought and displayed as before, and we sit once again to watch the ceremony and to receive gifts and blessings. The groom, Suresh—can you keep up?—circles through the crowd afterward touching the feet of each guest as a sign of respect and receives from them gifts of money. Giving 50+1 Rupees is considered a lucky gift. Suresh's friend Mohit and I are pressed into service as cashiers to collect, organize and count the money which totals to approximately 70,000 Rupees.

Meanwhile at the other wedding, preparations are being made for Ravikant, Bebu's groom to parade through the streets of Pushkar on a horse like a reigning Maharajah. This necessitates our moving Suresh's schedule forward, so that the catered dinner and staging of the other couple can be completed before the arrival of the original wedding party. Confusing, isn't it? Suresh gets a facial from a barber brought in, who also gives me a face massage as we dress in our best wedding attire. I wear a gold Indian wedding kurta, while Suresh dresses in a finely tailored custom suit. A catered dinner is served as evening begins, with sweets and hot milk as a feature. While photos are made on the stage, the dancing begins, quite enthusiastic and at times wild. A unique feature for this event is that two clowns have been hired to move among the guests to lighten things up a bit. It is a nice touch and gives this session a happy, celebrative atmosphere. We dance well into the night.

Distant Lands

This will be the night of the long ceremony for Suresh's sister and her wedding party when they arrive later, and it goes on all night.

It is a little before midnight when the sister's groom and wedding party arrive with great fanfare outside the gate of the temple next to Suresh's wedding venue. We go to greet them, the women of Suresh's family bringing gifts to shower on the mounted groom and food for the horse. Ravikant dismounts with great fanfare and enters the wedding venue, led by lively dancers from his family. They proceed to the same staging area, used a few hours before in Suresh's wedding. The young dancers have been dancing in the streets of Pushkar for over two hours but show little sign of tiring or slowing down. Dancing reaches a feverish pitch as the groom ascends to the throne chairs on the stage. Soon we hear another fanfare heralding the arrival of the bride Bebu, who again is looking quite shy and nervous as she is escorted to the stage area for more rounds of photos to be taken.

More dancing ensues and food and snacks are provided to the additional wedding party that has just arrived. I visit again with Drew and his girlfriend Jocelyn. I say visit; the music is too loud for any real conversation. I also meet another friend of theirs named Will who is from the Chicago area, now living in Jaipur, here studying Hindi. It is rare for me to see another foreigner at these weddings. It is a great opportunity for these students to learn a new culture and language.

I find it necessary to retreat to my room from time to time, to warm myself against the cold night air and wrap a scarf around my neck. The ceremonies continue all night, so I steal a little sleep at 2 a.m., only to be awakened at 3:30 for the final ceremonies, where the bride is given over to the groom's family. This part is a very sad occasion for the bride who goes from here to live with the groom's family. Family is such a huge part of the life and identity. She has lived with her parents and brothers, her aunts and their families and now she is being torn away from them. There is a ceremony in which the mother gives up her authority and care for her. There is a ceremony in which the groom attaches a tether to her and leads her away. There is a ceremony where the women of the bride's family give the groom's father a make-over, making him into a woman complete with shawl, lipstick, henna on hands and eye make-up. A child is brought for him to hold in his lap to symbolize that he now must become as a caring mother to his daughter-in-law. The final exodus is quite sad. The bride is distraught. The mother is weeping, along with the aunts, her brothers and, yes, me as well. Finally, the groom and bride depart with great fanfare to a waiting car, fully decorated as they drive away to the groom's household. We are left alone to return to our rooms for a little precious sleep. It is now 5:00 a.m.

The weddings soon continue, however.

Friday 7 December
Dancing the Streets of Pushkar

Preparing Wedding Attire for Suresh

Day 6: After a fairly quiet day recovering from the activities of the two weddings, we prepare ourselves for the grand procession of Suresh's wedding party through the streets of Pushkar tonight. It takes time to get the groom outfitted in his royal Maharajah gear, glittering with gems and royal detail including turban, taking four or five of us to do the job. Once everything is ready, a band of drummers begins a royal fanfare as we march toward the street to the waiting horse. Money flies everywhere as various relatives and friends do the money twirl over him. A young relative is put on the horse with him and the procession begins. The procession includes a generator-powered loudspeaker, a corps of drummers and a brass band. The noise is deafening. I insert cotton in my ears when I can find it, or if not, pieces of newspaper and even rose petals. It helps. If I am not deaf by the time I get home, it will be a miracle. Off we go, dancing feverishly to the loud noise, flanked by two lines of lamps on either side to provide light. It is a challenge negotiating our way through these narrow streets, with traffic trying to continue. Fortunately, it is night and there are fewer vehicles about. We dance and make merry for over two hours, stopping a couple of times for hot milk or cold drinks served by friends. At some of the stops, the horse is made to dance as well, which makes Suresh nervous at first, but he soon warms to the idea of riding a dancing horse. We make multiple stops for the horse to show off its stuff, and continue through the streets until eventually coming to the Ambay Palace Hotel, where the procession ends. After Suresh dismounts, they invite me to mount the horse for a brief turn about the streets.

It is the custom for the groom not to return to his home, so he spends the night in the hotel with a few of his closest friends, including me, even though my things are elsewhere, but I go with the flow. We order food to be brought to the room and banter with each other and the new groom about his marriage. Everyone is exhausted from the multiple weddings and we sleep late. Tomorrow, we go to the village of Nimaj, traveling in a decorated car to begin a whole new series of wedding ceremonies at the bride's village.

In the distance bands are still playing for other weddings. It is the wedding season. The celebrations continue with great enthusiasm.

The Pushkar/Nimaj Weddings

The Wedding moves to Nimaj

Day 7: After spending a night at the Ambay Palace Hotel with the groom and his best friends, we load ourselves into the decorated car for our trip to Nimaj, some two hours distant. My friend Neeraj from Jaipur has come to join us, making eight in the car for the trip. It is a merry group with much to joke about along the way, concerning marriage and life in general.

Nimaj is a very old city contained within walls adjacent to the Nimaj Palace, built by a reigning Rajput some centuries ago. We stop at an Indian Guest House, a large structure with many rooms reserved for the groom's wedding party to board, but will also to accommodate some of the bride's family as well. We are given a room upstairs to begin preparations for Suresh's ride through the streets on a horse. The room gets crowded as every cousin and relative tries to get dressed simultaneously. It takes at least five of us to get Suresh properly outfitted but the effort is successful and he looks the part. I am attired in a black and gold Indian wedding kurta.

Keith Dancing in Streets of Pushkar

Distant Lands

Finally we make a grand procession down the stairs, as we move toward the waiting horse. Once Suresh is properly mounted, the procession makes its way through the narrow streets of Nimaj. The narrowness of the streets, even more so than in Pushkar, enhances the already over-the-top volume of the loudspeaker, the drums and the brass band. I desperately find something for my ears to lessen the sound a bit but on we go with great merriment, winding around streets by the palace and on to the wedding venue next to the bride's house, where we enter and Suresh ascends the stage surrounded by his close relatives occupying the seat that the bride is to use as they await her entrance. Presently she comes forward also with fanfare and ascends the stage. The relatives challenge why she should be given the chair saying "He is our brother. What right do you have to this chair, unless you love him?" Apparently she answers the question properly for they yield the chair to her to sit next to her groom. Photo sessions begin, along with the food and dancing also.

We eat and dance in the cold night air. Luckily a shawl is found for me in the bride's house to wrap around my shoulders.

Once the photos are completed the wedding couple is fed and we join in feeding each other sweets as is the custom. The party adjourns to the bride's house for ceremonies for the rest of the night, with a spot found for me next to a wall, joined by Navneet and Mohit, best friends to Suresh. In the center of the room, a small fire burns, fueled by cow dung. The bride and groom sit on a pillow facing the pundit, a member of the family. By 3:00 a.m. I'm having great difficulty keeping my eyes open and ask to be excused to sleep. A place is found for me not far, where a couple of relatives are sleeping. I'm ushered into the room and crawl under a blanket to sleep, but little sleep is to be had, because once the ceremonies conclude, friends come to gather around in the room to talk. Eventually I get a little sleep and sleep until 9:00 a.m.

The Pushkar/Nimaj Weddings

Wedding Number Six

Day 8: Today begins Wedding Number Six. It is the wedding of Prashant Parashar, brother to Deepika, the bride of Suresh. Don't worry if you can't keep up, for sometimes I have trouble also. This wedding also takes place in the village of Nimaj, the ancestral home of this family. By now Suresh and his bride are on their way back to Pushkar, having completed his wedding by taking the bride to the home of the groom's family. However in this case, they will return tomorrow to participate in the final wedding events for her brother.

I finally get to change out of my wedding attire that I had slept in overnight. My friend Navneet suggests that we get more sleep, which I desperately need by this time. However, my friend Vicky Parashar arrives to take me for a tour of Nimaj on his motorcycle and doesn't want me to miss the opportunity. We travel through the narrow winding streets of the village, as he points out the various gates leading out of the village and in the course of the day we take each one of them. We stop at various shops to introduce me to his friends. It is a beautiful day and the fresh air does feel good as we gad about on the motorcycle. We stop at a temple surrounded by a garden and take photos. We even stop an ox cart for me to ride a short distance, while he shoots a picture. It is a good time and I enjoy the outing.

Later I manage to get a little rest before preparing for tonight's dance venue, which is primarily for the family members. Many of the kids and women have particular dance routines they demonstrate for us. When the groom comes to dance, much to the delight of everyone, he spots me, grabbing my hand to pull me to dance with him and we dance in front of the group. Again, everyone seems delighted, although my dancing would not qualify for Dancing with the Stars by any stretch of the imagination. We just enjoy the moment.

Navneet wisely suggests that we cut the evening short tonight to get some rest. We make our exit a little before 11 p.m. and return to our pallets on the concrete floor for sleep. By now, I desperately need it.

Final Wedding Day in Nimaj
Day 9: This is the big and final day of Prashant's wedding in Nimaj. We eat breakfast with the family and later an afternoon lunch. The wedding venue has been transformed into a new look for the grand finale. Prashant's bride comes from the village of Niwad. (Remember? It is the first wedding I attended.) Niwad is quite some distance, so the family uses the same guest house we do to serve as their home which makes it the destination to which Prashant rides his horse tonight through the streets.

I get outfitted in my best custom-made Jodhpur-style suit, wearing a gold turban this time. The groom is outfitted and the horse is ready. Once again with great fanfare, we accompany him to mount the horse. How many times have I done this? The music is overly loud and cotton is found for my ears. We start the procession through the streets of Nimaj from Prashant's house to the Indian guest house, the reverse of the route taken by Suresh two days ago, when we went from guest house to the bride's house. We dance feverishly as usual. I have been involved almost continuously since 27 of November, counting the three weddings I attended in Jaipur. This is wedding number six and my body is telling me it is enough! Suresh says he admires my stamina. I suppose it is not too bad for a 73 year-old, at least I haven't collapsed on a street somewhere. This has to be it for a while as I need time to recover. We dance until we reach the guest house. Prashant is tall and regal-looking in his outfit. He dismounts and enters the compound. The women of the bride's family surge forward bearing symbolic gifts. Soon they try something else. They try to reach high enough to tweak Prashant's nose. With his height, few are successful, but occasionally one is able to tweak. It is part of the sometimes humorous side of events attendant with these ceremonies.

The Pushkar/Nimaj Weddings

Once this is completed, a car comes for the groom to return him to the wedding venue back at his house. Suresh and I along with his cousin Vicky are invited to join him in the car. Once at the venue, he assumes the throne. Again, his relatives occupy the bride's chair. Eventually she enters to great fanfare and dancing and ascends the stage to meet the challenge of this set of relatives who want to know if there is true love there. Again they yield and she is seated for the photos to begin.

Food is served from various catered tables, all quite good. We enjoy the meal and then more dancing. Once again the ceremony moves back to the guest house for the all night portion of the ceremonies. I opt out this time. Sleep however is impossible as the room where I am sleeping always becomes a gathering place for various family members, including the groom himself who pops in for a time. The ceremony goes on into the wee hours.

Six weddings are a bit much for anybody and especially for my body! I have reached the limits of my endurance. Tomorrow, I plan to take a day off. I'd like nothing better than to be by myself, without any ceremony or occasion. I've hit the wall of enculturation once again, but this is India and that is not to be.

6

"It Ain't Over Until It's Over!"

Sunday 16 December
Pushkar, India

Post wedding Events

The weddings are finished, or so I think. I find that there are now several post-wedding events to keep us involved for days. First, there is the thanks-be-to-god-and-family post-wedding dinner. It is no small affair in itself. There is a ceremony at the Ganesh temple with Suresh's family, from which we return to feed about 200 extended family members as an expression of thanks for their participation. Guests sit on strips of cloth in the courtyard of an Indian Guest House and are fed by family members in appreciation of the family for a successful pair of weddings. I can't imagine in Western culture adding a "small" thank you dinner for a mere 200 to the already over-the-top wedding venue, but this is India.

Next, there are exchanges of dinner invitations. We are invited to Bebu's house (Suresh's sister) for a dinner which she gives for a chance to show off their new room fashioned with the furniture given in the dowry. It is a nice large room with bed and dresser. Bebu now wears saris as the appropriate dress for a married woman and she seems totally happy and quite out-going once the wedding has been completed.

"It Ain't Over Until It's Over!"

We then receive family members from Suresh's wife's family who have come from the village of Nimaj to receive blessings and gifts from Suresh's family. They arrive by bus after a two and half-hour journey. We feed them and house them for the night. Most of the guys gather in my room at the hotel and we reserve an additional room for spill over as we all sleep family-style in the two rooms, talking until way into the early morning hours. We get up early for them to catch a bus back to their village, in time to receive us, for we are going there to receive their blessings along with additional gifts. I just thought the weddings were over! Gift-giving it seems, knows no end.

We hire a car and stuff it with cousins and ourselves for the trip to Nimaj and stop a time or two along the way for snacks and such and make a final pause near their village at a busy stop to give the family time to arrive by bus in order to welcome us. Once they are in place, we proceed to the small village and are duly welcomed and dined and gifted before we load up to make the return trip to Pushkar. We arrive into the night. Am I being redundant in saying that I'm exhausted?

Finally, I get to spend a couple of days just hanging out before Suresh, Deepika and I make a trip back to Nimaj for her to stay a few days while Suresh and I plan to go to Jodhpur for a couple of days. They have arranged for me to stay at the Nimaj Palace here, which I anticipate, so I can live the life of a Rajput for at least two nights. Bring on the servants!

A Couple of Nights Luxury
Nimaj Palace was built in the 1600's by the reigning monarch or Raj of the area, one of three or four major Raja's in what now makes up the state of Rajasthan in northwest India. Other palaces are located in Jaipur, Jodhpur and Udaipur. Nimaj is a small walled city anchored by the palace. As it turns out, I am only one of three guests in the whole place. The other two are a couple of guys visiting from Holland.

Distant Lands

My room is located beside a porched area and decorated ornately, with a couple of single beds. My friend and Deepika's cousin Vicky Parashar made the arrangements for me. His grandfather had spent his life working at the palace and they are able to get a discounted price for me. Vicky and his cousin Ajay both Facebook friends accompany me to the palace along with Suresh. After I check in, my room becomes a hub of activity, with various family friends dropping by along with some of the hotel staff, who seem to relish hanging out with me. I begin to feel a little like a celebrity. I'm sure the other guests wonder who the heck I might be.

Otherwise, Nimaj Palace provides a quiet get-away in luxurious surroundings that I welcome after all the weddings. I spend time lounging at the swimming pool. The water is still ice-cold, but the sun is bright and I enjoy sunning on the veranda, along with the two other guests. We share dinner together with a set meal of chicken, mutton, potatoes and vegetables, all deliciously prepared and served by various waiters. It is a welcome break from the strict vegetarian fare, since arriving in India in mid-November. A cultural program of music and dancing is presented before dinner on the first night of my stay.

During the day, I take meals with the family and various visiting various relatives. My friend Vicky's family prepares a delicious lunch for me. Suresh's in-laws also feed us and I make a visit to the home of one of the uncles. All of them extend invitations for me a place to stay during any future trips.

Nimaj is small enough to walk around. Streets are barely wide enough for a car to navigate adding to its charm. After a couple of days, Suresh and I along with our driver head for Jodhpur where we visit another palace and a fort high above the city, setting on a bluff. You may wonder why Suresh is breaking away from his bride so soon after the wedding, to take a couple of days' vacation with me. I wondered about that too, but he and Deepika both insisted that we should go. She said "Mr. Keith is here for a short time. We will have lots of time for ourselves. Please go with him." I think that perhaps both of them were as exhausted as I from the marathon of weddings, so we agree to it and make contact with a friend of his there, a doctor who is a bone specialist, and together we enjoy a nice meal in a restaurant called "On the Rocks," which I recommend if you are ever in Jodhpur. Jodhpur is a military city, an outpost for the Indian Army's Desert Corps and is noted for its contribution to fashion with its famous Jodhpur-style clothing. The time provides a great interlude for both of us. We make a brief stop in Jethana to visit Suresh's mother's family, before returning to Pushkar.

21 December 2012
Pushkar, India

The End of the World
Today is the winter solstice, the day the world is supposed to end, or so some have predicted, who have studied the calendar of the ancient Mayans and because their calendar indicated no date past this date, some so-called prophets predicted the world's demise. I wake up this morning not particularly worried about the projected apocalypse. After all at 73, I've lived through several other predictions of imminent finality and ruin. It's a great cottage industry for seers, who make fortunes and gain followings of otherwise intelligent people. It sells books and makes money for these prophets. I don't waste time buying their books, nor do I read them and I certainly don't reorder my life based on their predictions.

The sun shines bright on this the shortest day of the year even in Pushkar, India. Here the sun rises of a range of peaks to the east side of the city. I go for a walk through the city as merchants prepare their kiosks for business and chai (tea) sellers ladle the national drink of India into small paper cups for people hunched against the early-morning temperatures, notably oblivious to the world's end. My favorite chai merchant Trilok is all smiles and anxious to serve me. After chai, I take

Distant Lands

a circuitous route around part of the city, passing the cremation garden where the dead are brought for their transformation into ashes. No one has died today apparently. Maybe they're holding off, anticipating company in the great cataclysm. I stop at the Om Shiva restaurant to enjoy a nice breakfast of eggs, potatoes and salad with coffee. If it is to be the end, one wants to be well-nourished.

I spend time with my Indian family and later with a friend who has opened a new store. They are worried about a small boy, a cousin, who has fallen while trying to retrieve his kite. It is kite season and the kids go wild with them. It seems he jumped from one building to another, chasing his kite, but when he jumped back, his slippers did not grab hold properly and he fell two stories landing on his back. It was feared he might be paralyzed, but apparently he has not sustained such serious injuries, although more tests must be made. Kiting is a dangerous sport here.

As I write this, it is dark here but I am aware it is still daylight in the Western Hemisphere, still time enough for the world to end on today's schedule. I think I will go to sleep and just let it happen, hoping it isn't a too noisy enough affair to awaken me. After all, I reason that I may have more ends of the world predictions to live through. I know my world will end one day, which is not of major concern to me. My concern rather is to live each day with full joy and abandon, saving my money for good books to read.

Soon it will be Christmas and that is a day I welcome.

7

A Sad Christmas and a Happy New Year!

25 December

Christmas Mourning

My Christmas in Pushkar is marked sadly by the death of family members here, not only my family but also of the family of another friend, which I discover it as I walk early on this Christmas Eve morning and meet a procession coming from the cremation garden at the edge of the city. It is the family of a young friend I had made before. The young Sonu tells me that he has just lost his father. I had met both of them on my previous visit and had spent some time with Sonu. The other death is that of Suresh's maternal uncle who has died in the small village of Jethana. We had visited him just three days ago. He was in critical health then, so it was expected. Suresh and his family leave immediately for Jethana for the cremation which takes place almost immediately loading up sacks of flowers to be sprinkled in the procession toward the cremation. Everyone is quite sad and crying over the loss. I stay in Pushkar for now but will go with the family the day after Christmas to share condolences. We will be among other family members who will gather for the same purpose. I go to see Sonu who invites me to his house for tea and I express my sympathy there.

Needless to say, these deaths have left me feeling sad and alone, missing my family in the USA at Christmas. It is not exactly how I wanted to celebrate Christmas here. I had hoped to give my friends a small party in order to share our family customs for celebrating Christmas. A party is out of the question as inappropriate for the time of grief, which makes my Christmas here an altogether different experience than anticipated. There is no Christmas music, no lights adorning houses, no choirs singing, no children's programs to attend, no cookies being made, no gifts to wrap or family and friends to visit to wish a Merry Christmas, no chance to see "It's a Wonderful Life," nor to hear the resounding Hallelujah Chorus, no Rudolph the Red Nosed Reindeer. The only thing I hear is a much too silent night. India is between festivals and all is quiet, somber and cold here in a village untouched by Christmas.

While the families are involved with their grief, I take a camel ride into the desert to spend Christmas Day, alone with my thoughts, emulating the journey of the wise men of old, following the star from the east. I tell the story of the journey of the Wise Men to my camel driver as we head out into the surrounding desert, but he understands no English. We take brief breaks and sit upon the sand to share tea that he has brought with him. "We three Kings of Orient are, bearing gifts, we've traveled thus far, field and fountain, moor and mountain, following yonder star." The song plays itself in my head. I wonder what those men felt as they traveled in search of the new king, wondering what I can do to celebrate His birth. It is just after sunset when we return in the quiet stillness of an increasingly cold night

In my sadness, I have failed to appreciate the goodness of the human spirit. My two dear friends Mohit and Suresh are sensitive to the importance that Christmas has for me and despite their situation of grief, have conspired to give me a proper Christmas. They are on hand to greet me as I arrive from my camel ride and gather me up on their motorcycles for a brisk ride through the cold night air to Pushkar Fort, a resort just outside the city. There is a nice restaurant there and they have arranged a table for us in the back of a packed restaurant. They have also arranged for a cake to be brought decorated with a single candle bearing the inscription "Happy Birthday Jesus!" As per Indian custom, they ask me to make a wish and blow out the candle. We feed a piece of cake to each other. Word spreads through the crowd and people begin asking waiters what is going on. They explain that it is Christmas and these men are celebrating the birth of Jesus with a friend from America. Suresh and Mohit have brought gifts, decoratively wrapped in red and white paper. We order dinner first and after we eat, they present the gifts to me. Again the entire restaurant crowd follows what is happening, watching as I open the gifts at the table. Now it is feeling more like Christmas. They give me a nice pair of walking shoes and a beautiful sweater to wear. I realize anew that good friends are among life's greatest blessings and that one is never really alone if there are friends like these around. Mohit asks me to tell him the Christmas story, which I promise to do when we return to my room. They stay the entire night with me. I place calls to my family in the U.S. It has been a perfect day. Jesus said "Blessed are those who mourn, for they shall be comforted." In spite of our grief, we have managed to find joy. "Joy to the World, the Lord has come." I tell the Christmas story.

Saying Good Bye to the Deceased, Welcome to the Birth
The day after Christmas, I join with Suresh's family in Jethana to "sit with" the family of their uncle who has died the day before Christmas. Family and friends gather in front of the family home. The men sit on a canvas spread over a small area. The sons of the uncle have shaved their heads. The cremation had taken place the day of his death now on this third day, we gather for a day of solemn remembrance and expressions of sorrow and condolence. The women gather inside the house, weeping copiously, while the men sit outside in stoic silence, with no one speaking. After some time, a family member stands to tell of the life of the deceased after which we all then stand and bow for two minutes of silent prayer and move to the displayed photo of the deceased, to gather rose petals to be sprinkled over the photo. No one says a word. After that, we form a procession through the village to the various

shops owned by family members which were closed immediately upon the death of the deceased. A brief ceremony takes place in which we scatter grains of seed on the shop to officially declare the shop to be re-opened. We make our way through the village to the sweet shop operated by the son Tanu, who sits each day making sweets of which I have partaken on my many visits. The last shops we visit are electrical shops operated by the brothers of the man who has died. Finally, the family members stand on a small ledge near the shop to thank all who have gathered. One of the brothers asks me to stand with the family since I am considered a family member but I politely decline this time.

The son Tanu and one of the uncles will take the next few days to carry the remaining ashes from the cremation on a long journey to the Ganges to scatter the ashes retaining some to be brought to Pushkar, where a few days later, we meet with them for a final ceremony at the sacred lake. I sit and watch as water is dipped from the lake after prayers. This is water for his father to have in transition. It is all very solemn. The party then comes to the house to share a meal with us before they return to the small village. Tanu will then be declared head of his family and given the responsibility of providing care for his widowed mother and his younger brother.

I spend the final days in Pushkar visiting friends, eating with them and flying kites on the rooftop. It is the season for kites and the young nephew Happy with his grandfather are at it every day. I take my turn from time to time. The air is warm in the afternoons but the nights remain cold.

On the day of my departure, I have dinner with Mohit's family. At Suresh's house, his mother presents me with a garland of flowers and applies the *tikka* blessing to my forehead. On the way out of town we stop at a small hospital to see a new nephew who has just been born. He is only three hours old when they hand him to me to hold. This family had lost their son this past year at only six months of age, so there is great joy with this birth. The father presents sweets in appreciation for my visit. It is good for my journey to end on this note of joy and new life. I take my leave holding a new life in my arms.

Suresh and I make our way to Jaipur, where we will celebrate New Year's in great style.

New Year's Eve in Jaipur
Most of my New Year's Eve celebrations have been fairly quiet ones, but this year is definitely an exception. We have come to Jaipur to visit our friend Neeraj, whose brother's wedding was the first I attended on this trip. Neeraj is a great host, happy and friendly and always ready to show us around. We visit Jaipur's City Palace and the adjacent Observatory during the afternoon. From there we spend the late afternoon flying kites from the rooftop. It is great fun and the guys really get into the spirit of adventure and competition as they seek to cut opponents' kites from the skies. They are practiced at it, enjoying a great time with cousins, neighbors and friends. We dress to attend a big New Year's Eve party atop one of Jaipur's largest shopping centers, where Neeraj has arranged free passes for two of us and we pay for just one. The band is playing as we arrive and the rooftop quickly fills with people dancing. The night air is cold, so if you didn't dance, it would be quite chilly, despite two wood-burning fire chimneys set up to help break the chill. It is all fun and we have a grand time dancing under strobe lights of green and purple, accenting the young crowd. At midnight, fireworks go off spectacularly around the city.

We spend our New Year's Day sleeping late. Neeraj and I catch the train from Jaipur to Delhi, where he is starting a six-month training program in hospital accounting. I will then catch a flight tomorrow to Nepal to visit with Manish and family. His mother had died quite suddenly in November, while I was attending the weddings in India, another grief to add to this mixture of celebration and mourning.

8

Sympathy in Nepal and Mountain Village

3 January 2013

Kathmandu in January

I arrive in Kathmandu not knowing where I might be staying, as my contacts with Manish have gone unanswered. I am not worried about finding a room, since this is an off-season for trekking. Since Manish's mother died, he may not want me to stay at his house as I've done before. I place another call but he does not pick up. Just as I tell the taxi driver to take me to a hotel, Manish calls back to tell me to wait, for he is coming to the airport. We greet warmly and he explains that he had not checked emails for over two weeks and my attempts to call had not worked. He also tells me that he has to leave town for five days for a trek, beginning early in the morning but insists that I stay at his house, telling me his brother will take care of me. His brother Sonu had been seriously hurt in a motorcycle accident just a couple of days before their mother had died, learning of her death while he was in the hospital. It was a tragic time for both brothers and a sad one for me as well, since I had stayed many times with this family.

I greet Pinkey and Vicky who are happy to see "Keith Uncle!" Both are school age children. Pinkey is growing into a young lady and must now take more responsibility for her younger brother since there is no

Sympathy in Nepal and Mountain Village

mother in the house. Manish's dad takes care of them too and prepares the meals. We talk awhile before Manish takes off. He assures me that he will be free in five days. I tell him not to worry that I am flexible and will be fine. There are several other friends I plan to see while here.

Sonu and I arrange a taxi to take me to Thamel. It will be some time before Sonu can ride his crashed motorbike. He still has several pins in his right arm. In Thamel we meet up with Tara Mainali, who I had met briefly four years ago during my first trip, staying at the hotel where he was working.

The days are warm in Kathmandu even in January, with the temperature plummeting at sundown. Power is off most of the time, coming on only later at night at nine or ten o'clock. After sundown, we are in the dark, except for candles. We huddle against the cold in the concrete structures with no heat. It is always a challenge but always fascinating.

Visit to Farming Village
Tara invites me to visit his family in a small farming village in a remote area of Nepal. We go by motorcycle for a four-hour ride over a couple of mountain passes. The last ten kilometers require passing over a steep mountain pass, a major off-road challenge and quite treacherous. We take three spills as we attempt to get up this mountain on a road with powdery dirt and loose rocks. We aren't injured, luckily. I have to walk at times, as the terrain proves too difficult for the two of us on a bike. Eventually we make it over the top and begin a steep descent to the small village below. I realize that two of us will never be able to make it back up this steep incline. I will have to climb this mountain when we return.

We meet his mother at his parent's two-story farm house. She is busy cutting corn stalks into fodder for the animals but greets me warmly and continues her work. Tara gets busy gathering Kori and fresh peas for our dinner. He shakes an orange tree for oranges and we eat several fresh ones from the tree. The village is at the head of a small valley with a magnificent view across to the mountains to the far side. The village consists of just a few houses located on small terraced farms clustered together. His father returns before dinner, after walking some distance, a sturdy man with big hands reflecting the rigors of farm life. Dinner is prepared over an open fire in the dirt-floored farm house. Smoke fills the house as dinner is being prepared. They raise several goats, a cow and calf. The cow provides the milk. They raise most all their food. Vegetables are still growing. Surprisingly, these Himalaya valleys are blessed with ample sunshine, allowing some things to grow even in January. Such valleys gave rise to the fabled Shanri-La legends of old, told by early explorers who had crossed mountain passes steeped in snow to find veritable Gardens of Eden in remote Himalayan valleys.

We enjoy a dinner of rice, Kori and fresh peas. Kori is somewhat like potatoes, once the prickly skin is peeled away. We mix dahl, the gravy made with lentils, over the rice. The goats are brought into the lower floor at night and given bunches of leaves tied in bundles suspended for them to eat. We eat at one end of the room, while the goats busily eat at the other. It is typical farm fashion in much of the world and probably similar to growing up in the Middle East as described in the Bible. I feel honored to be an over-night guest here. After a big dinner, we climb the small ladder to the next level where we will sleep. Tara has a pallet, but they give me a small bed and I huddle under thick comforters against the cold night air. Outside the stars are magnificent. With no toilet, we make do outside.

The next morning after a breakfast of omelet, apples and a cereal of some sort with chai (tea), we hit on a great plan for me to get me back up the mountain. A milk truck comes today to gather milk from the farms for the market in Kathmandu. Perhaps I can hitch a ride with them. The beat-up old truck arrives about 8:30. Milk is brought in large containers from several farms to a central area, where samples are taken for testing for fat content and the price is determined by that. It reminds me of my growing-up years on the farm when we took cream once a week to the market for money to buy staples. Once the milk has been gathered, I join three others passengers, cramming ourselves into the cab, along with the two milk handlers, making five in all. It proves to be a good thing to be so tightly squeezed in, for the ride to the top becomes as rough as any bronco ride in a rodeo. We pitch and lurch and twist as the truck hammers its way to the top over the nearly-impossible road. One false lurch or turn and we could just as easily plunge down the mountainside.

Without me as extra weight, Tara had no trouble getting his bike to the top. We pay the driver and we are off on our return. It was still rough for us going down the other side, but much easier than before, with no spills this time. We enjoy the view of the high peaks of the Himalayas, visible off to our right, as we return to Kathmandu.

In and Around Kathmandu
My days fall into a pattern here when Manish returns. We do daytrips in and around Kathmandu. We visit the "Reclining Buddha" temple one such day. In the center of the temple is a vat of water in which the reclining Buddha lies peacefully and is protected by carved, writhing snakes. Legend has it that a farmer was digging and accidentally hit the buried Buddha's toe, cutting it and causing blood to spurt from the ground. The farmer rushed to tell the King of Nepal but the king dismissed the farmer as crazy. The farmer goes back and digs a little farther away only to hit the Buddha's chest this time and milk spurts from the ground. Again the farmer goes to the king and is dismissed again as crazy. One of the twelve snakes slides out of the ground vowing that when the Buddha is carefully dug up and venerated, the snake will protect the enclosure in case the king should visit. The king will be bitten and die because of his disbelief.

We visit the ancient village of Sakwo, notable for its old buildings of brick and wood, some of which sag and lean from the ravages of time. It is quaint place with shops, vegetable markets and many shrines attesting to its once wealthy status. A temple with fertility carvings adorning it stands in the temple. Small boys take delight in pointing out the erotic carvings on the temple. Nothing hidden here! We have lunch at a nearby bluff overlooking a green valley of farms. It is a peaceful time. While I am eating, a dove comes and lights on my head. While Manish takes a photo with my camera, the dove makes a deposit on my head.

Nights in Kathmadu are a bit boring without electricity, with not little to do except stare at a candle. As a rule, we go to bed upon finishing dinner. It is cold in the house and best to stay under heavy blankets. It is cold enough one night that I sleep in my coat as well. When the power comes on at 10, 11, or 12, depending on a rotation system, I get up to check emails.

It's a simple life.

Ashram, Trout and a Police Station
With two days remaining, there is bound to be at least one adventurous episode in my travel. The day starts well enough. Manish and I take a trip to an ashram, a quiet resort for meditation located in the mountains to the west of Kathmandu. This ashram is one of several started by the popular guru named Osho, who has several such retreats located in the U.S. as well. Guests check into the ashram for ten days of quiet meditation, surrounded by a peaceful setting, which sounds appealing actually, because for me it would be a superior place in which to write.

Manish takes me higher up the mountain to a restaurant featuring freshwater trout that one can select from the restaurant's cold water ponds. The selected trout is then prepared for lunch. I seine for two, weighing in at one kilo. The restaurant charges by the kilo. They are then cooked, a little too much for my taste but still quite good, served with a plate of fresh vegetables.

Sympathy in Nepal and Mountain Village

Back in Kathmandu, Manish drops me at my friend Tara's, where his friend Bishwas has come to join us for an evening together, before I head back to the USA. We go to their apartment for a meal of mutton they have prepared. Tara's brother Gopal also joins us. They insist that I stay the night for more time to enjoy the full evening together. I call Manish to tell him. Tara decides that we should enjoy live music and dancing, which we do in Thamel, renting a room at nearby guest house so as not to walk the streets late at night. Thamel can be unsafe in the dark of the night, especially with little or no power to light the streets. When we return from the party, Gopal leaves to walk home alone where his pregnant wife is waiting, despite Tara's warning against it, but he is determined to go.

The rest of us return to the room for the night and prepare for sleep. After some minutes, Tara receives an urgent call from his brother telling that he has been attacked by three men seeking to rob him and beating him before he could get away from them. Tara and Bishwas quickly dress and run from the room to rescue the brother, telling me to stay put. They run as fast as they can through the darkened streets. When the police spot them running, they assume that they have committed some kind of crime and are fleeing from it. They try to explain that they were going to help their brother who has been attacked in a fight, but the police only hear there has been a fight. Though the brother is bleeding profusely from his head, the police dismiss him and put Tara and Bishwas in hand-cuffs and haul them away. It is arrest now and ask questions later! They confiscate mobile phones and throw them into jail cell along with 18 other prisoners. Unable to call out, Tara and Bishwas spend the night in jail, worrying about whether the brother got treatment for his wounds and they worry for me as their guest. Neither the brother nor I know this has happened to them. When Gopal was dismissed by the police he was told to get help for his wounds. He assumed the police would let the others go once they explained everything. When the Gopal arrives at the room, his head is wrapped in a cloth but is still bleeding. I get a towel to wrap around his head after examining his wound. He has a gash in his scalp. Scalp wounds tend to bleed a lot. He tells me he doesn't need treatment. I get him onto the bed in a sitting position, leaning against the wall to keep his head high. We spend the rest of the night, not knowing the fate of the other two, assuming that perhaps after explaining everything, the police would surely have released them. We even speculate that they have gone back to their place for the night, so as not to disturb us at the guest house. Since my mobile phone had run out of minutes, I was unable to call and verify their whereabouts. Early the next morning, I get a call from Tara. It is the one call he is permitted. He tells me they have been detained at the police station jail overnight. Gopal and I hurry immediately to the police station, finding them looking quite bedraggled and worried. We are not permitted in, but we can see and hear them. We are told that it will take time for the police to process their catch of the night, but if they pay a fine, they can be released later. Prisoners have little rights here. They are relieved that we are alright, especially that his brother had not bled to death. I arrange the money for the fine, slipping it to them past one of the guards.

The bureaucracy of the release takes time, so they tell us to go on to Gopal's house so we can clean the gash in his head. It probably needs a stitch or two but he should heal, though probably will be left with a scar. After 10:00 a.m. the two jailbirds are released and arrive at the house a little after eleven. They tell of their horrible ordeal spent in a cold jail with drunks and crazies unable even to have a drink of water or any kind of blanket, staying huddled together to keep warm. Had I not stayed in the room and had run with them, I might too have spent a cold night in a Nepali jail.

Heading to Washington, D.C.!
I say my good-byes to my friends in Nepal and head toward home. It is a long layover in Delhi, made longer with multiple delays in departure. Delhi's airport is a fairly good place to hang out if you have a long layover. I check into the use one of the sleep pods offered for rent by the

hour. The pods consist of small rooms with a bed and desk. It is what I need and I have just enough U.S. currency to provide four hours' worth, though I don't actually sleep. At least I get some rest. My 3:00 flight is delayed to 4:00 and then to nearly 5:00 a.m. They tell us that the plane had trouble getting out of Frankfurt because of an ice storm and when it approached Delhi, it had encountered thunder storms. Lightning had struck the plane on the approach to the airport. Before we board, technicians check out the electrical systems. Eventually we get airborne and fly through the morning hours to a cold and wintry Frankfurt, Germany.

I board another Lufthansa flight to Washington, DC, where I am looking forward to visiting a friend I haven't seen in 18 years. We had gone to college and seminary together and he had been in my wedding long ago. I hope to connect with David Massey and his wife Angela.

It is late afternoon when we arrive in Washington, DC. David is there to welcome me. It takes an additional two and half hours to get to his house, normally a 45 minute drive, but Washington's traffic is in hopeless gridlock on this Friday evening before the start of a 3-day weekend and the inauguration of President Obama for a second term. I plan to attend the inauguration.

9

Inauguration of a President

Monday 21 January

Inauguration of a President
I had never attended a presidential inauguration before. When I discovered that my flight home would take me through the nation's capital, I decided to add a few extra days and visit my friend David and his wife Angela, so I could attend the inauguration of President Obama for his second term. My visit with David and Angela was a real treat. They live in suburban Rockville, Maryland in a small house. Upon arrival David invited me to speak at his church on Sunday. He pastors the Grace Reformed Church near the White House, a historic old church, attended by President Theodore Roosevelt while he was vice-president and president. The sermon requires hasty preparation on my part, despite my half-zombie state from travel, but I make the best of it and enjoy the time with the people there.

On the Monday of the inauguration, I board the Metro from Rockville into Washington proper and circle around the Capitol itself. Security is super tight, with most entrances to the mall requiring a ticket. I had applied for a ticket through my congressman James Lankford but did not get one, so I join the masses on the mall to view the inaugural events on giant screens. Perhaps it was for the best for I wanted to experience it among the crowds who attend such an event. The amount of walking required is phenomenal. I am on my feet from 8:00 a.m. until 6:00 p.m. either walking or standing. The crowd swells to nearly a million, fully charged with enthusiasm and excitement. There are large numbers of young people, ranging from students to young professionals, along with large numbers of African-Americans and groups from churches of the area.

2013 Presidential Inauguration

As various dignitaries arrive to be introduced over the loud speakers at the inaugural platform, cheers ring out, sprinkled with occasional boos for certain personages of the opposing party. All in all, it is a jubilant crowd.

Following the inauguration itself, the crowd makes efforts to get into

Distant Lands

gates leading to the parade route. Security is extra tight and the entrances are too few. After two hours walking, thousands try to enter a gate set aside for those without tickets, with only three small openings available to process through security, taking us more than two more hours just to get to the security booths. By the time many of us get through, the president had already gone by on the parade route, disappointing the crowd not able to get in. I finally get through in enough time to watch about half of the parade. The bands are outstanding, high school and military, especially the Marine Corps Band.

Exhausted, I take the train back to Rockville, with legs and feet extremely sore, but I am happy to have experienced an element of our democracy, the transition of presidential terms.

The day after President Obama's inauguration, I knock around Washington to visit the Library of Congress and the Capitol Visitor's Center. The weather has turned extremely cold by now. Visiting the Library of Congress has been a long-term goal of mine. In previous trips to Washington, it had never worked out but this time I am not to be denied. The building itself is well worth the visit with its columns, murals and art. The Reading Room is a classic. Unfortunately, visitors are not permitted there but one can view the room from a balcony. Entrance is reserved for researchers, who apply for admittance. Many of these are the staffers of Congressmen and Senators.

There are plenty of exhibits to see. The highest on my list is the Thomas Jefferson Library. Jefferson had sold his extensive library to Congress after the Congressional Library had burned. At the time, Jefferson possessed the largest collection of books in the young United States. His interests were wide and varied. Books included works on business, architecture, philosophy, agriculture, politics, religion, history. I even spot a copy of the Koran on one shelf. One could certainly get a well-rounded education from reading from his library alone. There were other featured displays in the library on the American Civil War, the early Americas and one of the earliest printed Bibles, The Bible on the Mainz. Many high schoolers who had marched in bands yesterday in the Inaugural Parade are there as well.

Home at Last!
After a good dinner and a night of rest, I catch the earliest train available to Washington's National Airport. I arrive on time, but there has been a snafu in my ticket made by the airlines. I am delayed trying to get through security and make three trips from security back to the ticket counter in order to get things corrected. By the time I get through security, I have missed my flight. I quickly book stand-by.

The house is cool with a stack of unopened mail and Christmas cards to greet me. They will have to wait. I am home at last! I thank God for a wonderful trip which allowed me to see friends, to celebrate weddings, to mourn deaths, to discover new things, to see new sites, to watch a President inaugurated, to speak in a historic old church, to laugh, to cry, to enjoy varied food as I experienced the world. I consider myself richly blessed!

Part Four
2013 Rafting the Himalayas, Whales in the Desert, Camels in India

"Beyond the east the sunrise, beyond the West the sea, And East and West the wanderlust that will not let me be; I works in me like madness, dear, to bid me say, good-bye! For the seas call and the stars call, and Oh, the call of the sky." –Gerald Gould, Wanderlust, c.1905

It is not that I don't have a life where I live. In intervening months between travels, I maintain my residence, requiring constant work in both yard and garden. I direct a study group at church for older single adults. I tutor young children in an after-school reading program called Whiz Kids. I make occasional trips to see my children, grandchildren and other family living in distant parts of America. I keep up with a bounty of nieces, nephews and cousins, both near and far. I love to read. I take daily walks to maintain health. I love to be in nature. I am involved with astronomy and marvel at the nature of the universe. Through social media, I keep in frequent contact with friends all over the world, with whom I share joys and sorrows. Travel has made me aware of our shared humanity. It has taught me much about the nature of religious faith. I marvel at the simple teachings of Jesus. That I respect the ancient practices of Hinduism, the philosophical aspects of Buddhism and the broader implications of Islam does not diminish my faith. In today's world of global integration, we can ill afford to ignore one another or remain untouched by the aspirations and sufferings of our fellow human beings. Humanity is a family affair. Our faith should help us be more human, not less.

1

Rafting Nepal; Hot Days in India

21 April 2013

A friend of mine in Mississippi and I had recently re-established contact, made personal when I stopped by Booneville, Mississippi on the way to attending an annual conference of religious educators in Atlanta. I visited with Mike Hatfield, who had lived in Florida for a number of years and had recently returned to his home area near Booneville. He arranged for me to stay at his parent's house overnight, joining me there so we could catch up on our lives and travels. Mike works with Wycliffe Translators. He tells me he was anticipating a trip to India and Nepal. As we talked, we found that we shared similar ideas about travel—both enjoying meeting local people and learning the cultures. I had always dreamed of meeting a fellow traveler who shared the same approach to travel and thought it would be neat if ever it worked out to share a trip. Mike suggested that I join him in Nepal or India, but I deferred, mainly because of the number of recent trips and my need to recover financially. Yet, I didn't exactly say "no." Upon my return home, I checked possible flights, but again talked myself out of going. Inside my heart kept saying, "do it." There were complications. I had committed to tutoring, plus I hadn't seen my grandchildren in Wyoming since last summer. I contacted them and agreed to come in June, a good time to go there. I found a substitute for tutoring. On

Distant Lands

a whim I hit the "purchase" button for tickets and was soon on my way. I called Mike to tell him and we arranged to spend almost a week together in Nepal, when he finished work there. I gave him contact information to meet some of my friends, one in India and two in Nepal.

The adrenaline of travel preparations kicked in as I made the necessary arrangements. The flight to Abu Dhabi was not full and this time I had empty seats to stretch out on and watched the movie "The Life of Pi" during the transatlantic flight. I had earlier read the book and was interested to see the movie. Ang Lee did a superb job telling the story of the Indian boy lost at sea, trapped with a wild tiger in his small boat after their ship, carrying zoo animals had sunk. It was a contest of wills between the boy and the tiger. I arrived a little after 6:00 in Abu Dhabi, disappointed that the friends I had hoped to meet there were unable to come to the airport to meet me.

We landed early the next morning in Kathmandu with a resounding bump, hitting the tarmac on Kathmandu's short runway. Tara was there to greet me with a garland of flowers and the red *tikka* blessing for my forehead. We drive to his brother's house near Bahktipur to shower and crash while he returned to work. In mid-afternoon we go to Thamel for pizza and he takes me to a barber friend Anand, who goes to work on me like an Edward Scissorshand, clipping away. I had said "Take just a little," indicating with my fingers what I meant, but he translated it to "leave just a little." It is one of the shortest haircuts I've ever had, but he makes up for it with a wonderful head and back massage.

We head for Mike's hotel in time to catch him at the finish of his day of teaching and join him for dinner, where he introduces us to some of his colleagues. Later on the roof of his hotel, Mike and I have a chance to talk and he tells me about his travels. He had been able to meet Neeraj in Delhi and enjoyed meeting him. We discuss plans for the next few days after he finishes his assignment, planning to go to Pokhara and to Chitwan National Park. Tara will make the arrangements.

Rafting Nepal; Hot Days in India

I sleep like a baby resting from my travels. Tara and his sister prepare an omelet breakfast for me. My luggage had not arrived with me and still has not arrived. For some reason, it had not made it out of Chicago, an occurrence that has happened many times before on these trips. They say it will arrive on the next flight sometime in the early afternoon. We go from the airport to his brother Gopal's small apartment near Thamel, and meet his brother's wife who is busy preparing lunch for us. Tara leaves me in her care, to make arrangements for our trip. They have a new baby son and a daughter who is now seven. You may remember that Gopal was the brother who had been beaten on my previous trip. After a nice lunch, Tara and I return to the airport to retrieve my derelict luggage which has arrived by now. It is torn, but nothing is missing and we take it back to Bahktipur. Tara returns the bike we had been using and catches a bus back while I take a nap, still resting from my trip. He returns with a young cousin Sachin, who is in the tenth grade and quite interested in sports and hires a taxi to go to a restaurant called the Taj Mahal for dinner. The driver knows of a dance place not too far away and Tara insists that we go there. The singers are good and dancing fair, but I am still tired from travel. We stay late despite knowing that we plan to leave early in the morning to go white water rafting.

Rafting the Himalayas

I had only been on one white water rafting trip before, on the Bozeman River near Yellowstone National Park. I wasn't sure I was up to rafting the Himalayas but Tara assures me that I would be fine. The alarm jars us awake this morning, waking with a major headache from last night. The driver had already arrived, allowing little time to arrange things before taking off. The road out of Kathmandu is a challenge anytime—sharp curves, chaotic traffic over winding roads. My headache turns into a queasy stomach and rafting a wild river isn't likely to make it any better. I might have thrown up, except there wasn't anything on my stomach. We finally stop for breakfast, once we clear the difficult mountain pass out of Kathmandu. Tara orders an omelet for me, but all I manage is a nibble on plain toast. The thought of getting onto a raft to be tossed about is beginning to sound like a nightmare. Slowly I begin to feel better and by the time we reach the casting-off place, I am feeling somewhat normal. Still, I have little on my stomach, which might be a good thing. After being outfitted with life jackets and helmets, our rafting guide walks us through the necessary instructions about rowing. They place me at the front of the raft, which is the wildest place to be. The guide also tells us what to do if the raft capsizes or if we are thrown from it, which doesn't lift my spirits. I begin to question why a 73-year-old guy, with better sense, is doing rafting the Himalayas. Why can't I be like everyone else my age and simply do cruises? The thought of being on a cruise quickly jars me back to reality. Better to be thrown from a raft with five people than to be dead in the water with thousands, a recent happening on Carnival Cruise Lines.

Rafting in Nepal

I take my place at the dangerous front as we ease out into the river, deceptively placid here. When the guide shouts "All forward!" we are instructed to row forward in syncopation. It is a peaceful and deceptive beginning, until I hear the roar of rapids ahead. Have I got everything right in my will? Will they retrieve my body, and if so, what will they do with it? Cremations are readily available here, or if like the Tibetans, it could be a sky burial where they cut the body into pieces and feed it to the birds. The first rapids turn out to be exciting but not too bad, psychologically important in keeping a tourist from losing it. The guide checks to see how I'm doing. So far, so good! Soon the rapids turn into drenchers, dowsing us with water. Each set of falls become rougher than the last. On one precipitous dip, the guy rowing parallel to me is sent cascading into me. My hand hard against the oar breaks his fall, but his teeth imbed themselves into the back of my hand. It's a wonder that I hadn't knocked his teeth out. The next rapids send me to the floor of the raft. I don't know what I hit, but a large hunk of skin peels from my index finger from where the knuckle joins the hand, leaving skin dangling and me bleeding profusely. In a bit of quieter water, I retrieve a handkerchief to wrap around it. The guide decides to move me to the safer center of the raft and tells me to hang on as we approach the roughest of the rough. The last of the rapids is wild. In spite of it, we manage to arrive at our camp site in one piece. Thank God.

We set up tents for sleeping and build a campfire. Two of us walk to the village just above us, where we find a pharmacy. The pharmacist removes my dangling skin and cleans the wound, wrapping it with gauze. Back at the camp, we gather driftwood for the fire to skewer chicken for our dinner. Sleep comes peacefully with the white sound of the rushing river nearby.

Early the next morning, we go for coffee and pack our gear to return, stopping later for an omelet for our breakfast. A truck has gone partly over the edge of the road, blocking it, causing a long delay of snarled traffic. We make it back and rest a bit before picking up Mike's luggage in preparation for our trip tomorrow to Pokhara. It begins to rain.

Distant Lands

Sunrise in Pokhara and Twin Elephants in Chitwan
In Pokhara we stay in a nice hotel Tara has arranged, a bit more expensive than we had hoped. Mike, like me, has to watch expenditures for this part of the trip but Tara doesn't hold back. We enjoy a nice dinner and leave very early the next morning in order to catch the sunrise atop a nearby mountain, arriving at the top in the dark. Others are waiting there as well. It is well worth the wait. Mike gets some good snaps of the sun rising over the high peaks in the distance, an awe-inspiring occurrence. On the way down, we stop to explore a bat cave, later taking a boat ride on Lake Fewa, a nice quiet experience, especially after my recent rafting venture. We take in Davi's falls, exploring both above and below ground, as we head out of Pokhara toward Chitwan.

Three Friends—Keith, Tara and Mike

I had been to Chitwan several times before. We opt for a boat ride down the river and time to see the elephants, where I get re-acquainted with twin elephants I had seen just after their births five years ago. Being male, they are soon to be separated from their mothers, to live on their own. Bulls are separated out. At night, we take in a series of cultural dances performed nearby and the next day, we take an elephant safari into the jungle. Riding elephants is not all that pleasant a ride, with a lot of bouncing back and forth. Tara insists that we take an elephant shower, performed in the river. We remove our shirts and shoes and empty our pockets to sit on the head of an elephant, which dowses us with water from his trunk. My trainer decides I need to be dumped in the river and gives a command for the elephant to roll over into the water, sending me into the deep. I remember seeing crocodiles on this river before, but I guess they were scared away. I am happy to report that I didn't end up as their dinner today. It is all fun and we enjoy the time, much to the amusement of onlookers. Mike spends time with Tara as they get better acquainted, while I talk with the others. The bills of our adventures mount up and we tell Tara we must temper the activities.

1 May

Indian Stogie
We gather with Tara, his friend Bishwas and his brother Gopal for a final night in Thamel, enjoying good food, time at the Buddha Pub an live music at a place Tara had picked for us. It is late when we return to a hotel nearby. Bishwas, Gopal and I share a room and Mike and Tara another and we oversleep. Tara comes knocking at the door, waking us to return to Bahktipur with little time to get our things packed before Mike and I have to head for the airport to check into our separate flights to Delhi. Mike is transitioning back to the U.S. while I plan to spend time in India. I check into a hotel in Delhi and send a message to Neeraj who is on the way from Jaipur to meet me. Mike takes a hotel near the airport for his flight later tonight. It was a short but good time to spend with him in Nepal.

An exuberant Neeraj shows up. We share time, exploring the local area,

Distant Lands

eating at a small Indian restaurant where the food is good and quite inexpensive. Later we go shopping near Connaught Place. Neeraj is always fun to be with. We pass a cigar vendor and on a whim he stops to buy one, which he presents to me, saying "Here, this suits you. You should smoke cigars. It fits your personality." I never smoke, but it does remind me of my father who always smoked a pipe but later gave it up, until at a wedding he was given a cigar and started smoking them much to my mother's disapproval. Neeraj lights the cigar and hands it to me. Picture me smoking a very sweet stogie, walking the streets of New Delhi! Don't worry, unlike my dad, I didn't pick up the habit. Neeraj is delighted that I tried it, and we laugh about it.

We watch a game of cricket back at the hotel before we sleep.

While Neeraj returns to his training session, I spend the day at the hotel pool, updating my journal, reflecting on my friendships in Egypt, Nepal and India, friends who express unadorned affection and seem to revel in my presence. Mike and I talked about the phenomenon, which he has also found. Part of it has to do with a curiosity about all things Western, yet it goes deeper than that. These are very relational cultures which value close friendship. It is a warm comradery, where age makes little difference. They relish my presence in much the same way as they would with their own age group. They share their dreams, hopes and ambitions and often seek my guidance on various issues affecting their daily struggles. It is a strong bond that develops between us.

I send greetings to my youngest grandson Zack for his fourth birthday today. I pack my bags in preparation for our departure by train this afternoon for Jaipur. When Neeraj comes, he takes me to a gem shop, insisting that I buy a gem of coral for a ring, which he says I should wear based on my birth. We select an elongated coral gem to take with me to Jaipur to a guy who will fashion a ring of silver for me to place it in. The shopping makes us late for our departure. We rush through heavy traffic to the Old Delhi station. We grab our luggage and rush through security, climbing stairs for the walk ways over train tracks and down to the departure platform just in time as the train is pulling away. I am wet with perspiration and tell Neeraj, "Don't do that to me again!" Though the train has air conditioning, it takes time for it to get going and by that time I'm ringing wet. We settle in for a five and half hour ride to Jaipur, arriving there at 8:30 p.m. in the dark. A rickshaw takes us through Jaipur's chaotic traffic to Neeraj's family home to be welcomed and graciously served dinner. It is good to see the family again, which includes the brother and wife, whose wedding I attended last fall. A bed is prepared for me in the dining room and a pallet for Neeraj. It is the one room with an air conditioning unit. May is Rajasthan's hottest season.

"Shoot Out at Valdada"
Neeraj decides it is time for me to experience the Cinema in India. It is a Bollywood action drama entitled "Shoot Out at Valdada." The theater is filled with young Indians, an experience in itself. The place is already packed and noisy as we find seats in the middle of the large theater. The crowd is mostly young males, though several girls are there as well. Everybody has their mobiles, which they keep busy, chatting even after the movie gets underway. Neeraj calls his cousin Gaurav and insists that the come and join us. Others do the same while the drama unfolds. New arrivals have to crawl over seats in order to hook up with their buddies. It is like a zoo. The movie we watch is an action thriller, based on a true story of gangs in Mumbai in the 1970s with lots of action, gore, blood and emotion as the hero, who is sort of anti-hero gang member, is being sought by the other bad guys and the corrupt police as well. In the middle of scenes of intense action, the cast breaks into Bollywood dances. It is a prerequisite for all Bollywood movies. In the drama portions, the camera lingers on faces of the actors undue lengths of time, to wring from them the most excruciating and over-done emotions of fear, anger or revenge, much to the excitement of the audience. In the final scene, the hero gets gunned down in a shoot-out, taking bullet after bullet for a full two minutes of film before falling to his knees to die. Maybe it isn't the bullets that kill him, as much as all

that air rushing into bullet holes! Finally he succumbs and the heroine rushes to embrace the dying and dead hero for another full two minutes of anguished expression. It is a hoot. I suppose Hollywood action movies are just as silly. It was more fun for me watching the dynamics of the audience, expressing themselves with each scene.

We leave the movie house for dinner at the Copper Kettle before returning to the house. Gaurav spends the night with us. Neeraj tells me he will leave early to return to Delhi for his training.

When I awake later in the morning, I see Neeraj's legs poking from under covers on the pallet. He tells me he has decided to go later, allowing him time to accompany me to the bus station for my trip to Ajmer to connect with my friend Suresh.

7 May

Pushkar

Today is my grandson Emiliano's 10th birthday and tomorrow, my granddaughter Olivia's birthday. I send them messages of Happy Birthday. Mitty, who is 12, and Suresh come to my room to use the shower. Unfortunately the water is off with just enough in a bucket to manage for the three of us. I spend time in the restaurant area upstairs where there is a breeze. Chennu the owner comes to chat and orders tea for us and calls one of the hotel boys over to give me a shoulder and neck massage. I give him some money. Many of the staffs at these hotels are young boys from poor families from surrounding villages who come for work. They are given housing, food and small pay, which they share with their families when they return for short visits.

Suresh and I visit with Summit, Mohit's younger brother who plans to get married November 25 and insists that I come for his wedding. I had attended both his brothers' weddings and will find it difficult to refuse.

Rafting Nepal; Hot Days in India

Deepika outdoes herself with our dinner, serving spinach paneer, butter paan, dahl, rice, salad, lemon drink and chocolate banana for dessert for dinner. Her younger brother Tony joins us, visiting from Nimaj. Suresh, having fasted all day, eats with gusto.

The days are extremely hot in Pushkar during the month of May, forcing me to stay in my room at the hotel when there is air conditioning or at Suresh's house which is cooled by a water cooler. We have been invited to Deepika's uncles for dinner and we dress though the uncles sit around in undershirts and a cloth wrapped around them, a preferred mode of dress in the summer in households. Generally dinner is not a social occasion as in the West. Meals are consumed hurriedly and with little conversation. With Suresh on his fast, he consumes his quite hurriedly

Sunday: Triple Spicy Pasta
I find a spot near the lake and sit to read from Isaiah, a passage about justice and care for the poor as part of authentic worship. Priests come to offer me flowers with the expectation of my joining in prayers at the lake, but I decline to have my own meditation. These moments are important for me to maintain equilibrium in my travel. Immersing oneself in another culture day after day can overwhelm even the most seasoned travelers. It is necessary for me to pull away in order to keep my bearings.

Deepika prepares a special pasta dinner for my final night in Pushkar, partly to impress me. The power goes out making the kitchen quite dark and she over compensates adding spices in the darkness. When Suresh and I begin eating the pasta our mouths are on fire. I try to mask it at first with drinks of banana lassi, which she has also prepared, but is too much, even for Suresh, making her quite embarrassed, of course. We assure her it is ok. I drink lots of water to alieve the burning tongue and throat. Later, we joke about it. A five year old cousin comes along and scoops up a big mouthful but with little reaction. Apparently he likes super spicy food. Suresh drapes a garland of flowers around my neck. Young Mitty arrives to join us for the trip to Delhi, with three of

Distant Lands

us and luggage crowd into a single sleeper compartment, a tight fit, but we manage. It is Mitty's first trip to Delhi.

Mitty: Keith Uncle, Are You Hungry?

We arrive early in the morning and walk to a Metro station to catch the Metro to New Delhi to check into the Prince Polonia in Room 204. Mitty is intrigued with the idea of room service and enjoys calling in orders for water or snacks for us, a novel experience for a boy from a small farming village. Suresh and I relax on the bed watching cricket matches, while Mitty calls room service from time to time. In the afternoon, Neeraj also joins us, coming from his training event in Delhi, staying the night, the four of us sharing the large bed and more cricket to watch on the television. Mitty keeps asking "Keith Uncle, are you hungry? Keith Uncle, do want some chai?" Each enquiry is met with a "yes," much to his delight, which means he gets to pick up the phone to order from room service. And so it goes. "Keith Uncle, are you sure you're not hungry?" It is hard to keep up.

Pool Fun—Mitty, Neeraj and Suresh

Rafting Nepal; Hot Days in India

Suresh has some clients to meet and Neeraj goes to his training, leaving Mitty in my care. We explore the area for souvenirs, stopping at a shop of items manufactured by a school for the blind. I buy a carved elephant, a carving of the Taj Mahal and antique jewelry, getting a bit caught up in buying. I purchase an outfit for Mitty, to wear for special occasions. In the afternoon, we spend time at the pool, joined later by Neeraj and then Suresh for a grand time, refreshing on a hot afternoon. We have a final dinner together and set the alarm for 2:00 a.m. for me to get to the airport in time for my 4:30 a.m. flight. Suresh and Neeraj get up to accompany me to the airport, leaving Mitty to sleep there alone. It is hard to say good-bye to these friends.

I fly to London for my transition to the U.S. Security is especially tight and I am patted down thoroughly by a security officer, to the point of his checking inside the bands of my underwear, a first. Finally, I'm passed through. I'm seated with a family from Pakistan, on their way to Tyler, Texas to visit her parents. The one-year old son is a delight and a handful to keep contained. On the other side I chat with an IBM executive from India. I soon fall into a deep sleep, unusual for me on flights. The lines for immigration in Dallas are long and slow. I run into Oklahoma U. S. Congressmen James Lankford and Frank Lucas at the gate. James and I worked together before my retirement and we chat about my travels before we are called for our flights.

My faithful friend Hap is there to pick me up in Oklahoma City. Even though we arrive after dark, I can tell my lawn is in need of cutting. It will be my first task after a night's sleep.

18-20 May

Tornadoes Take a Toll

A message greets me on my return. My sister-in-law Cinda sends a message that her mother has passed away asking me to conduct the services. I mow my yard and clean up downed branches from trees. Strong winds during the night have blown down additional branches and power lines in Edmond. I meet up with Cinda's family on Saturday morning in my home town of Watonga, taking flowers there for my wife's grave in preparation for Memorial Day. On the way back from Watonga, alarms begin sounding on the radio warning of an approaching severe storm with the possibilities of tornadoes. I see darkening clouds forming off to my right. By the time I reach home, the thunder is so loud it shakes the house. The storm is approaching in all its fury south of me with tornadoes in the air not yet touching the ground, passing a short distance away. If they were to drop to the ground, they could potentially devastate a large area of north Oklahoma City and Edmond, but they remain aloft until they reach the eastern side of Edmond, where they drop, doing extensive damage to a newly built hospital and some homes there, and continue on toward Shawnee, hitting a trailer park, killing some people. One elderly couple, caught on the highway, are sucked from their vehicle and cast on the roadside, severely injured.

2013 Moore, Oklahoma Tornado Destruction

Rafting Nepal; Hot Days in India

It is only the beginning. On Monday, another storm forms to the southwest and builds in intensity, spawning a killer F-5 tornado, which hits the town of Moore, a suburb of Oklahoma City, making a devastating path, destroying thousands of homes, two schools and a hospital. The destruction is horrific, with children killed in the schools. One of the schools is where my grandchildren attended when they lived in the area. With dire warnings, many people find shelter. Twenty-four are killed. The estimated damage is measured in billions of dollars. Touring the area later, I am astounded by the damage. The path of the tornado paralleled a similar path to the one fourteen years before, taking a higher toll with wind velocities the highest ever recorded on earth. It was the same week that my wife Barbara had died. The memories flood me.

The next day, I make my way to the small town of Fay to conduct the funeral services. As we move to the cemetery for the burial, dark clouds quickly form over us. I hasten to conclude the service of burial. We barely make it to our vehicles before a hail storm hits.

Messages pour in from friends around the world upon hearing the news of the tornadoes. They inquire of my safety. It is a somber conclusion to my journey.

2

Whales in the Desert

Saturday 21 September 2013
Edmond Oklahoma, USA

To the Other Side
It seems to come regularly for me, trips to the other side of the planet. This will be my third time in 2013. The demands of editing and producing my first book of my earlier travel have dominated much of my time over these last few months. It is a bit harder than I thought, considering all the editing and re-editing but I believe we are about to get there.

Again, I spend a week with my family in Pittsburgh. It's increasingly a challenge to keep up with my far-flung family, with two sets of grandkids in Wyoming and one set in Pittsburgh. I had gone to Wyoming in July.

Pittsburgh is one of America's premier cities, founded at the confluence of three rivers, the Ohio, the Monongahela and the Allegheny and steeped in history from the days of French traders to English dominance and finally the American Revolution. Here George Washington achieved his first fame during the French and Indian War, as an aide to the British general, who was shot in the battle. Pittsburgh later became famous for its booming steel industry which brought great wealth to the likes of the Carnegie and Mellon families. It was then a dirty place to live and work. Now the air is clear and the downtown is modern and fascinating, as it transitions to a new economy.

One of the best views of Pittsburgh can be seen from the bluff of Mt. Washington, where my daughter serves a Presbyterian Church as pastor. We go there Sunday and I take a photo of downtown. It is easy to be reminded of movie scenes from movies such as *Silence of the Lambs* and *Batman* which were filmed there. I spend a few days enjoying my two grandsons, who are now ages 10 and 16.

I head for the ancient and currently troubled land of Egypt, flying through Istanbul.

Monday 30 September

Istanbul's Ataturk Airport
The stop in Istanbul this time is only a transition to Egypt Air's flight bound for Cairo. Ataturk airport is always busy with many flights transitioning to numerous other locations throughout the Middle East, Asia and Africa. I wait in a transit lounge which is always busy and congested. I secure my boarding pass for the Egypt Air flight.

Boarding is already in progress by the time I reach the gate, having to run across the airport.

Surprisingly, the flight is comfortably filled, leaving only a few empty seats. Most of the passengers appear to be Egyptian, with only one other couple appearing to be European. My seatmate turns out to be a young doctor from Cairo, returning after a month's-worth of surgery practice in Istanbul. He tells me he is in the final stages of qualification for his doctoral program. We chat amiably about times spent in Istanbul and discuss the events now happening in Egypt, although I am careful not to probe too deeply. He recounts Egypt's ancient history as a civilization which has led him to study the nation's long past. We exchange contact information to stay in touch, which we do.

The flight goes smoothly enough, across the Anatolian peninsula, the Mediterranean Sea and south into Cairo. What awaits me in Egypt, I am not sure. However I look forward to meeting my friend Karim who has promised to meet me at the airport.

Cairo Welcome
After landing, I pay the $15 for a visa at a money exchange counter. I am not required to fill out anything, just told to hand over the cash in US dollars, please!

Outside I spot Karim who welcomes me, introducing me to his friend Khaled from Yemen, who is here for some type of medical attention. We load my bag in a car and head into Cairo to the Bedouin Hostel. All seems relatively quiet in Cairo

It is dark by the time we arrive, a location familiar to me as I had been here three times before. The Bedouin is a small hostel located up three flights of dark steps, run by Karim, who like most Egyptians, has schemes in his head for hapless tourists like me to get involved in unique Egyptian adventures, all for a price of course. Yet, it is good to see him.

Karim makes plans for us to go to el-Fayoum, the desert oasis southwest of Cairo and from there to Wadi el-Hitan to see whale fossils imbedded in the desert sands and on to the Bahriyah Oasis for a night in the White Desert. It will involve four nights, assuring me that we will get me back in time for me to catch my flight to Qatar. This is to be a short visit.

We talk until late before I beg off for a little sleep following my long flight from the USA. Tomorrow is another day. At least I've made it to Egypt!

The streets of Cairo are noisy and crowded as we make our way across the Nile River to the west side into Giza. Our driver's name is Ahmed along with a young assistant called Ali. Traffic in Cairo is impossible most of the time and today is certainly no exception. Leaving Giza, we make our way out of the Nile Valley passing through new suburban development to the open desert. Plastic bags blow about in the wind among the waste dumped alongside the road. Urban development is seldom a pretty picture. The road divides and we take the one to the southwest, toward el-Fayoum, passing the City of the Dead off to the right, a large metropolis of burial crypts, along streets and avenues of the ghostly city populated by millions of dead Cairo residents. It is one of Egypt's fastest growing cities! Past that, there is nothing to see but barren landscapes.

The Fayoum valley is an ancient place, once inhabited by the early Egyptians and later by the Greeks and Romans. Karim buys fish, freshly caught from the lake to grill for our dinner and we stop to ,pick up Karim's father-in-law, Musoufa, who is to be our host at a guest house he owns in a development by the lake. It is not where he lives but he rents it out or uses it for entertaining his personal guests. It is a large house, though not that well-kept. A swimming pool remains empty and trash filled, suggesting a more prosperous day. We relax in the shade on a grassy area and drink tea. A relative comes with a grill and we grill the fish we had brought, with some help from me. Vegetables are prepared by Ahmed, who is to be our driver and cook for the expedition into the Sahara. Ahmed, it turns out, is good cook.

When all is ready, we sit cross-legged on a blanket spread for us on the grass and eat our fill. Pieces of the round Egyptian bread are used to dip into the various dishes. We pick delicious white meat from the fish, careful to sort out the bones. It is all good. Tea is served and we relax for the evening, sometimes picking again at the food left over. A group of neighbors drop in for tea and conversations with Musoufa, Karim's father-in-law.

Karim and I sleep on pallets on the floor, while the others return to their homes.

Wadi el-Hitan, Egypt

Whales in the Desert and a Starry, Starry Night

With camping gear loaded, we head out in the desert to the west. Our party consists of Karim, Ahmed our driver and cook, the young assistant Ali, father-in-law Musoufa, making his first venture into this part of the desert and me. The paved road turns into a dirt one and when that runs out we follow only tire treads through an open desert, crossing sandy areas and up and down ridges. Occasional markers tell the seasoned Ahmed where to go toward the Wadi el-Hitan, an ancient sea bed located far into the desert. It is beginning to feel a little like an Indiana Jones adventure, as we race our Land Cruiser across open spaces.

Ahead a series of sandstone cliffs marks the rims of an ancient canyon. Eventually we approach a few small mud buildings which is the entrance to the park at Wadi el-Hitan. After paying a small fee to gain entrance, we get out to hike marked trails through various dunes and outcroppings to sites of fossilized skeletons of ancient whales. It's hard to imagine whales and fish being in this forbidding desert but this was once a sea, thriving with life, with whales living here between 42 and 37 million years ago in what is now being called the Tethys Sea. We locate several skeletal remains, lying exposed on the ground, gathering blowing sand. We hike some distance, discovering several more to view and read about from markers, before finishing the three kilometer trail. As we start back, a park ranger comes to offer a ride to the farthest point where one of the larger whale skeletons can be found.

Whales in the Desert

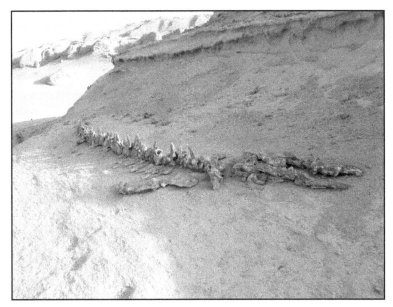

Whale Skeleton in the Sahara

It is by now drawing toward evening and we will camp here, just outside the park area at the face of a remote canyon. As Ahmed prepares our campsite, I hike to a series of outcroppings and climb to a peak for an incredible view of the desert, just as the sun is setting. A couple of Saharan foxes come to visit our camp site, hoping for food. They keep vigil a short distance away then sneak up to snatch something.

Ali prepares a campfire as the sun sets, while Ahmed prepares our dinner. We lounge around on carpets placed over the sand next to a vertical sheltering carpet, attached to the Land Cruiser to help block the desert winds. It is a peaceful setting. As darkness settles in, we eat the deliciously prepared food, including chicken grilled on the fire. After tea and some talk, we get into our sleeping bags. I lay there in the night totally mesmerized by the scene unfolding above me as millions and millions of stars silently become plainly visible. It is a moonless night, making it ideal for star gazing. I have never seen so many stars as I am now seeing in the Sahara. The Milky Way is so obvious! I can see deep into our solar system and am able to make out a few galaxy clusters beyond. My mind tries to wrap itself around the immensity and beauty of this universe, but it is impossible. We are but a small speck in the scheme of things. It is quite humbling.

The language of the stars tells us much about the God who made them. It is so daunting that I am humbled, curious and more determined than ever to better understand. I can hardly sleep tonight with views so spectacular. I count no less than 17 shooting stars in the course of the evening, indeed a starry, starry night. The song about Vincent Van Gogh keeps playing in my head as I doze.

Bachriyan Oasis, Egypt

Crossing the Desert

I climb to nearby bluffs early before the others awake. When Karim gets up, I wave to him from above and he climbs to join me. We locate large layers of seashells. Karim makes it all the way to the top but I content myself to avoid some of the more difficult climbs to reach the higher layers, fearing that I might have trouble getting down. Agile, yes for my 74 years, but not quite as agile as the 30 year-old Karim! He yells from the top layer marveling at the desert spread out before him.

We come down for breakfast and tea before breaking camp, after a transforming night spent in the desert under a moonless sky. I can only imagine what it might have been like when Jesus spent forty days in a similar desert wilderness at the beginning his ministry, searching and tempted by his call. We are often too numbed by lights, noise and constant entertainment that our spiritual senses remain dull. One starry night spent in the Sahara desert proves transformative.

Once packed and loaded, Ahmed guides the Land Cruiser across the desert. If there is a trail it is barely discernible to us, but to his more practiced eye he knows where to turn, which knoll to ascend, what dunes to plow through and at what speed to avoid getting bogged down by the sand. I commend him for his sand-worthy driving skill, quite different from ordinary driving. Where I grew up, we also dealt with sandy hills and sand-filled roads. City cousins who visited our farm sometimes would be unable to handle the kind of driving needed to negotiate their vehicles through the sand and end up stuck and fearful, complaining that we lived too far "from civilization." For me, it was a great place to grow up, taught by the wind and the blowing sand and the brilliant stars in a dark sky. In fact, the Oklahoma City Astronomy Club now operates its observatory from the very farm where I grew up. I am a member of that club, an interest that stems from those growing up years.

We plow ahead through sand and rocks, zooming and sliding our way across the desert, eventually to a railway running next to a highway, leading southwest toward the Bahriayan Oasis, some 200 miles distant from Cairo.

After hours of driving on an improved road, we drop down into a valley, lush and green covered with date palms. It is a large oasis that must have looked like heaven to early caravansaries when they came across it. Eventually we enter a village and cross to a small resort called Camp Badry, which is presided over by a man named Badry, a friend I had made from my last visit. We are welcomed to the camp and he again assigns me to stay in a thatched kiosk-style cottage with a single bed. I am happy to find a clean shower building nearby, and clean the desert dust from my eyes, nose, throat and ears. We relax the rest of the evening in this idyllic setting, where the air is cool in the shade and stirred by a gentle breeze. A table looking out over the oasis provides a perfect place for me to catch up on my journal. The interlude also gives me an opportunity to wash out some clothes. Ahmed is busy preparing dinner in a small kitchen just before dark. We spread a sheet on a grassy area to sit and sip tea, joined by our host Badry for a time that he and Karim can catch up on tales.

Distant Lands

White Desert, Egypt

Desert Sand Storm

I go for a walk through the palms and meet workers who are busy gathering dates from the palms. They shimmy up the trees and cut the seed fronds which fall to the ground onto a canvas which is spread. Others pick up loose ones that fall away from the canvas. They put me to work helping them. A woman appears and serves tea, while they encourage me to try the dates which are sweet to the taste. Delicious!

Later in the morning we load for our trip to the White Desert, heading southwest across more of the barren Sahara, stopping for lunch at another oasis next to an irrigation pump that is pumping fresh water from the ground, shooting a large stream into a concrete tank. Karim decides to swim and strips to his boxers and plunges in. Since the other tourists have yet to arrive for lunch, I also plunge in similar fashion enjoying the refreshing water and swim. We get out to let the desert wind dry us before joining the tourists who have arrived by now for lunch, which is served inside a mud-framed building next to the tank.

After lunch we speed cross the volcanic Black Desert before turning off the pavement and cutting across the sandy landscape toward the White Desert, nearly getting stuck in the sand at times but eventually make it to a gorge opening onto the White Desert below us, notable for its chalky-white formations, stopping to revel in the stark beauty of surreal formations before continuing to the far side of the desert in areas I had not been before. We select a large formation as a backdrop for our camp tonight. The wind becomes increasingly strong, enough to make ripples in the sand as it blows. Ahmed arranges a carpet wind barrier, which he attaches to the Land Cruiser. I walk about to get photos of the sunset hoping the cooler darkness might calm the winds, but it does not happen. Ahmed is driven by the wind to prepare dinner in the back of the Land Cruiser to shelter the flames of the propane cooker. We seek shelter behind the carpet barrier, but the wind keeps whipping around and blowing sand in our faces and into everything we have brought with us. Instead of dying down, the wind only increases, developing into a full-scale desert sand storm, forcing us inside the Land Cruiser to eat our meal and discuss whether we should stay or go. I give my permission to go, as the wind seems only to be increasing in velocity. With great difficulty in the howling wind, we break camp and hurriedly load everything into the Land Cruiser in the dark and make our way blindly in the darkness and blowing sand to escape. How Ahmed finds the way is a mystery to me, for it is nearly impossible to see anything like the usual landmarks to determine our way. We make it eventually to the highway without getting hopelessly lost, which is indeed a miracle.

We are forced to drive all the way back to Bachriya Oasis, a long ways, arriving well after midnight with eyes and ears filled with sand, which I hasten to wash out. The desert storm has destroyed our plan for another peaceful night under a star-filled sky. We were just lucky to have made it out of the storm.

A different kind of storm awaits us in Cairo.

Egypt's Political Storm!
We take time before making the return trip to Cairo. Ahmed and the others decide to harvest a supply of dates to take back. We join them in the oasis to gather boxes of fresh dates. I have in mind that we are leaving after that, but as is often the case, I am wrong. It seems our host Badry has invited us to his house for lunch and hospitality demands that we go. Before lunch we arrange a car to return us to Cairo, instead of the mini-van we had used. Karim is worried that the van will gain the attention of the military, which is stopping vans moving toward Cairo. He hits me up for more money to help pay for the car. We had already paid full price for the van. It causes an argument between us because it is beyond our agreement, but in the end I help with a portion of the additional cost. I know he has safety in mind. We go into the town to Badry's house where he has prepared a feast of various meats

Distant Lands

and vegetables, breads, honey and jellies. I am gaining weight in Egypt! The food is always exceptional.

We have a young driver at the wheel for the trip to Cairo. He looks to be no more than a teen-ager. It's a long drive back. The winds are still blowing sand across the highway and the air is cold. A cold front triggered the desert storm. These Haboobs of the desert are infamous. We stop briefly at a rest stop but continue without interference. Approaching Giza, we encounter one of the worst traffic jams imaginable. It is virtually grid-locked, as we inch our way along. I soon discover the reason. All the traffic using the entrance to a freeway leading around Cairo is required to make a sharp U-turn in order to enter the main highway. Large trucks, buses and taxis get snarled trying to make the sharp turnaround. It is testimony to the stupidity of whoever planned such a thing! After hours spent in this gridlock, we finally make it onto the freeway only to exit within a short distance to enter Giza. Karim takes us to the stables owned by his brothers for something to eat. He stays there but sends three of us by another car into Cairo to the Bedouin Hostel. There is concern about this being the eve of the 6 October Holiday which celebrates Egypt's 1973 victory over Israel in regaining the Suez Canal. More demonstrations are anticipated.

We pass by Tahrir Square, where these riots have taken place over the past months with more expected tonight and tomorrow. I may have picked the wrong day to be leaving for the airport. The whole of Tahrir Square is cordoned off by police and numerous military vehicles standing guard over the now-empty square. Diverted traffic has caused more snarls but we finally make our way to the hostel to spend my final night in Egypt.

I leave early for the airport to allow time in case of riots. Fortunately, traffic is still light on the morning of this holiday. The protest crowds have yet to form. I learn later that several indeed take place and that more than forty people are killed in the demonstrations. It's good that

Whales in the Desert

I left as early as I did, though it made for a long wait for the ticket counters to open at the airport. I have to wait in the outer area for the Qatar Airlines desk to open, sticking close to my luggage all that time.

I plan to spend tonight in Doha, Qatar before going on to Kathmandu.

3

Qatar, Oasis of Wealth

Monday 7 October

Qatar Oasis of Wealth

Arriving in Doha from Cairo I purchase the necessary visa and clear customs and hire a taxi to a hotel I had reserved online. Hotel prices in Qatar can be astronomical but after much searching I found a cheaper one and am anxious to see what it might be like. Obviously, it isn't meant for the rich and famous, who often frequent Qatar's new hotel industry but I find it adequate for my needs, being a simple traveler.

Qatar has the distinction of being the richest country in the world per capita. Oil wealth has made this small peninsula what it is today. The city skyline is visible just across the bay from where I am staying, and I plan to visit there tomorrow.

I get up to explore too early to visit the nearby *souk* where I want to see what kinds of market goods are on display. Instead, I spot the Islamic Museum and Cultural Center and decide to give it a try. I am greeted and invited to visit displays of Islamic history, organized around the five pillars of Islamic faith. A staff member graciously brings me tea. The educational displays are impressive. A young man in the white robe attire of Qatar approaches to welcome me and asks me to join him for "a few minutes" to talk about Islam. I am certain that it is a proselyting effort, so I respectfully decline. He insists but is sensitive to my decline and we let it go at that. I continue my tour of the exhibits. One of the aspects of Islam that has most fascinated me was the historical period when Islamic scholars are credited with preserving ancient Greek culture and science, which might have been lost to us had they not done so. Europe at the time was still wallowing in the Dark Ages, but Islamic learning was soaring. They established the first universities in the world, which became centers of learning and exploration. It was the Crusades that brought Europeans into contact with classical, scientific learning. I take time to enjoy the exhibit.

Modern Skyscrapers of Qatar

A friend recently met in Pittsburgh advised me to visit the new and impressive Islamic Art Museum while in Doha. He had visited and worked there before, so I arrange for a driver for the museum visit as well as a tour of Doha. He proves to be an interesting companion, telling me that the Islamic Art Museum is one of his favorite places to go

Distant Lands

"when I get lonely or bored," he says. From Bangladesh, he has come here to find work driving oil trucks from the desert which he says was a hard and dangerous job and now works doing taxi service. The museum is an impressive building, designed by the famous architect I.M. Pei. The queen of Qatar had persuaded Pei to come out of retirement to design this project, and what a wonder it is. We are greeted by a large atrium, tall with windows looking out across the bay to the Doha skyline beyond with its crowded skyscrapers, most of which were not even there 10 years ago. A large fountain anchors the atrium, giving the refreshing sounds of water, with a feeling of light and openness. On each side various floors contain exhibits of art of all types, from pottery to furniture, doors, ancient carpets, textiles and jewels, including gold and diamond encrusted swords and scabbards. It is all quite impressive. We take our time walking through each one.

Skyscrapers are still being built downtown. One is called the "Tornado Tower," designed like a swirling tornado, which I dub as the "Oklahoma Tower." Beyond downtown is a planned city called Katari City, home to upscale malls, luxurious condos with convenient harbors for the yachts of the wealthy. One yacht must have cost multiple millions. The Qataris seem to be enjoying their wealth.

The visit is brief but good. Qatar reflects vividly the growing disparity between rich and poor. Menial jobs are done by low-wage foreigner workers. Wealth derives from the poor who get little benefit from it.

Speaking of the poor, it is time for my flight to Kathmandu, not exactly a center of wealth.

4

Nepal for Dashain

Tuesday 8 October

Arrival in Kathmandu

It is after dark when I process through immigration, now getting a bit routine for me. I pay my $25 in USD. A young couple in line behind me has run out of cash. The money exchange desk is closed and ATM machines are not working. I overhear them pleading with the immigration officer. As a compromise, he suggests that the girl stay here while the guy goes by taxi into the city to find an ATM and return to the airport to pay the bill. I see the worried look on the girl's face and ask how much they need. Fortunately I have the $20 needed and pass it to them, the least I can do. They tell me they are from Jackson Hole, Wyoming, not so far from where my twin daughters and grandchildren live in Cody, Wyoming. They gladly accept the money and I wish them well. This is their first trip to Nepal.

Outside, my friend Lokman is waiting, having come on his motorcycle and patiently waiting two hours for my arrival. Since the bike is not enough to carry both me and luggage, we hire a taxi to his house. They give me a room upstairs in a study center that has been set aside for girls seeking an education. The girls have now gone back in their native villages for the Dashain festival coming up.

Distant Lands

I stay two days with Lokman. He is a manager at the Kathmandu Prince Hotel, where I first stayed five years ago. While he is at work, I take daily trips into the Thamel area near the hotel and connect with my friend Tara. We are planning to journey again to his mountain village, this time for the Dashain festival.

Night with Friends
After two nights at Lokman's, I transfer to a hotel that Tara's friend Bishwas has booked for us for tonight. Bishwas invites us to join him for dinner with foreign tourists he is guiding on a trek starting tomorrow. The dinner features a sampling of traditional Nepali food. The tourists are from Switzerland and a delight to meet, a trio of friends from university days, gathered for this trip, mostly in their late 50s and early 60s. With the meal, we are served sips of the native rice wine, dramatically poured into small clay saucers from a great height for toasts, which we do. It is strong stuff and clears my allergy-congested throat, making it good medicine!

The guests return to their hotel. Tara, Bishwas and I join Tara's two brothers at the Buddha pub to share a double apple shisha together. One of Tara's brothers, Youbaraj, is here from Tokyo where he lives with his Japanese wife. The other brother is Kumar.

We will all travel together to their native village, except for Bishwas who will guide his tourists on a trek.

A Remote Village
A car is arranged to take us to Tara's native village, quite remote, requiring passage over a steep mountain pass, possible only with a four-wheel drive vehicle for the difficult climb. The driver neglects to mention that the four-wheel part is not working, which we will discover later. It's a beautiful drive through the mountain, offering spectacular views of the high peaks of the Himalayas. The trip goes well until we depart the main road to begin our ascent, on more a path than road, with deep ruts or

Nepal for Dashain

loose powdery dirt defying traction. The car is insufficient for the task, lacking both power and traction for the steeper inclines. We get out to reduce weight. I start hiking up the mountain, while Tara and Youbaraj help the driver make multiple attempts, backing the car up for new runs at the incline. I end up walking for two hours, breathless at first due to the high altitude but gradually I get my wind and am able to maintain a slow pace, still keeping me ahead of the car. After much effort, I arrive at a small village of three or four houses near the top, desperately in need of water. The car catches up but cannot stop until it reaches a more level spot higher up. Before I can reach the car to get water, they tell the driver to go on to the top and the car speeds off. I am dehydrated to a point that I can't go on. Tara has to make a quick hike to the top to bring water back for me. I have reached my limit and may be risking a problem, so I wait until he brings the water, a concession to my nearly 74 years of age.

Refreshed with water, we walk slowly to the top, load up and make the steep descent to the village, a cluster of a few farm houses and a school. I had visited here on my trip in January. The house is shared with goats on the main floor, where the cooking and eating is done and we sleep on the second floor. The family is quite happy to see their son Youbaraj, who has not been home in three years. It is a good family time together for the festival, when families usually reunite. I will be an interested observer.

We eat dinner together. The three brothers sleep on pallets, with a small bed provided for me. During the night, their cousin Tej from Kathmandu slips into bed with them. I don't hear him come in and am surprised when I wake the next morning to find him there.

Celebrating Dashain

It is time for the Dashain festival, celebrating a victory of good over evil. The family is united. The fourth son arrives to join his wife and two children, who have been in the village for some days. His name is Gopal.

Distant Lands

A goat is selected to be sacrificed. Across Nepal thousands of goats are being sacrificed during this festival. We had seen herds of goats corralled outside Kathmandu for sacrifices in the city.

Here the process is up-close and personal. The family gets involved and the deed is done. The goat is washed and sprinkled with spices as a sign of blessing. Flower petals are scattered. When the goat shakes itself of the water, it signals that it is ready to be sacrificed. Kumar, the more muscular and stocky of the four brothers, takes a long knife, finely sharpened, as the father stretches the goat's head and the other brothers hold the goat's back leg to begin the sacrifice. Kumar makes a swift and decisive blow, severing the goat's head. The brothers quickly upend the kicking body to let blood drizzle on a small altar nearby and then to drain into a bowl. The blood will be fried and eaten first. The head's eyes meanwhile are still blinking. The father pours water to wash it and gently closes its eyes its one final of life. The head is then placed on the altar.

Water has been heated nearby on an open fire. A sack is spread and the goat's body is scalded by the hot water while the family jumps in to begin pulling hair from the body. Even the little girl assists her grandfather who brings the head to be cleaned of hair. It is hard work. Finally razors are brought and the remaining hair is shaved, until the skin is clean.

The carcass is brought inside where an uncle with sharp knives does most of the butchering. Nothing will be wasted. The body cavity is cleaned of internal organs. The liver will be cooked first. The intestines are stripped and cleaned to be used as well. Legs are cut away and then the chopping begins without distinguishing "cuts" of meat, chopping everything into small pieces for cooking. Soon there are piles of small pieces—meat with bones, intestines, tail, skull, everything!

We eat the fried blood first and later the liver.

Nepal for Dashain

Dashain, Rains and Down the Mountain

Dashain's main day follows the initial goat sacrifice we made with the immediate family. Now we move to the uncle's house for a more complete ceremony involving another sacrifice of still another sacrifice.

In the yard, an altar has been prepared with banana leaf stalks planted in the ground. The household god is brought from the house and propped against a rock wall. Coconuts and other food offerings are brought. Marigold blossoms are strung to make garlands, placed around the altar. Tara tells me to sit nearby. I am not to interfere, just to observe, which I do.

Uncles and family members gather dressed in their finest. The ceremonies begin. Tara and a cousin are chosen to read from ancient Sanskrit texts. The uncles blow sea shell horns similar to sound of the ram's horns described in the Old Testament. Singing and chanting begin. People move about, talking or even joking, sometimes fully participating. Their idea of sacredness does not to require silence. The ceremonies go for some time as the rain begins to fall gently and gets heavier but not enough to drive anyone away. The goat is brought and sacrificed and butchered as I described before. Kumar wields the knife. The blood is sprinkled on the altar and on the food offerings. The head is placed before the god with eyes pointed toward it. There is more chanting and reading and the blowing of horns. When one reader gives out, another cousin takes his place. When it is all over, the food offerings are gathered and distributed among us to eat, including me. We break the coconut into small pieces and eat the sweets.

We take our leave. The rain, by now, is increasing and does not let up for three days, creating a problem for our return trip back to Kathmandu.

The rainy days keep us inside the farm house amidst the smoke of cooking, setting off my allergies big time. We play cards. The brothers are quite competitive, playing a card game with complicated rules, I just observe. I ask only that Tara include me every so often in conversation, to let me know what people are saying, but he gets so caught up in the moment he forgets. I remember how it was with my brothers back home during holidays playing our hard-fought games of Monopoly and such, so I don't remind him. For days I hear no English, resigning myself to go with the flow. We eat the goat with rice and dahl. It is their time to enjoy.

The rains do not let up and we cannot leave as planned, waiting until we can walk down the mountain to the main road. On the morning of the 15th, the rains let up to a light drizzle and we decide to go for it, packing bags to carry on our backs. Tara, his brother Youbaraj, brother Gopal and his family, including the little baby and I begin the hike down the mountain. The rain has made the rocks slippery and the earth unstable. We fear landslides. They give me a tall walking stick to help me steady myself on the descent. Part of the way is by trails, but much of it consists of descending steps almost straight down. I have to be careful. I don't want to make a fall. I would not want them to have to carry me down. We descend for an hour before taking a rest break, still looking straight down. We continue. I am amazed by dexterity of the mother with the baby on this difficult descent. Once or twice I slip on the rocks and land on my bottom, with slight scrapes to my arm but I am lucky, for at another place or two it could have been much worse. By the time we reach the bottom the muscles of my forelegs have given it all they can. I don't think I could have gone another step.

We walk to a small village to await a car to take us to Baktipur near Kathmandu.

It has been an interesting time, challenging and difficult, giving me a unique experience with a Nepali family. I loved it.

Leaving Nepal
Back in Kathmandu, I am ready for a hotel with a hot water shower, but there is no hot water. Though it is cold, at least I am able to wash

Nepal for Dashain

five days' worth of village off me. My allergies are really intense, settling into my bronchial tubes.

My next stop is India to participate in an educational and cultural project in the farm villages of north India.

It is dark when the plane successfully lifts from the short runway in Kathmandu but there is a brilliant glow in the towering clouds above emanating from the distant sun casting its last rays in the west.

5

Utter Pradesh

Wednesday 23 October

The Villages of North India

I arrive in Delhi by Spice Jet from Kathmandu and check into the Prince Polonia Hotel in New Delhi. Due to an ongoing problem with my room, the staff offers me the use of the owner's suite, furnished with a large table, comfortable seating areas and even a library. I am now a happy camper. They also promise the use of this room next weekend when my friends come to celebrate my birthday.

Returning to the airport, I greet our team arriving from America. We load into two vans for the trip north to Utter Pradesh through impossible traffic, taking nearly five hours for the trip. We check into a hotel and meet the next day at our host's house to receive orientation. A young translator assigned to me for our projected visits to the villages, where we will meet the people to learn about their lives, hopes and dreams. My translator is a nineteen year old young man named Rahul. We hit it off immediately.

Utter Pradesh

Perfecting Sugar Cane Eating Technique

Rahul and I hail a bus and then travel some distance by rickshaw, where we are let off to walk from the main road to our first village. In the small village, we meet a man who serves us chai and takes us around to introduce us to his relatives, most of whom are potato farmers, who are busy sorting mounds of potatoes, sacking them for shipment to Indian's markets. We drink lots of chai. Over the following three days we visit in at least three villages, mostly peopled by the Tyagi caste, one of the many Indian sub-groups. It is all quite interesting and educational. I learn a lot, and grow to love the people I meet, who invite us to have lunch in their homes. It is a good experience for my young translator, who had not been into that many small villages before. Between times we joke together and laugh. Back in the city, I meet some of his friends. We debrief our experiences by sharing with our group. Seeing the "real" India up close and personal in this way is quite a vibrant experience, even learning the skill of eating sugar cane from the stalk.

I meet an ambitious young man in our last village, who insists that we spend more time together. He invites me to spend the night in his village on this our last night here, so I let our team leader know, who gives his blessing. I am always willing to try something new.

Night with the Buffaloes
I'm with neither toothbrush nor anything else, but what is life if one doesn't seize the moment? My translator returns to Meerut to be with his family. My host Rumal promises that a young nephew who is taking English in high school will stay with us to help translate.

Rumal is a bright young man, hoping one day to go into Indian politics and does not plan to marry at this time. It is the first time I've encountered an Indian intent on living as a bachelor, at least for some time. He explains that many of the leading politicians in India remain unmarried, due the demands of the political life, which makes it difficult to give proper attention to one's family.

Rumal introduces me to his extended family as we make rounds throughout the village, including uncles, cousins and nephews, many of whom walk with us as we go from house to house, drinking chai at each stop. We walk to the edge of the village to wait for a car to take us to the nearby city of Hopur, where again, we meet various relatives operating a variety of shops. One runs a pharmacy. His best friend happens by on a motorcycle and gives me a spin around the city, stopping for various snacks. Back together, we order skewered chicken from a street side cafe to take back to the village for our dinner, which we eat on the rooftop of his shop, sitting on cots. Other items are brought for dinner for about fifteen of us to eat and enjoy the time, including his wiry grandmother. I am probably the only foreigner to have visited the village. If not, I'm sure that I am the only one who has stayed overnight.

Following dinner, blankets are brought to be spread over the cots, where we will sleep tonight on the open on the roof. Below us, water buffaloes are tethered to each farm house which has one or more

Utter Pradesh

buffaloes, living as part of the house. We talk way into the night, the young nephew helping us to communicate, while relaxing on our cots. The night air is cool and by four or five a.m., I'm getting quite cold and ask for extra covering.

This morning I shower at the house, partly discrete behind the flimsy curtain, using a bucket of water. Toilet facilities are basic here, typical of farm villages but I manage. His sister prepares breakfast on a buffalo-dung fire, cooking chippattis on a flat burner, then thrown into the fire to puff them up, using the same tong to pluck fresh buffalo patties to stoke the fire.

Ruhal my translator comes for me at ten. We had earlier promised a family we visited the first day to return today to attend the funeral ceremony for their 96 year-old father, who had died just before we came. They send a car for us. We arrive to a large feast, staying only a few minutes after eating, to listen to a band play the father's favorite primitive Indian music. I wish I could have stayed longer, but we are due back for our return to Delhi.

Getting off the tourist track in these small villages is a great experience, if one is willing to forego a little comfort. How else do we learn? The real India awaits those who are willing.

6

India Birthday

Sunday 27 October

Birthday in Delhi

We arrive back in Delhi on October 25 to meet my Indian friends come to celebrate my birthday on the 27th, marking the fourth birthday celebrated in India over the past five years

Mike from the USA arrives from northeast India, where he has been on a teaching assignment in Nepal, India and Bangladesh since August. He plans to return to the USA on October 31st after a brief trip to Bangalore. We are good friends, sharing many of the same interests in travel, meeting local people wherever we go. Mike is an easy-going gentle spirit. Next to arrive is Suresh from Pushkar, a friend I've known since my second trip to India. Last to arrive is Neeraj from Jaipur. I had met Neeraj at the Pushkar Camel fair two years ago.

With everyone in place, there is time for catching up and enjoying being together. Suresh invites a friend from Australia to join us. He and I share the same birthday. His name is Brad.

In the afternoon, I am ordered to leave the room so my friends can decorate it.

India Birthday

When all is ready, Brad and I are led into the room to an amazing display! Rose petals cover the large table, incense is burning and candles lit. The guys gather hands full of rose blossoms to shower on us as they give us each a big hug and sing "Happy Birthday." Photos are taken. Candles light a dual cake—one with "61" for Brad and one with "74" for me. Another candle is lit, which flashes and begins revolving, quite spectacular. The cake is cut and we feed each other pieces of the cake. According to Indian custom, some of it is smeared on our faces, all in good fun.

After the cake celebration, we are joined by the hotel staff to enjoy snacks, seated in the large area with couches. It is a great time.

Country Bumpkins at Rambagh Palace
The three of us, Suresh, Neeraj and I, catch the early morning train to Jaipur, where Suresh and I check into the Diana Palace Hotel. Neeraj stays for breakfast but returns to his home, coming later to join us for dinner at the Copper Chimney, quite popular with tourists.

After dinner, Suresh insists that we visit Jaipur's luxurious Rambagh Palace, Jaipur's very exclusive resort, which none of us can afford. We arrive at the great palace by car. Valets are on hand to park our car and we make our way a welcome desk. Suresh explains that we are here just for a snack and drinks, whereupon we're directed to the posh Polo Club, located past opulent dining areas with alcoves for seating. At the club, it is obvious that we can't afford much listed on the menu, even hors d'ouvres, but we order a few along with mocktales and such for drinks, feeling a little out of place. The waiters appear often asking if there is more we'd like to order. After we finish and pay our bill using all the cash we have, we call for the car to be brought, only to realize by then, that none of us has any money left to tip the valet. No doubt we were pegged as the country bumpkins adrift in the big city, which in fact we were. Maybe we will return another day for a more impressive exit.

Suresh and I catch a bus the next morning for Pushkar.

Birthday in Jethana

Returning to Pushkar is like coming home. Everyone seems to know me, greeting me on the street by name, sometimes by people I hardly know but who know me. We make a journey to Jethana to celebrate another birthday for young Mitty, who turns 12 birthday on October 31. I had attended several of his birthday parties before. I join the kids on the roof, blowing up balloons in preparation for the party, while ladies are cooking a celebration dinner. Birthdays are big occasions in India.

Mitty's Birthday Party

The neighborhood kids gather in the single room decorated with streamers and balloons. A cake is brought and we sing "Happy Birthday," while Mitty blows out the candles and feeds everyone a piece of cake, starting with his mother and soon me as well, since I am "Keith Uncle" to him. After the party and dinner, I stay the night at another uncle's house, who has three sons named Aman, Shaman and Naman, always a delight. Naman shares his favorite music by mobile before we sleep.

India Birthday

Diwali Festival in Pushkar

Diwali, also called Deepiwali, is one of India's biggest and brightest festivals. We return to Pushkar to make preparations, following the custom of buying new clothes for the festival. At my hotel owner's suggestion, I chip in to help buy a set of clothes for one of the young boys on the staff, who proudly models his purchases for me.

I buy new shirts for myself to go with a pair of slacks I brought with me, so I can be appropriately dressed for the main night of Diwali. Homes are decorated with lights and candles in every room. Suresh's wife Deepika has beautifully decorated their room with lamps and rose petals. I join for the prayers at the beginning of the celebration, his parents first with their poojas, then Deepika and Suresh. I join the younger brother Kumal for the *tikka* blessing. Fireworks go off around the city, making it a spectacular and loud night.

Suresh Praying at Home Altar

Distant Lands

We sit at the street to receive greetings the next morning from a constant stream of people coming to pay respects, who touch our feet as a show of respect. I sit with Suresh and his father. We then do the same making rounds to other houses, drinking chai and eating a rich variety of sweets. Everyone is dressed in their Diwali finery.

Fireworks continue all during the day and into the second night. It is a joyous time.

Rajasthani Moustache
The annual Pushkar Camel Fair is a world event, quite unlike any other. Thousands of camels and their herders are camped just outside the city on the desert sands. Horses and cattle are brought in also. It is a time to barter, to buy and sell camels, horses, cattle. It is a fair and exposition of animals, featuring camel and horse races in the Mela at the edge of town. Cultural dances are performed each night. A midway of Ferris wheels and countless other rides give it a fair-like atmosphere. People have come from all over the world and India. It is difficult to maneuver through the crowds, given the sacred cows, the vendors, motorcycles and display carts vying for space. Hawkers call out for passers-by to look at their wares. The fair offers all kinds of amusements. Perhaps most interesting are the camel safaris. The fair coincides with a season of religious pilgrimages as worshippers come for ceremonial bathing at the Poojas, starting early in the morning well before sunrise. My friend Suresh is a Brahmin priest who helps with the Poojas. He arises at 2:30 to begin his day.

The official first day is marked with a parade of colorful floats, dancers and bands. The various gods of Hindu mythology are costumed and featured. Flower petals are thrown in extravagant abundance as the parade inches its way through the crowded narrow streets.

A Rajasthani man displays a long moustache proudly showing its full length, surely a world record. He holds it in the length of both outstretched arms, letting its ends drape to the street and demonstrates how he carries it, winding it up to form a knot on the top of his head, which he then covers with his turban. Interesting! Moustaches are a Rajasthani trademark.

India verses the West
Random events are held across the breadth of the arena, like the one I observed today, a contest between an Indian team and a Western team. The object is for each team to build a human pyramid three layers high and once established, the man on top is given a cane stick to knock a clay pot from a pole. The Western team is formed made up of visiting tourists—Europeans, Australians, Americans and Israelis. The Western team is muscular enough, young men in their twenties but they are neither as limber nor as agile as the Indian team. The crowd cheers the Western team as they attempt the feat, only to end up failing. The Indian team quickly constructs its pyramid and knocks down the clay pot, much to the delight and cheers of the crowd. Being sports minded as they are, the crowd insists on giving the Western team a sympathy round. Once again they try, finally succeeding, much to the approval of the crowd!

Crowds pour into Pushkar as the fair progresses toward the final day, the holy festival of the full moon. One can hardly stir through the crowds. Pickpockets have a heyday, even picking the pocket for the wallet of a policeman. The policeman comes to a friend of mine, asking what he should do as his ATM card was inside the wallet. My friend tells him he must cancel his card. Evidently he didn't know to do that.

India is nothing without its many festivals and rituals that excite the senses and overwhelm with its countless numbers of people, showing exuberance for life.

I will miss it when I return to my quieter, well-ordered existence!

More Indian Weddings

I can't escape India without participating in a couple of weddings. This trip is no exception. I previously attended the weddings of my friend Summit's two older brother and now it is time for his wedding. Suresh is heavily involved in the preparations, negotiating with various vendors in behalf of Summit's family. I plan to attend the initial ceremony of Summit's wedding and then make a trip to the village of Nimaj to attend a wedding in Suresh's wife's family.

Before the wedding, I attend Summit's investiture ceremony at his house for investing him a full Brahmin. It was quite something to see. He sits shirtless, wearing a white *dhoti* for trousers, as his family leads him through the ceremonies which I have described previously in reference to Suresh.

A large venue is selected for Summit's wedding at the edge of the city. Kiosks for serving food to the guests are set up with vendors busy making preparations. My friend Honjoerg arrives from Germany, who like me has attended all the family's weddings. We visit while everyone else runs around making preparations.

The groom's wedding party arrives to great fanfare and the initial ceremonies begin. Now Summit is outfitted in the full regalia of a Maharajah. His wife is adorned in a sari and bedecked with jewels, from a ring on her nose to bracelets and anklets of gold and silver. Indian brides wear the wealth of their dowry.

At night there is the big event of the groom's wedding dinner. We change into our best clothes. The late fall air is cold. We were greeted at the entrance by Summit's brothers and directed to select food from various tables around the perimeter of the wedding venue. I had brought a gift and was ushered to the stage where the bridal couple holds court, seated on their thrones. I present the gift, duly photographed. We are photographed together about three times during the

India Birthday

course of the evening. The photos go into the wedding album, which will be shown to family and guests for years to come.

The next day we go to Nimaj for the wedding of Deepika's cousin. The wedding venue is set up in an area next to the family home. The groom's party arrives, treats are served and the family is welcomed, some two or three busloads of them, arrived from another village. The second night is the bride's family's dancing night and we enjoy dancing. I join with a young cousin do a version of "Lungi Dance," a popular song at the moment. They seem to enjoy my participation, which of course, leaves a lot to be desired, but it is the spirit of the moment that is celebrated. I put my self-consciousness aside and experience the moment, good advice for anyone participating in Indian celebrations!

Winding Up My Trip: Time to Leave
Back in Pushkar, I get ready to head home, deciding not to continue on around the world as I thought I might. I am ready to head home for Christmas to be with my family.

My friends are downcast at the prospect of my leaving, as I knew they would be. It is hard to leave them. Suresh decides to accompany me by bus for the long trip to Delhi, delaying the good-bye drama. His friend Navneet also comes with us. I make the usual rounds of good-byes before leaving Pushkar, starting with the hotel, and Jonty who insists that I sit awhile with young backpackers at his small restaurant, where despite the difference in ages, I am accepted and welcomed by the group of mostly young Israeli and Australian backpackers.

I am given the *tikka* blessing at Suresh's house by his mother. His brother takes me by motorcycle to the bus stop and Suresh comes separately with the bags. We board a sleeper bus. I get acquainted with the only other western occupant, a young man from Israel. We sit and talk for some time before crawling into our respective sleeping compartments, crammed with luggage and the three of us, including Navneet. It's a long trip through the night to Delhi.

In Delhi, we check into the hotel and then attend a special 50th Anniversary performance held at a stadium in Delhi for a production of John Bunyan's Pilgrim's Progress with songs, narrative and choreography. It is the work high school youth, students of Anita, my niece's mother. Suresh and Navneet both enjoy the presentation as well.

I board a Gulf Air flight to Bahrain and on to Frankfurt, Germany, then Dallas and finally to Oklahoma City—a 36-hour marathon. In Frankfurt, I am detained by security to be thoroughly searched due to suspicion about my cowboy hat. It seems to have something to do with the materials from which it is made. I had purchased the hat in Wyoming. Security informs me that the hat was made from palm leaves which grow in Central America. Had they already analyzed the fibers? Satisfied that it does not pose a major threat to American society, they turn their attention to me, patting me down in a way that leaves nothing to the imagination. They remove every item from my carry-on bag for careful examination. Finally, they allow me to proceed, leaving me to wonder what that was all about.

My friend Hap is once again there to pick me up in Oklahoma City, having just returned from Ft. Worth where he spent Thanksgiving with his family.

Part Five
Fourth Trip around the World—Istanbul to Tokyo

"I am no longer bounded by locality, the habitat of a confine. I free myself into world spaces. Vastness is in my adventure.. I am a world-person, a sky plainsman, a maker of spirit trails." –Muriel Strode (1875-1964), "Songs of Freedom," A Soul's Faring, 1921

1

A Night in a Turkish Fire Station

Wednesday 3 September 2014
Deer Creek Edmond Oklahoma, USA

Ready to Go...Again!
Bags packed. Bills caught up. Kids notified. Neighbors alerted. It is becoming my usual mantra.

I'm off again for my fourth solo adventure around the world. Travel indeed is addictive, but in a good way. There is so much yet to learn.

This time, I plan to visit Turkey, Nepal, India and Japan, Lord willing, to connect again with friends I have made along the way. My friend Nurettin plans to greet me in Istanbul. He is has arranged for me to spend a night in the fire station, which should be an interesting experience! Istanbul is an incredible site for history and culture. From Turkey, I plan to fly to Nepal, where a friend from India plans to join me to explore Nepal's natural beauty, after which we will travel to India to be with my lovely friends there. My final destination is Japan, to stay with a Nepali friend I made last year, and his Japanese wife.

Solo travel can be a challenge but pays rich rewards in adventure and experience. I prefer to go where few tourists go, staying with locals, living among them to experience the daily rhythms of life.

Along the way, I will celebrate my 75th birthday, entering the fourth quartile of life. You are welcome to join me for another adventure!

Friday 5 September 2014

Istanbul: Prayer at the Fire Station
I am informed by the airlines agent at the Oklahoma City airport that I will need a pre-arranged visa in order to enter Turkey, news to me. I had not needed one to fly before. The harried United Airlines clerk finally issues a boarding pass, as much to get rid of me as to help, I think. Clearing security, I begin to worry that Turkish Airlines in Chicago might not allow me to board. A quick check online produces only confusion on the subject. I cast my lot to fate and go on.

I hasten to the International Terminal to the Turkish Airlines desk in a friendly manner and say to the agent that I hope that she is good at solving problems. She assures me she is as she asks for my passport, quickly stamping my boarding pass for Istanbul. "And what problem can I help you with?" Accepting the boarding pass, I say lamely "I guess visas are still available at the airport on arrival." She smiles and says "Of course, no problem." My worry had been needless.

My seatmate is an elderly-looking man from Macedonia and chatting, we discover that he and I were born the same month of the same year, only 6 days my senior! He is on his way to Belgrade to visit a brother. He is widowed like me. As we talk, he confides that he is envious of my travels.

In Istanbul I message Nurettin, waiting outside the airport, that I just need to retrieve one checked bag, but the bag never comes. It takes time to file reports. Nurettin picks me up and we head to his apartment

A Night in a Turkish Fire Station

to greet his lovely young wife Sibel, who has dinner waiting for us, and a fine meal it is.

The next day Nurettin introduces me to his buddies at the fire station, along with his chief. I present the chief a patch I brought from my local fire station and he presents me a commemorative plate and t-shirt. I have arrived at prayer time and I am invited to attend prayer at the nearby mosque, with several of the firemen and others, to participate with them kneeling and touching my head to the floor. I feel a little awkward, but they are gracious about it and I make my prayers. Afterwards, we enjoy tea together.

After a short visit, Nurettin takes me to the Metro station so I can go to my first hostel. He heads for the airport to travel to a swim meet some distance away, assuring me that we will stay together at the fire station once he returns from the competition.

Luggage and New Friends
It is my third day in Istanbul when I receive a call from the airlines that my luggage has arrived and can be picked up at the airport. A friend of Nurettin's had connected with me on Facebook this past year. His name is Atalay. He suggests that I stop by his print shop, near one of the Metro stops, to meet me and take me to lunch. By the time I retrieve the luggage, fill out the necessary paper work, return to my hostel and deposit my luggage I am quite late. I leave the luggage with the desk clerk to be taken to my room and hastened to the Metro to meet Atalay, wondering if we will be able to spot each other in the crowds. I needn't have worried. Atalay, with a sharp eye, calls out to me from across the Metro tracks. He is with his twelve-year-old son Ozgur (Oscar), with smiles to greet me enthusiastically. We walk some distance to his print shop. The shop has an office upstairs, somewhat like a small apartment. Atalay prepares lunch for us—pasta, Turkish meatballs and a salad, suggesting I get comfortable, finding a pair of shorts and an undershirt for me to change to be comfortable in the

warm weather. We enjoy the tasty lunch and we relax the remainder of the afternoon. On Saturday, he works only a half day, so we are free to kick back and relax which I welcome, having been keyed up about my luggage. It doesn't take long for us to establish a rapport with these guys. Ozgur and I work on English words together. He is taking English in school. Atalay calls a friend named Inaj to join us. They had recently been in an English class together and Atalay knows he would like to practice English skills with me. He too is enjoyable as we spend time practicing, while Atalay picks fruit, quince and figs to eat, from a small orchard.

Toward dark, we pile into Atalay's Toyota to deliver a package to the Sultanahmet area close to my hotel. After the delivery, the group takes me the Terrace Café, located on a roof with a commanding view of Istanbul's harbor, enjoying tea and hookah. Inaj excuses himself briefly for prayers at a nearby mosque, returning to discuss with me our various beliefs. In the distance, fireworks shoot skyward, a perfect evening. I don't know when I've enjoyed a more relaxing time, especially with new friends just met.

They kindly drop me back at my hostel for the night.

Hagias Sophia and Topkapi
Sunday is a perfect day to visit the historic old church, *Hagias Sophia*. It has long been at the top of my list of historical structures, which I most want to see in the world. Built in the 600s, it has survived invasions, earthquakes, and religious remakes. For a thousand years, it stood as the largest enclosed space in the world. Today it is a museum that never ceases to awe by its beauty and endurance. It was the religious center of the Byzantine Empire (Eastern Roman Empire). Emperors were crowned here. Thousands of curious tourists visit each day. The aging beauty requires continuous restoration, including the ongoing restoration of the priceless mosaics, covered over during the period it served as a mosque.

A Night in a Turkish Fire Station

The nearby Topkapi Palace, the home and seat of the Sultans' administrations, was built in a pavilion style with many rooms and chambers, including the Harem where the Sultan's wives, concubines, consorts and eunuchs lived. It housed the Sultan's personal living quarters, quite impressive, especially the treasury where treasured objects of gold, diamonds, and other jewelry are displayed. A 85 carat stone of great beauty is displayed. Another room displays Islamic relics: Moses' staff, Joseph's turban, David's sword and relics of the prophet Muhammed—a footprint, along with various objects, even a clipping of his beard.

It is my day for history.

Spending the Night in an Istanbul Fire Station

Atalay helps me identify the correct metro bus to take to the Pelican Mall near Nurettin's fire station. In spite of confusing directions by people on the street, I finally find my way to the fire station to greeted warmly by a waiting Nuri and the crew, arriving in time for dinner, served upstairs, meeting several of the fire crew. Following dinner, the fire crew sets up nets for a volleyball game, a way to fill time between emergencies, asking me to join, but I decline due to my age. I could already tell they were a fiercely competitive bunch. The game gets under way once Nuri climbs a nearby tree to shake down some walnuts, which he offers to me and the others for a snack. An injured fireman in a wheelchair is enlisted to serve as referee and scorekeeper. He was injured in a recent automobile accident. That the game is fiercely competitive is an understatement! After a break following the first game, the teams heatedly argue over certain calls but still maintain a good nature about it, though they seem quite serious.

Even with gathering darkness, the competition is no less intense. Afterwards the losing team treats everyone to slices of fresh watermelons, while continuing their sparring over the outcome. It is all fun to watch. We sit around a table and talk into the dark, with many of the guys asking questions about my Christian faith and comparisons with

Islam. I answer as best I can. In the process, we have a good-natured and instructive discussion, the way such discussions should be. When one earns people's trust and friendship, it is easier for barriers to dissolve, allowing a climate where both can learn together.

The fire crews sleep in dormitory rooms upstairs, outfitted with single beds. Nuri and I, along with another guy, share a room. The night is warm and we leave the window open with the traffic noises keeping me awake for some time. We get some sleep once the night cools.

As far as fire calls, it is a quiet night without urgent alarms for fires, traffic accidents or animal rescues except for one which occurred during the volleyball game when a cat got stranded on a roof. Five of the players made a quick exit to rescue the cat. Nuri had promised that I could go on a run if it was not for a major fire, which in that case, I would probably have been in the way. I do not go on the cat rescue.

After breakfast, I take my leave, having had a great time and adding new friends to my Facebook. It is another event added to my travel adventures. What happens next, though, affects the rest of my trip.

Last Day Spent at a Police Station!
Well, it was bound to happen. Crowded metro buses come and go, people shoving to get on. One, two, three, four buses pass me by. I tell myself to get a little more aggressive about getting on. Forcing my way, I squeeze on bus number five when a fight breaks out next to me with those trying to get on and those trying to keep them off. The door squeezes closed, leaving me clutching desperately to hang on, while holding onto a hand rail above my head and clutching my small bag in the other hand, which I also hold above my head. There is no other room. We lunge forward in these crowded conditions until I exit to transfer to the tram back to Sultanahmet and my hotel. I can't wait to have a shower and shave. As I exit, I feel for my wallet. It is not there! Panic! In the fight to get on the bus, some opportunistic thief

A Night in a Turkish Fire Station

must have reached into the front pocket and lifted my wallet, without my knowing or feeling it happen. All my money, credit cards and driver's license are gone in that instant. My medical cards...everything! Horrors! It is a sickening feeling to lose one's wallet, especially this early in my journey. Why didn't I remove it? Why had I stopped at an ATM just before going to the fire station? I should have waited. I pile on questions of regret.

The deed is done. I scrape together enough coins for a metro token to take me back to the hotel; even my metro card is gone! At the hotel, I spend several anxious moments making phone calls, navigating endless credit card menus, getting cut off four or five times, only to start over. Eventually I get all the cards cancelled. The next step is to file a report with the police.

The hotel clerk directs me to the local police station in Sultanahmet. When I reach there I am told that I must return to the area of the crime to file the report at a police station there! Fortunately, that station is located near Atalay's print shop, so I stop by and he promises to accompany me to help translate for the police. The police captain tells us that it isn't in their jurisdiction either, since it happened on the bus. It is a run-around. We persist, finally persuading him it is his jurisdiction, whereupon we take time to laboriously fill out all the required forms. It brings back memories of my first trip to Turkey in 2009, when I had spent my last night in another police station, into the wee hours making reports concerning the theft of my cousin's friend's purse. Maybe it is my destiny to spend final days in police stations. A weird symmetry is at work—one night in the fire station and one day in the police station.

Poor Atalay probably thinks he will never be rid of me! Yet he is so kind and ready to help. After the report is completed, he invites me back to the shop for lunch and tells me to relax. I owe this friend big time for his kind hospitality! Again, he gives me comfortable clothes to change into and orders tea and snacks for us. After lunch, he continues works at his presses, offering me the use of his computer so I make notifications. He also offers the use of a small bed on which to relax, and puts on music by Louis Armstrong and Ella Fitzgerald for us to listen on his computer. After dark, he takes me to his apartment for dinner and to meet his wife and again see his son Ozgur. Well into the night he returns me to my hotel. We will be friends for life!

My flight is not until 5:00 p.m., so I have time to visit the bay for some final photos. The hotel is kind enough to loan enough money for tokens on the tram. I walk around enjoying the salty air of the bay, busy with ferries and other boats. Istanbul is such an interesting place!

One of the hotel boys assists in carrying my luggage up the hill to the tram station for my trip to the airport where Nurettin is on the way. I had promised him an autographed copy of my last travel book, in which I described our first meeting in Australia, but by the time he arrives, I had already cleared customs, so we can't actually meet, but a security guard is kind enough to allow me to pass the book to him through one of the side doors.

I board the Turkish Airlines flight to Delhi.

2

Nepal with a Friend from India

11 September

Traveling Nepal with a Friend
My friend Neeraj has come from Jaipur to join me for a trip to Nepal together, with a different hair style and I almost do not recognize him. I am anxious to see how he responds to Nepal. Indian citizens are not required to obtain visas for Nepal, so he waits while I obtain mine.

Lokman is waiting for us with a taxi to take us to his hotel. Neeraj snaps photos right and left as we thread our way through the traffic. At the hotel we are greeted enthusiastically by the bellboy named Raj Kumar, who always remembers me when I come to visit. We set off to explore Thamel area of Kathmandu where tourists stay, stopping for *mo mo*s at a shop to my friend Tej, who is busy making them upstairs. While he continues his work, we enjoy cold drinks while his brother brings fresh steamed *mo mos* for us to eat. They are so good, the best in Kathmandu. Tej takes a break and joins us for a time. At night, Neeraj and I take dinner in an outdoor café overlooking one of the main streets in Thamel, anticipating meeting my friend Tara in the morning to make plans for travel.

Tara has been working on requirements for certification as a travel guide. He discusses hiring a car for travel to Pokhara. I explain my problem with the stolen wallet and ask his help in locating an American Express agency to get a replacement card. Unfortunately, the address we are given is one that has been shut down. We discover another one, associated with one of the larger banks in Kathmandu only to learn, after multiple phone calls to American Express, that American Express no longer sends replacement cards to Nepal! The only way I survive is using a temporary back-up debit card, which thankfully I had brought with me, kept in a separate pouch. It is my only means for obtaining cash for the remainder of the trip. I will have to pay cash for hotel bills, flight and train reservations. Bummer!

Fortunately, I did bring extra American cash tucked away separately this time, not my usual mode. Raj Kumar offers to exchange large bills for me, which too can be a problem here. He tells me that his son has broken his arm. I count out six $100 bills to give to him for exchange. When he returns with the wad of Nepali bills, he lets me know that two of my bills were stuck together and I had actually given him seven hundred instead. I appreciated his honesty. The exchanged bills make quite a wad of Nepali money, which I don't want to be carrying around, so I place the bulk in a security box at the hotel. We will need that money for our trip to Pokhara. I give Raj 5000 rupees to help with his son's medical expenses.

Trip to Pokhara
We plan to leave this morning. Raj Kumar looking downcast tells me he had taken his son to the hospital overnight and that he was not doing well. I give him another 5000 to help, for which he is very grateful.

Nepal with a Friend from India

Trying Out a Nepal Waterfall

Tara's brother Gopal accompanies us on the trip to Pokhara. I pay the driver and we are off before breakfast. I want Neeraj to experience the waterfalls on the way, where I had stopped before. We strip to basics and enjoy the cascades of water flowing over us. Neeraj scampers to the rocks above like a monkey. We are like school boys playing in the water. I give Gopal my camera to take pictures. It begins to rain and soon everybody is soaked, with no good way to dry off before continuing our journey, like drowned rats.

We share a room in Pokhara and take a walk by the lake and listen to music playing from nearby open-air restaurants. I order skewered chicken for snacks and later the other two have *dahl baht* at a Nepali restaurant. Gopal tells me the hotel staff doesn't have a room for him, as they usually do for drivers and guides, so I invite him to stay with us.

The day is a calm and humid. We ease a row boat into the water at the lake, with Neeraj sitting in the front with an oar, me in the middle, and

Gopal at the back with an oar. Neeraj has trouble learning the proper technique of rowing, so I give him instructions, as we row along the far shore under overhanging vines in which we sometimes get caught. Otherwise it is a nice outing on the beautiful lake.

Serene Lake Fewa, Pokhara, Nepal

I exchange positions with Neeraj to guide the boat a little more efficiently so we can make our one-hour deadline, after which we hang out for the afternoon. Gopal asks for advance money and takes off for the afternoon. In the evening, we are unable to find him and he does not pick up his phone, so Neeraj and I go ahead with dinner at lakeside, listening once again to the music of the evening. Two Chinese ladies sit at table next to us and Neeraj, always the charmer, invites them to sit with us, telling us they are from Beijing, working as secretaries in some kind of business, and have just arrived in Pokhara. We watch native dancers performing traditional dances who invite guests to participate. Neeraj tries to get me to join him but I decline encouraging him to go ahead. He makes a hit with the crowd, as he is a good dancer.

Dhampus Mountain Village
For the first time, the weather clears enough for us to see the high peaks of the Himalayas, both the Annapurna and Fishtail Peaks. The peaks are playing peek-a-boo with the clouds. We leave a little after 11 in a four-wheel jeep we've hired for a climb to the mountain village of Dhampus, heading west along the White River before beginning the ascent over a rough trail paved with stones. The jeep is capable enough and we have little trouble. We take a break at a place with a great view of the valley below before continuing the ascent to the top of the ridge to the village straddling a trekking path with an old guest house, where we check in and sit for a while drinking tea under a covered patio. It begins to rain. The trail and village look somewhat familiar to me, causing me to wonder if perhaps this had been the trail Manish and I had taken in 2009 on my first trek in these mountains. I confirm that it indeed was the same trail, which gives me a feeling of nostalgia, remembering it from five years ago.

The rains continue off and on throughout the afternoon and into the evening. Power is out and we eat by candlelight in a common area of the guest house. A young man plays a guitar quite well, in a classical style, so good in fact that I ask him if he had performed professionally. He says he had and was offered professional opportunities but chose instead to remain in the small village to play as he likes. We enjoy snacks and drinks for a great evening with the small group gathered. Two young men appear with the acquisition requested by Neeraj of the local plant, which is prepared and shared among the group, making for a happy evening and talkative mood on the part of the guys. One of them wants to discuss religion with me—Hinduism, Buddhism, Christianity and Islam, so we do. He tells me that many Hindus in Nepal harbor animosity toward both Islam and Christianity, because of over-proselytizing. The charge against Christians, he explains, is that Westerners come displaying wealth which entices the poor to convert in the hopes of financial gain. I listen respectfully and counter the perception as best I can, although some of those dynamics are at work, even if unintentional. It is an informative and humbling discussion, amidst the gaiety of the evening.

When presented the bill for the guest house, I discover that many of the things consumed last night by others were added to my bill. Even with correction, I am short of cash. Gopal takes what money I have and promises the owners to bring the rest when he comes again. We head down the mountain returning to Pokhara, rejoining our original driver so we can find both money exchanger and electricity to recharge my mobile.

I had visited Bandipur many times before and wanted Neeraj to experience it as well. We check into a hotel on the far side of the village. Neeraj and Gopal explore while I relax in the room until we have dinner at the street café eating by candlelight as darkness descends. Neeraj and I share a room. He is in an especially giddy mood.

It is a foggy morning when we head toward Kathmandu, joined by a young Australian trekker from Melbourne, who had asked to go with us. Casey is a bearded, skinny and pleasant young man, bumming his way around the world. We stop to visit the Manakamana Temple atop a mountain, accessible by cable car, while Casey and the driver wait below. Neeraj prepares an offering but is turned off by the slaughter of animals.

Nepal with a Friend from India

Back in Kathmandu Lokman has arranged a room for us at the adjacent hotel.

I sort through the money issues to make sure I have enough for four days' worth of hotel bills. An issue has developed between the car owner and Tara, claiming that we had not paid enough for the car, because we had stayed an extra day. I reminded Tara of our agreement concerning the number of days and the amounts to be paid, which he had not fully understood and is now caught between the owner and our agreement, leaving him to make up the difference. I suggest a compromise letting the owner and I split the difference, to which he agreed. I did not want Tara to have to pay.

3

A Month in India

19 September

Nepal to India

It rains hard during the night with much thunder and lightning. I give Tara money to cover our expenses and the extra payment for the car trip and pay our bills at both hotels. A weather front has moved in with causing delays from the airport. Once we reach Delhi, which is quite hot and humid, we check into a hotel with a room next to the pool and are quick to plunge in for a refreshing swim.

The next night, due to multiple delays along the train track, we are quite late arriving in Jaipur at the Diana Palace Hotel for the night.

Meeting Devansh

Devansh, a student I had met through Facebook, promises to meet up with me at 12:30 p.m. I spend time at the roof for my Bible reading on this Sunday morning. Neeraj and I have been discussing spiritual things of late. Neeraj believes in the value of good karma. As in Nepal, we discuss religion as friends with a shared humanity. It is the "pure in heart" who seek God, as I read this morning from Jesus' Sermon on the Mount.

A Month in India

Neeraj takes leave to visit his family and friend while I wait for Devansh. The bell rings and two young men present themselves, Devansh and his friend Aseph. Devansh is a nice young man, eager to get acquainted with me in person. He tells me that his friend Aseph had injured himself on the way on his bike. They were delayed due to stopping at a clinic to have his wounds cleaned and bandaged, but still he has some bleeding. I insist on seeing his wound. He drops his jeans to reveal a raw wound above the knee, tender to the touch, along with four or five scrapes. I order food for lunch, vegetarian for Devansh and non-vegetarian for Aseph, who is Muslim. After lunch Aseph takes his leave while Devansh stays longer, inviting me to visit his native village a little later on. Neeraj returns and we relax together until after dark and go to meet his parents.

I buy a general boarding pass for my trip to Ajmer but board the reserved seating car at Neeraj's suggestion and pay a small upgrade after the train leaves. It's a good plan for there are plenty of seats, costing only an additional 15 rupees for the upgrade. We cross the arid landscape of Rajasthan to Ajmer station, where I greet a smiling Suresh rushing toward me. We place my luggage in a car and stop by a clinic to pick up his wife Deepika, who is getting a check-up. Suresh offers two hotel possibilities for me in Pushkar, one still being renovated, so I select the Mama Luna where I had stayed before. We enjoy a falafel dinner at a restaurant he has found which he likes. After dinner I stop at Jonti's small café to sit with trekker friends, meeting a guy from Jaipur working for Bollywood. The group has a lively time and never seems to mind my presence.

25 September

Trip to a Baghara and Bundi
The van is a bit old, with springs not that good and shocks worn out, quite noticeable on the rougher roads. We stop in the village of Sarawat to meet a friend of Suresh's, by the name of Arvind, a young, bearded guru and member of a political family, who shows us around the small

city, famous for its ancient mosque. We are required to perform certain ablutions before removing our shoes and entering. Everyone is required to wear a head covering. My cap will serve that purpose but Suresh must borrow a scarf from me to cover his head. Hawkers are busy selling souvenirs. We go through a process of prayers and offering of flower petals, even though we are two Brahmins and a Christian. The mosque is located by a lake commanding a beautiful view. Busloads of visitors have come from faraway places.

We stop in the small city of Kekri to find lodging and rest there before going on to Devansh's village, some distance away. Devansh joins us in Kekri to show us the way to Baghdera, over particularly rough roads, guiding us through the village's very narrow streets to his family compound, where we meet his parents, his grandmother and his grandfather's sister, two stately ladies with weathered faces. We drink chai, enduring the hot humidity of a small room. His father works as a nurse at a clinic. Devansh is also studying to be a nurse. Following tea, Devansh shows us around his village. We are joined by several friends of his. He leads us to a beautiful Jain temple with a large marble room containing an altar surrounded by 24 statues of venerated and naked gurus. They apparently teach stark naked, sitting in lotus positions. The statues re of black marble, standing on either side of the room, fully exposed in nakedness. I'll have to research more about the Jains later.

We visit a Hindu temple dedicated to the goddess that Suresh is currently honoring with a 9-day fast, allowing no food during the day, only juice. He prepares an offering there. The goddess represents a particular event related to the fasting. Devotees chant readings from Sanskrit pages. After this visit, we move on to climb rock outcropping to a small cave half way up to see where a guru resided for years. We bend low in order to enter the cave where there is a small statue and altar dedicated to him.

A Month in India

A group of boys are competing below, lifting a 50 kilo stone over their heads with one hand. Devansh tells us that he has done it before. He leads us toward a river and we board a boat to row us across to the other side. The small skiff serves as a ferry, shuttling villagers, goats and produce across. We assist with the rowing. Devansh stands at the helm imitating Leonardo di Caprio in the famous scene from the Titantic, allowing for some dramatic photos just at sunset.

The road to Bundi the next day is smooth with not much traffic, until we turn off to a narrow pot-holed stretch crowded with cars, trucks and buses that leads us into Bundi. We check into the Dev Newas Hotel, a palace at one time, quite nice and Suresh talks me into taking the luxury room for 3400 rupees a night. It is a spacious room with a huge bath, and opens onto the plaza. Due to the heat of the day, we venture out only after 4:00 p.m. visiting the markets and shops lining the streets. Suresh buys *saris* for Deepika, digging through hundreds pulled from shelves and spread out for him. I sit to one side and watch, only helping when he's close to deciding. There is a fort at the top of the hill which I want to visit. On the way we run into Jonti and his entourage, a lady from Israel and friend from Gujarat. They are on the way to see a waterfall out of town and insist that we go them, although it is getting toward dark. We drive and drive over rough roads, losing our way at times and stopping locals to ask for directions. By the time we arrive, it is already pitch dark. We make our way toward the falls through herds of monkeys, only to discover there is no water in the stream. It has dried up! There's nothing to do but turn around and head back to Bundi, making it a wasted evening!

A Real Waterfall
The Israeli girl also wants to see the fort, so Suresh accompanies us as far as the ticket office to assist with getting the tickets. The two of us then climb the steep steps, only to pay extra in order to take photos inside. There is nothing inside to see but a courtyard overgrown with weeds and more steps with only pigeon droppings. Nothing had been

done to restore the place for tourism, hardly worth the extra cost for photos. I am disappointed.

The group decides to go to a real waterfall this time. I really don't want to but Suresh insists, telling me it is "on the way." I reluctantly agree. We pile into our rickety old van for the trip. It is on the way only in the sense that the North Pole is on the way to the South Pole. In other words, the opposite direction!

The roads are horrible! We feel the impact of every pothole. Eventually we arrive at an area of granite outcroppings and turn onto a side road, traveling up and down hills and gulches until we reach the falls. This time, the falls do indeed have water, with a stream pouring over the cliffs to a nice pool below, like a miniature Niagara Falls. It is so hot out that everybody wastes little time stripping down and plunging into the pool. I'm a little reluctant to swim only in underwear in the presence of the Israeli girl, so I borrow shorts before joining the swim. We frolic in the water and enjoy the surrounding scenery, climbing steep steps back to our van.

I sit in the front of the van for the bumpy ride back to Bundi, less bumpy than sitting in the back. By the time we clear Bundi and continue toward Ajmer, I know I will be late in meeting up with my friend there. We are hungry and must stop for lunch at an Indian restaurant, which displeases the Israeli girl no end, who will have nothing to do with it. Jonti rolls a piece of flat bread into a ball and squashes it into his food and offers her a bite, making her almost gag at the thought of it. We are all hungry and eat away, but she is not a happy camper.

By the time we reach Ajmer I am about two and a half hours later than expected. Vikram (not his real name) and his friend are staying at a hotel for the weekend and I am dropped to meet them there. I pay for the van before leaving, without quite enough money and give them what I have. This has become an expensive trip for me. Suresh makes up the difference and I promise to pay him later.

A Month in India

That isn't Goldilocks in our Bed!
We go upstairs to the large room that Vikram and his friend have reserved for us for the weekend. I look forward to the time of relaxation after the difficult trip. I had gotten to know Vikram mostly on Facebook, although I had met him briefly once before. He had shared with me the ordeal of losing his father by suicide and the difficulties that had brought about for his family. There were times when he seemed quite despondent and times when I worried for his well-being. It was with eagerness that I looked forward to spending time with him. I share with him some of the ordeal of this trip, and that I ready for something a little less stressful for this weekend. He assures me that it will be that kind of a weekend. I head for the shower to wash off the grime of travel. As I exit the shower, I am surprised and shocked to see a young woman lying in the bed. My mouth drops open. She appears to be about twenty, and my first thought is that she may be his sister come to visit. Before I can recover to ask, Vikram's friend says, excuse me and undresses and crawls into bed with her, pulling covers over the two of them. Just then, Vikram responds to a knock at the door and a hotel boy enters delivering snacks and drinks, followed closely by three of Vikram's friends, arrived to hang out. Vikram introduces me around to everybody and invites them to sit, ignoring the motion going on under the covers. The only place for me to sit is on the far side of the large bed. This is surreal! What should I do? I am without money to pay for a taxi.

There is another knock at the door and my good friend Yuvraj enters, recently come from Dubai to see me. Now we are five guys sitting around talking, while the covers go up and down on the bed. Talk about bizarre! When the motion stops, the friend slides out, dashing to the toilet, whereupon Vikram takes his turn under the covers. The girl is fully aware of the group sitting around, but seems unfazed by it. Hotel staff comes and goes multiple times with snacks. I'm at a loss for words. I've been in a lot of situation but never quite like this. When Vikram finishes, he like his friend makes a mad dash to the toilet, offering me a turn. "We've already paid, so it's free." I refuse of course. In time the girl arranges her clothing and slips quietly outside, all in a day's work.

Dinner is brought and spread out on newspapers across the bed. It is a large bed. It is where the three of us will sleep, with me hugging the far side. The two guys pretty much ignore me as they talk among themselves in Hindi. I tell them that I must return to Pushkar in the morning, even though I don't have money for bus fare. I feel like a fifth wheel. This is not the weekend I had envisioned!

Days in Pushkar
We sleep late but I want out of here as soon as possible. Suresh sends a message that he is coming to Ajmer later this morning with his wife for a checkup. However, Suresh informs me that I can't return with him because he has brought only his bike this time and asks Vikram to arrange transportation for me. They take me to a bus stop to wait for a local bus, paying my fare. The bus is extremely crowded and hot, but thankfully it gets me out of Ajmer! As I walk from the bus stop in Pushkar to Suresh's house. Neeraj messages that he has come from Jaipur and agrees to meet me there and we walk to my hotel. The ordeal of the trip is over. I tell Neeraj all about it. Later we stop at his cousin Gaurav's house and visit with Gaurav, his brother Saurav and their father.

Suresh and Neeraj prefer to hang out in my room for naps in the afternoon. Something I ate for lunch has not agreed with me and my insides begin to rumble. I need a quiet evening at my room, but just as I prepare for bed Neeraj and his cousin Gaurav appear, announcing that we must go for dinner to discuss "important things." Just then Suresh arrives with urgent news that his brother-in-law Bablu has taken some medicine and is experiencing a severe reaction and must be taken to Jaipur for tests. He seeks Neeraj and Gaurav's help, initiating a flurry of calls. Just then Bablu himself arrives with a friend and the

A Month in India

group goes into a frenzy of talking all at once. Calls are made to a doctor in Jaipur that Neeraj knows. They consult with Gaurav who is a dentist. The doctor agrees to see Bablu in the morning, provided that they bring a certain sweet from Pushkar, of which he is fond. After the conversation with the doctor, it occurs to them that the sweet shop doesn't open until 9:00 a.m. and it is two and a half hours to Jaipur. Imagine someone having a heart attack, but before the doctor will see him, he must stop off and buy special sweets which the doctor craves.

Such excitement has apparently triggered their hunger, so we all head to the top of the Blue Moon restaurant for dinner. Though I had already eaten, they insist I eat more. Their "important things" turns out to be obtaining my assistance to get Gaurav into the U. S. As they don't have money for dinner, I end up paying for it. We go back to my room and I collapse onto the bed while the others leave. For the first time in some time, I sleep alone.

1 October

A death has occurred in Suresh's larger family, the father of his uncle's wife. The family has been to the Ganges and is on the way back but first stop at Pushkar Lake for a ceremony. I come to the house for breakfast and am introduced to the family. While sitting upstairs, the ceremonies begin downstairs with chanting, singing and incense. Male relatives have shaved their heads.

Preparations are in full swing at Suresh's house for a festival beginning this evening. It is a beehive of activity. Baths have been taken. An auntie sitting on the floor in front of a cooker is busy frying bread. When she finishes, she places a cow patty on an open flame for a fire for the altar. When all is ready, the entire family gathers and begins sing-song chants as they ring bells. Fire is brought out from the altar and waved about in syncopation with the chants. When the chanting is done, the children are served sweets and gifts, including plates with money.

I sleep the night alone. I mention this because it is unusual for me in India.

Burning Man
People have already gathered, including kids in abundance. A camel caravan enters the arena, bearing a sword-swinging fighter at the lead. It is a dramatic battle re-enactment follows between good and evil. I move in closer to the action. Various dignitaries are welcomed and the drama begins with a great display of battle skills involving swords, bows and arrows. The forces of good (Ram) are victorious in defeating the forces of evil. Fire is lit to giant effigy representing evil. Fireworks embedded in the huge effigy go up in flame with loud bursts of explosions. People standing a little too close have to flee in order to avoid being burned. The flames shoot high into the air, eliciting much cheering and excitement. Good has triumphed over evil!

I again visit Gaurav's dental clinic, facing onto the street with a large glass panel slid back. Dust from the traffic wafts into the clinic. Little attention is given to sterile conditions but I guess most have endured such things all their lives. Gaurav is enamored with the idea of going to America and sees me as an avenue to make it happen. While I'm there, he again wants me to assist with a patient, to whom he introduces that I am a visiting American doctor. He wants me to make the injection, which I again refuse, but sit and watch. He calls me over to examine the patient whose mouth is opened wide. I make a few grunts—hmmm, uh-hum and so on, before he proceeds to make the extraction.

Suresh drops me at the Monkey Temple in the evening, located at the base of the mountain across town where I meet there a young man who goes by the name of Lotaguru. Today is the conclusion of the 9-day fast which has involved the young Brahmin men and they are all gathering tonight for a *dahl bhoti* feast called *Gaumuhk,* being prepared at the temple higher up. It is dark by the time Lotaguru and I reach there. The cooking is in progress—potatoes roasting nestled in hot coals. Dahl is cooked in huge pots over an open fire. Bountiful rice is cooked and heaped high in a large bowl. Sweets are rolled into balls by four men sitting nearby. I am greeted by the guys, some I know and others I don't. To one side, a few are smoking pot. When all is ready, the chanting begins and we find places on concrete to sit as plates are distributed and the food is served. Hot potatoes are tossed to us. There is much merriment among these men, relieved of the ordeal of fasting. All are quite hungry and consume their food in a matter of minutes. There is nothing leisurely about this meal!

Nimaj
Suresh announces departure for Nimaj is to be at 8:00 a.m. so I hurry to be on time, obviously quite a Western response. He tells me the driver is on the way. Eight turns into nine. Nine turns into ten. Still we wait. Finally, the car arrives and we load up, still missing one passenger who is "on the way." The car is too hot to sit in and I get out and stand in the shade. Finally at 10:30 the last one arrives and we leave, stopping along the way for Suresh to eat something, still recovering from his fast. It is after noon when we arrive in the village of Nimaj, the home of his wife Deepika.

My young friend Vicky joins us at Prashant's family's house for chai and snacks and then for lunch a little later. They have arranged for me to stay again in the Nimaj Palace nearby. I am assigned to Room 502 in the historic old palace, a spacious room for me with a large bath area.

Vicky and I join some local youth playing volleyball in a school yard. After the match, several of the guys get together for a trip out of town a short distance to an abandoned old temple to hang out for a time.

My breakfast at Nimaj Palace includes a buffet. The other guests are a group from Australia. It is rare for the palace to have an individual guest like me as most come as part of tour groups.

Distant Lands

Vicky sends his friend Rohit by motorbike to pick me up to return me to the school yard. School is out for the Muslim holiday *Eid*. Nimaj has a strong Muslim community. Vicky's team is preparing for a big district volleyball match set for tomorrow night.

My dinner at the palace is a feast fit for a Raj—tomato soup, chicken, rice, chick peas, chapattis, bread plant. I hardly do it justice. After dinner I join the family at their house just finishing their dinner. We join some friends and walk to a tree-covered yard they know about for smokes. Hanging out with a bunch of twenty-year-olds is not exactly a Sunday school picnic, yet they are a lot of fun to be with.

I get up early for my morning for a walk before having breakfast and coffee alone at the Palace and spend a quiet day swimming at the pool, which I have all to myself. The other guests have left. There is something a little spooky about being the only guest in a large hotel, but I manage to enjoy myself anyway.

At 4:30 Rohit picks me up for the long-awaited district match of volleyball to be played at the school yard. I am welcomed as a visiting dignitary and given the title "Special Guest," which I discover has a job attached, officially welcoming the teams at the beginning of the match. I shake hands with each of the combatants lined up on either side of the court, asking each his name. I am given a special seat at the center sideline of the court. I shout "Let the games begin!"

The Nimaj team acquaints itself quite well in the first round, against a superior team from across the district, but eventually they lose the match. I congratulate the winning team, again with handshakes around, feeling like a celebrity.

Tonight is birthday party time at Prashant's for his young daughter. We dress in our finest and arrive at the scheduled time, which is a little earlier, given India time. Cake is brought and we sing "Happy Birthday" to Prashant's little daughter and present gifts. After the celebration, they bring dinner for me, served on the roof under a brightly-lit moon. The family is quite gracious. Prashant gives me a lift on his motorcycle back to the hotel, telling me that we are to depart at 4 a.m., so I pack my bags in readiness.

A Death in the Family
I'm at Prashant's house by 3:45 a.m. Everyone is up. We are heading to a funeral celebration in Surayapur for the funeral of the relative who has died. Prashant's father is going with us, a pleasant man, administrator at a nearby school. I have no idea how far this place is but it turns out to be a long drive. We stop at the bus station in Ajmer to pick up the rest of Suresh's family coming from Pushkar—his father, mother, sister and her baby, making it a crowded van when we all load up. The drive seems endless over the rough roads and the day is hot. I sit in the front seat allowing at least some leg room, but it is a terrifying place to sit facing Indian traffic. We stop for spicy road-side food, which doesn't set well for my stomach. Eventually we arrive at a good-sized town and head for a *dharamsala* (Indian guest house) where the funeral event is taking place. Hundreds have already gathered and are seated. Apparently, the relative had some standing in the community. I am the only Westerner present, so they see fit to bring me a chair to sit in. The brothers and sons of the family are seated in a circle in the center of the crowd. Turban material is brought and a large turban is wound around the head of the oldest son to symbolize that he is now to be the head of the family. Much of our time is involved just sitting, sometimes in silence, but often with noisy chatter. Suresh arranges a motorbike to be brought and we take a break to see the sights around town. A resort is located at the edge of town, catering to wealthy travelers. Suresh tells the guard at the gate that I am an important official from America, who wishes to see the place for future reference for a visit. The guard calls the main office and we are allowed entrance. The grounds are manicured and the guest area consists of an old palace outfitted for modern guests, but quaint in style. The man in the office is the son

Distant Lands

of the family that has owned the place for generations and appears a bit skeptical, quizzing me about my work and past accomplishments. Coffee is ordered and he shows us to one of the older structures, where we sit and drink chai in comfort, with uniformed attendants serving us. He gives a tour of one of the vacant rooms upstairs, outfitted with period furniture. We inquire about prices and it obvious that I will not be staying here anytime soon, but I don't comment. We walk to the swimming pool where a few European men are swimming. The pool is set in the gardens, complete with a service area and changing rooms. We thank our host and walk back to the gate, mount our bike and return to the funeral still in progress. No one seems to be in a hurry.

A meal is served. Small boys crowd around for me to take their photos. A young waiter takes a liking to me and is thrilled when I snap his picture. He is keen to serve me, making sure I get a sample of every food. Following the ceremony and feast, Suresh's uncle, whose father-in-law is the one deceased, ushers us to a side room where a few pallets are spread, so we can take a rest. I am tired from the journey for sure. Suresh and I lay on the floor, along with two or three others. It doesn't take long for me to doze off only to awaken with someone curled up beside me, with a hand resting on my waist. A few boys standing in the doorway are giggling and watching. I lie still as the hand begins to wander. I catch the eye of one of the boys, who is highly amused, giggling. The person becomes aware of their presence and gets up to shoo them away and pulls the door closed to resume his position. The boys simply move to another window to watch, which by now becomes a bit funny. Suresh awakes and everything stops. We get up and go outside. It is time to go. The boys gather around me for pictures.

It is a long, long way back to Pushkar.

Each morning on my walks, I have encountered the same old, thin will-of-the-wisp *sadhu* I've seen before. I usually find a coin or a 10 rupee note to give him. He is bearded with finger-nails grown long. I don't know how he survives. We do not speak. I just clasp his hand in greeting, slip him the coin and continue my walking.

I check the status of my money, worried that I might not have enough for next week in Utter Pradesh. Money has been a challenge ever since my wallet was stolen in Turkey. Suresh presented me a new wallet to take its place and we count out enough money to pay for the hotel. At least I have enough to cover that expense.

12 October

My friend Mike messages to say his schedule has changed and will not be able to hook up with me in Delhi, leaving me some unplanned days in Delhi. I will have to see how the money situation goes, thinking I should have booked a flight home. Travel's luster has grown a bit thin, leaving me thinking that I should plan shorter-duration trips in the future. I don't know, maybe it is just a funk at the moment. There are still places I want to go. Maybe I have tried to see too many friends and family members each time. My weekly times of Sunday meditation help me regain my spiritual anchor, and keep going.

It is a first. One of the Brahmins at the lake organizes a sweeper brigade to sweep trash and other debris from the steps and platforms by the lake. I had talked about that need with them before. We gather in a group and brooms are brought and we join together to do a thorough cleaning of the lake area. This is significant because sweeping is the lot of the lowest caste. Brahmins rank far above that, making this effort revolutionary. They justify it as being related to the temple, but it times past that has not mattered. The organizer of the event refers to me as Mr. Writer. I encourage them onward. The activity garners publicity and they seem delighted by my participation. I feel a victory has been won! Now, if we can get the rest of India on board, it will be truly historic.

Distant Lands

Finally I am able to get my back-up bank card to work again. I had had trouble making it work and had paid out the last of my American money to the hotel, leaving me unsure how to function for the remainder of the trip. I am now able to arrange the train trip from Ajmer to Meerut, leaving my plan open for my time after Utter Pradesh. Suresh begs me to come back to Delhi and to return here.

I've promised Kamal a night spent just with him, so we go to the Om Shiva for dinner. His English is very limited making conversation difficult, yet he is in a talkative mood. Suresh comes later and eats what we have left on our plates. When Kamal leaves, Suresh and I walk to a friend's shop where he gives me ice cream. Suresh is getting very clingy as we approach the time for my departure, never an easy time for him.

Deepika and Suresh are under increasing pressure from family and friends about having a baby even though she has had miscarriages early into pregnancy. Friends chide Suresh, saying "Who will inherit all your earnings, if you don't have a baby?" It is unfair and hurtful. I've been counseling them to ignore these pressures as best they can and relax about it, that it likely will happen eventually.

Today is my last day here. I had promised to do poojas with Kamal before I leave. I give a donation but I have to watch my money, yet it is expected.

At the last minute, Suresh decides to go with me to Jaipur. He can't bring himself to be separated. The bus ride is rough. I prefer to travel by train but Suresh takes over the arrangements. In Jaipur, we check into the Diana Palace Hotel, waiting for Neeraj to come which he does late, and it is raining. We have dinner at an Indian restaurant. When I check, I learn that my bank account has been devastated by an error in a bill payment, which somehow got doubled leaving me a zero balance in my account. Navigating through the interminable menus long-distance is difficult and frustrating, only to be told they can't help. I call again to get a supervisor who is able to sort out the mess, or so I think.

Neeraj spends the night with us.

Travel Tip: Don't Throw Up When Greeting Your Host
I look forward to seeing Neeraj's family once again. They have invited me for dinner but on the way, my stomach begins to rumble and by the time we reach the house, I'm in a bad way. We enter through a courtyard downstairs, but I have to sit down, feeling nauseated. I sit for a brief time which settles things somewhat, so I say I'm ready to go upstairs to meet the family. We climb the stairs and walk across to the door, where we are greeted and welcomed inside, but just as I enter the room, my stomach lets go with a big heave. I run as fast as I can toward the bathroom at the back, but don't quite make it before throwing up. I put my head in a sink and continue, while Neeraj and the others gather around trying to help me. It's a mess! I feel light-headed. After cleaning up a bit, they usher me to a nearby bedroom to lie down. They must have dinner without me; there's nothing else I can do. To say that I am embarrassed is an understatement. Who could imagine such a thing? It was like "Hello, Namaste…excuse me while I vomit all over your house!" It is not the most mannerly thing to do when you visit someone's house.

They make the best of it and assure me that it is okay. When I feel a little better I join the family for some soothing tea and meet the brother's young son. I had attended his brother's wedding a few years ago. It is a wonderful family and they have been good to me. When I get back at the hotel, the bug that was bothering my stomach now moves south into my intestines, making for a long night.

Neeraj spends the night with us, in spite of it.

Suresh leaves for Pushkar, crying and clinging. He and Neeraj conspire about plans for my birthday when I return from Utter Pradesh. They talk of a desert event of some sort. I hurry to nix that idea. I love these two but they can be over-the-top at times. Suresh returns to Pushkar and Neeraj comes for me lunch then takes me to the train station to settle me into my train seat for my trip to Delhi. I meet a young couple from New Zealand sitting across from me who work in Singapore. They have come to India for their first-time. It is nice to have someone to talk with who speaks English, a rare occurrence for me.

The Old Delhi train station is its usual mad scramble. My auto-rickshaw driver envisions himself as a race-car driver as we careen through the traffic-laden streets at break-neck speeds. I keep telling him to slow down. At the Prince Polonia Hotel I take the last room available, not a very good one, but they promise to move me to a better one tomorrow.

The room begins leaking water from above and the hotel moves me to a nicer room early. I spend time in the swimming pool. Some of the hotel staff drops by my room to spend time with me, always happy when I come. I check my extra luggage for the hotel to keep while I'm away for a week in Utter Pradesh.

4

Small Village Project and 75th Birthday!

19 October

Utter Pradesh

Our team from America is due to arrive in the early morning. I go to the airport to receive them only to get a text from the project leader that the team has had multiple delays and will not be arriving until after midnight. What to do? I decide to return to the hotel. They let me use of a room upstairs that had not yet been cleaned, so I stretch out on the couch for a time and then go to the lobby to hang out and wait. It is a long wait. Our leader then messages late in the afternoon for me to come to Nehru Place by Metro. I squeeze onto the crowded metro with my backpack. Women holding babies jostle against me triggering other passengers to warn me to watch out for my wallet. Apparently it is a favorite tactic of pickpockets. I really can't move. When we get off, these observant passengers check to make sure I have everything. Our leader is still at a hospital when I arrive, messaging me that one of his local crew has just given birth to twins early and that one of the twins is in jeopardy. I eat at a KFC, minus French fries which, it is explained, "are not available today." Our leader and his family arrive with their SUV loaded with luggage, having no time to eat, so I agree to stand watch while they eat lunch, after which make our way to Greater Noida and check in. He will return to the airport to receive the team late tonight. We book into the YMCA compound, where we will be staying during the project. I hope to be asleep when the team arrives after midnight.

Their flight was delayed once more and they do not arrive here until 4:00 a.m.! I'm glad that I didn't go back to the airport. Despite their late arrival, our orientation plans move ahead beginning at 9:30 a.m., even with a bleary-eyed group. A "Great Race" is planned as part of our orientation, to take place back in Delhi. We split into teams of two with a translator assigned and are dropped off randomly on a street in the city to follow a checklist of things to do, to acquire or to talk with someone about. It is a challenge. Josh is assigned to be my translator. Although American, he is living in India learning Hindi. I feel sympathy for the team who has just arrived from traveling all that time, but everyone remains positive and we have a good time with the challenge to test our ability to function in a strange environment.

We return to the YMCA for more orientation before dinner at the restaurant there. The team has brought new credit cards for me from home. I activate the replacement bank card and check my account once again, still showing a 0.00 balance. The correction I had called about before so many times had not been made, despite assurances to the contrary! I get on the phone once again and talk with no less than five people in an effort to get the correction made. Frustration! They tell me that it might take another three to five days before it gets fixed. It is amazing that in the electronic age you can easily spend money instantly but to correct an error takes multiple days. I transfer money from my dwindling savings account to replenish the checking account. It is so very frustrating.

Small Village Project and 75th Birthday!

Getting a Lift on a Motorcycle in India

We split into teams with Josh again assigned to me. He is a fine young man of 23 learning Hindi. We drive to the southeast with two of the other teams, passing through crowded villages, until the two of us are let off at a dusty road to find rural villages accessed only by such roads. We greet a group of men in the first village. Word spreads and soon the village leader arrives to invite us to his small house where two of his sons serve us lunch. A grandmother of the village joins us and informs us she is Christian and welcomes to talk with us. The village leader then takes us on a tour of a large house nearby he is having built. We continue along a street and meet a young businessman home from Delhi for the Diwali holiday which will start soon. He welcomes us for tea. His younger brother arrives by motorcycle to join us. He tells us he is working at a city near Lucknow in a bank. Since we are planning to go to another village, he kindly offers us a ride on his motorcycle, a pleasant young man who is pleased to take us there. Once we arrive to the path leading to the village, we thank him for his assistance. He starts away, but turns around and comes back to us, wanting my contact information. I give him my Facebook address.

In the next village, the village leader shows us his house, being painted for Diwali. People use Diwali as a time to clean up, paint up and repair. We meet a retired science teacher who engages us in a lively conversation. After a lengthy talk, we leave the village. Somewhere along one of the paths, we are given a ride to the nearest town and hire a *tuk-tuk* to return us some distance to Noida. Having these informal conversations in the small villages is quite educational. We debrief and enjoy pizza together with our group.

We drive out once again with two of the other teams, but are let off a bit early and we have to hire a *tuk-tuk* to take us farther down the road to our start. In the next village, we meet an elderly couple whose work is to care for the small temple. She is quite the talker, confessing her fears about what to expect when her husband dies and leaves her without a livelihood. Next we meet a large family at a house surrounded by a yard full of buffaloes. A hay grinder is noisily chopping up hay for them. The kids and the elderly invite us to sit on bed-like frames in the yare while they summon a young man, home for the holidays, to come out and speak to us in limited English. The young man is dressed only in his underwear, but a shirt is brought for him to put on. Through Josh's interpretation and his limited understanding, we are able to tell our stories to the audience of about 25 gathered around. It is fun talking with them. At the next village, we meet another family who engages with us and listens intently to our stories. When we are ready to return, we hire a *tuk-tuk* but it has a punctured tire and we must wait for it to be fixed. Once fixed, the driver takes us all the way to the YMCA in Greater Noida. Our group assembles again for debriefing. They all want to go to a Friday's restaurant in Noida for dinner, but I opt out in favor of a quiet dinner here. My friend Mike is in Bangalore and we chat for a time using our mobile apps.

Diwali
Today is Diwali, India's biggest festival. Family members return to their villages, even if they work far away. We decide to make one more village

Small Village Project and 75th Birthday!

visit before calling it a day and transitioning to Meerut. Diwali traffic slows us in reaching the village. Another team member has joined Josh and me for this visit. The three of us are welcomed to the village and invited to eat Diwali sweets in the courtyard while a huge meal is being prepared for Diwali. We drink water from the local wells which we consider safe enough to drink, safer than city water, and we have no undue side-effects. After the visit, we take a dusty trail to wait for our pick-up by the other team members. While we wait, we visit with a couple of local farmers who have come to an irrigation pump to water their crops. We join the team for the long journey to Meerut and have dinner with our host leader at his house, spending the evening on the roof watching Diwali fireworks, and shooting some ourselves in the streets below, quite noisy but fun.

We start early the next morning back to Delhi. The car I ride starts overheating due to a leak in the radiator, forcing us to stop to get water before continuing on, driving slowly and adding water every now and then until we get to Delhi. We stop at a market for souvenirs and hire *tuk tuks* to return to the guest house before dinner nearby at a restaurant called the Big Chill. The Algerian chicken is quite good, especially with their featured blueberry cheesecake for dessert. It is a non-veg splurge before returning to a veg diet for me. The group stays a short night at the hotel before getting up early for their trip to the Taj Mahal. Since I had been twice before, I stay and sleep in.

26 October

Lunch with Family in Delhi
It is Sunday. I join Anita and her daughter Janetta for Sunday services at the Delhi Bible Fellowship. They are the mother and sister of my niece Jennifer. The service is conducted in English. The pastor delivers a strong message on the unconditional love of God. Anita's cousin Joshua John is here from Hyderabad and meets us after church to take us to the Tamil Nadu State House for a lunch of South Indian cuisine. The House is located near the main government area and serves as a

place for officials from the state of Tamil Nadu to come to Delhi to do business with the government. It is impressive to get to eat there and the food is quite good. I hire a *tuk tuk* back to my hotel. One of the hotel staff comes to my room and hangs out for some time in the afternoon.

27 October

Birthday 75
Today is my 75th birthday, marking the fourth of the last five birthdays to be celebrated in India. Suresh and Neeraj arrive very early this morning from Pushkar and Jaipur respectively from all-night bus rides. I am still sleeping when they knock at my door. They are ready for showers after their difficult bus rides and join me for a little more sleep. When one is awake we chat, and then when the other is awake we chat, so I take turns talking with each.

Of course, they have plans up their sleeves for me. Suresh buys an all-white Indian outfit for me. He asks me vacate the room between 4 and 5:30 p.m. while they make special preparations, so I go to a nearby place for a Sprite and when I return at 5:30, Mintu of the hotel staff greets me in the lobby and leads me to the room. As soon as we open the door, the group bursts into singing Happy Birthday. A table has been decorated with rose petals and candles with a birthday cake inscribed with "Happy Birthday Mr. Keith" placed among the petals. Candles with the number 75 are burning on top of the cake. They invite me to sit as they sing Happy Birthday and I make a wish, blowing out the candles as confetti rains down over us. These guys know no limit when it comes to celebrating a birthday.

Train Blues
After breakfast at a small hole-in-the wall Indian place earlier, we catch the train to Jaipur. I caught a stomach bug and begin to get really sick, rushing to the toilet to throw up. There's no water for flushing, and I must throw hands-full of water from a sink to wash things down as best

Small Village Project and 75th Birthday!

I can. From my stomach, the "bug" moves into my intestines. At first I do okay but there is still no water for flushing or cleansing. We pull into Jaipur to make a quick transfer to the train to Ajmer. Neeraj brings sandwiches to eat, which seems good at the moment, but as we move on toward Ajmer, I start throwing up again and losing it from both directions, still with no water. By now my clothing is soiled. When we arrive in Ajmer, I rush into a small toilet stall, hardly big enough to turn around in, yelling for Suresh to bring my bag. Changing is totally awkwardly, balancing bag and clothes over a hole without dropping things in it, which proves nearly impossible. I'm frustrated to the nth degree and very angry. Why did I return here, when I could have stayed in Delhi! This is awful. The only pants I pull from my bag are the tight-legged Indian version, frustrating me more as I try to balance, pulling off the soiled ones and putting on the others. Later Suresh tells me that there was a larger toilet stall nearby, but since I had been so sharp with him, he just let me go ahead with this one. I could have killed him! Finally, I get changed. The *tuk-tuk* we hire to Pushkar is driven by young kids who made no attempt to avoid bumps in the road. I'm miserable. The police stop us at a security check as we approach Pushkar. *Tuk-tuks* are generally not allowed in, but Suresh orders them on. Fortunately, the room at the hotel I check in has a welcoming shower and I am finally able to get properly cleaned up. I was not a happy camper.

I later apologize to Suresh for my outbursts. I had reached the end of my tether!

Still weak today, I apologize again to Suresh when he brings medicine for me. Eating only plain rice, I manage to get vertical by 6:00 p.m. and go out onto the streets at dark. It is now the beginning of the Camel Fair. I greet several friends who welcome me back. Suresh and his friend Mohit come for a visit.

I feel better having completed the medicines and manage to book a train back to Delhi for tomorrow. I have invited a new friend that I met in Utter Pradesh to meet me there. Nothing has been easy about this trip. In the evening we attend the special ceremony at the lake where beautiful and intricate mandalas have been created by school children. Lights of oil candles are spread along the lake making it quite colorful. Brahmins have gathered to begin their chants. Fire is used. Milk is poured into the lake. It is quite colorful and impressive ceremony. A new friend we had met from Denver shows up accompanied by a couple of young ladies, one from Washington and one from Australia. It is 10:30 by the time we finish. I send a message of birthday greeting to my friend Hap back in the U.S.

1 November

Return to Delhi
October has gone. I give Suresh's mother a wool shawl for the winter. Her arthritis is becoming a problem for her. I say Good-bye to Pushkar not knowing when I will return. I must make some changes in my travel routines for the future. I feel that too much of my time is now being controlled by others. Though I am saddened to leave, I'm also relieved. I give Suresh two autographed copies of my books.

The *Shabutti* Express train to Delhi is much better than the one coming here. The food is good and the seats recline. The train makes a number of unscheduled stops and starts as we near New Delhi which eats up an additional hour. Anticipating my exit from the train in New Delhi, I move my things beside an open door for a quick departure at the station, but stand back a ways. A middle-aged Indian man comes and stands in front of me, setting a large briefcase on the floor. As the train slows before reaching the station, a hand suddenly reaches inside and grabs the case! The man is distraught. Apparently it was full of money for his business. Angry, he jumps out to chase the man but falls as the train speeds away. We don't know what's happened to him or what to do. It has happened so quickly. He probably was injured. What a tragedy. One has to be vigilant at all times.

Small Village Project and 75th Birthday!

I meet my new friend after eight at the Ramakrishna Metro station and walk with him to the hotel to check him in and we spend most of the day talking as he relaxes from his all-night ride. It is a short visit for he is on the way to the village where I had met him.

I move closer to the airport to spend a couple of days visiting with Mike at his hotel near there. We enjoy lunch together as we catch up on our respective travels. A friend of his who works for Jet Air comes by later for a visit. He is very nice and we enjoy time together.

5

Staying with Tokyo Friends

4 November

Today is Election Day in America. I anticipate that a friend of mine with whom I worked will be elected Senator from Oklahoma, filling a vacated term. Mike tells me they had roomed together once on a mission trip. He is a smart young man, though a bit too certain on his perspectives and not much open to compromise, I fear. He will be popular among most of my friends. I do laundry, repacking and check on the weather in Tokyo, my next destination. It will be cool there. Mike and I walk around a bit enjoying lunch at a Chinese restaurant, especially their spring rolls. We chat with a young man from Nepal who works in a spa nearby who offers to come to the hotel to give a massage tonight if we like. Later as a gesture of good will for my last night there, Mike calls him and invites him to come. Mike steps out to call some friends, while the young man gives a wonderful oil massage. Later Mike and I enjoy an omelet prepared by a vendor on the street. I call my friend Youbaraj in Tokyo to check on the train from the airport to his home outside of Tokyo. After recent ordeals with train travel, I find these few days enjoyable and relaxing, which restores me enough for continued travel.

Mike and I hang out in the room while I pack one more time. Friends

Staying with Tokyo Friends

of Mike's join us for lunch at a place called the Four Seasons where we share chicken biryani and Afghan butter chicken for a delicious meal. My flight to Tokyo departs at 8:20 p.m. Fortunately, the flight is not full and I actually have seats to stretch out on.

6 November

Tokyo

There had been a weather disturbance over the ocean and the skies are overcast and stormy as we approach Tokyo before sunrise. It is chilly and raining. Finding the right train is a bit confusing, but I make it onto the right one eventually. The ride from the airport to Tokyo is quite long, requiring switching trains at the main station downtown. I seek help from passengers which one to ride this one to its end and transfer to yet another train to Fussa where Youbaraj lives. It takes two and half hours to do all this, but Youbaraj is there to greet me. He is the Mainali brother from Nepal, living in Japan with his Japanese wife. Youbaraj hires a taxi to transport us from the station to his house, an apartment on the second floor. His wife Koku (pronounced more like Keishi, or maybe the nickname) and young son Ashish are waiting. She has two grown sons from a previous marriage and speaks English, while Youbaraj is more limited in that regard. They prepare a wonderful Japanese lunch and invite me to sleep for a time on a pallet in their room. Fussa is near an American Air Force base. Military planes fly over regularly. In the evening, they prepare a lavish Japanese dinner called *Nabe*, basically a traditional hot pot dinner. Her two sons join us—Yuya and the other one, who feels too shy to sit with us. Yuyu's girlfriend Judy also joins us. We enjoy a great time which they finish off with *saki*. I sleep on the pallet in their room while they spread pallets for themselves in the dining area, pushing aside the low dining table.

Youbaraj wakes early so he can take me for a walk a short distance to see snow-capped Mount Fuji in the distance as the sun rises, highlighting its summit. Later, we take a series of trains to the *Asa Kusa* Shinto shrine and temple complex, a favorite spot for visitors to Tokyo. A large arch leading to shops and on to the shrine itself greets visitors. Today is a holiday and the place is filled with visitors as many Japanese families and school children dressed in their uniforms visit the shrine. Incense fires burn and people gather around to scoop the smoke to inhale in a ritual manner. Devotees pray at the vintage temple. It is a beautiful setting with rock gardens and streams with Koi gold fish. It makes for a wonderful day.

Back at the apartment, Keishi prepares another Japanese dinner for tonight. When all is ready, she serves us shrimp appetizers, meatballs and mushrooms. Yuyu and his girlfriend join us once again.

Trek in the hills
We trek to a trail leading outside the city along a river and across to mountain trails to the heights beyond on this cool and somewhat misty morning, making for a good walk. Once we cross the river, we stop at the historic site featuring a Japanese house of an earlier era. Keishi has joined us by now, riding a bike with a basket on the front holding young Ashish. Yuyu and his girlfriend also join us. She has said little to me since I arrived. Japanese are especially shy with strangers. It is their custom not to make eye contact, which is a strange phenomenon for me. She just smiles and looks down. The house we visit was built in 1847, with a central fire pit, which is burning today and filled with period pieces, including tools. Youbaraj and I trek higher up the small mountain through dense forests with a view beyond while the others stay below. We plan to take the circular trail, but that section is closed for some reason, so we backtrack down in order to rejoin the others. Ashish is busy putting railroad tracks together in a children's room at the museum. We take a short-cut back through quiet neighborhoods to return to their apartment. I try to memorize the way so I can return for walks while Youbaraj returns to work tomorrow. The area reminds me a lot of the topography of Pittsburgh and the chilly, damp weather reinforces the comparison. Back home, we rest from the three-hour trek. Youbaraj confesses that it has been five years since he had done

Staying with Tokyo Friends

that trek, which is a pity for it is such a beautiful place for walking. He stays quite busy with his work and family. Keishi again astounds us with a dinner of fried goodies which we dip in a special sauce. Again, Yuyu and Judy join us for dinner.

Tokyo is cloudy with the threat of rain. I love the cool fall weather here. I look through my suitcase in vain for my Bible but cannot find it. I must have left it in India, but where? Probably, I left it in the hotel in Delhi. I check online and there is a Baptist church located near the airbase, which possibly could be reached by walking but I am unsure and do not know the service schedules. Their website did not reveal the schedule. It seemed more concerned with statements about fundamentalist doctrines and I didn't care for that. I walk around a bit using an umbrella Keishi has loaned me. Fussa has some nice neighborhoods and it makes it easy to envision living here. At a book store I can find no books printed in English. I stop by a Mr. Donut shop for a chocolate-covered donut with coffee and hang out for a time. The clerks are especially friendly and polite and even bring me a refill on my coffee.

I walk along the "red" street that Youbaraj had pointed out to me, lined with bars, clubs and restaurants but are all quiet on this Sunday morning. I spend much of the day just walking about and exploring. Yuyu and girlfriend return and Youbaraj returns from work a little after 6:30, tired from work after being off for three days. Yuyu, Judy and I eat dinner while Youbaraj relaxes. He prefers to eat later and chooses to wait until after eight or so to have dinner a little before his bedtime. It's more the Nepali way, but I don't care to eat that late.

I take a quick walk for a good glimpse of Mt. Fuji. The sun is shining today, making a nice view. Keishi, Ashish and I walk together to the markets. Later I walk alone to the river we had hiked along before. The sidewalks are filled with high school aged youth in their smart uniforms. It is good to see young people again. Otherwise, it has been mostly older people, grandmothers and grandfathers whiling away

Distant Lands

their time on the streets or in their yards that I have seen. Japan has an aging population, quite in contrast with India. The difference is quite noticeable. I reach the river and hike up a trail that follows its course. By the time I reach the pedestrian bridge spanning the river, it is close to sundown, so I drop down to the river and take some photos before tracing the route from memory, when we took as a short-cut before. As the sky darkens, some of the landmarks look different and I make a few false turns, but eventually manage to find a train station that gives me a proper bearing to reach home, which I reach just in time. When Youbaraj returns we relax and have a good time discussing things over snacks and juice, which is his usual ritual. He tells me that he hopes to return to Nepal someday and that he finds Japanese society a bit strange to what he is accustomed. Nepali people, like Indians, are quite relational and expressive, while Japanese are much more reserved. I can tell he misses the camaraderie of close friends, their touch and willingness to enjoy good times. It matches my observation as well—a generally touchless, don't-look-you-in-the-eye culture, isolated except for the small family unit.

Keishi has purchased a plate of sushi, a variety of raw fish, shrimp and salmon, rice balls and other sushi delights. I am not sure about eating raw fish, but decide "when in Rome…" and plunge ahead to eat them. They are good to the taste, though different. I'm sure it must have been quite a leap for Youbaraj when he first came to Japan. He seems to take to it now. Afterwards, they ask me to taste a sweet plum wine, which is quite good. By bedtime, I am feeling full and quite relaxed.

I sleep, but my phone beeps several times with messages and photos from Indian friends who are on quite different schedules, wanting to chat with me. Mike gets in on the act as well. Outside, I hear a loud siren and a loudspeaker. I fear some tragedy has occurred and ask Youbaraj about it, but he says it is only firetrucks responding to a fire somewhere.

Staying with Tokyo Friends

By now my intestines are in revolt from the raw fish I had eaten earlier. Perhaps it was not the right choice for me. I rush to the toilet, making subsequent trips during the remainder of the night.

Birthday Party for Yuyu

It is cold and rainy. I sleep late after last night's interruptions, eating only plain toast for breakfast with some ginger tea. Keishi later gives me a creamy soup to eat and hot milk to drink.

I begin to feel a little better and get up and walk, spotting a McDonald's. I decide to replace the sushi with something a little more familiar, so I order a small burger with French fries and a coke. The system seems to return to normal. It wasn't just that it that I ate raw fish but how much I had taken that proved too much of a change for the system.

Today is Yuyu's twenty-second birthday and a celebration is planned for the evening. Keishi has prepared a good dinner and a birthday cake. Yuyu arrives with his fiancée. Later the younger brother arrives with his girlfriend and for the first time seems comfortable around me. He begins cooking a mixture of something using a wok. His girlfriend also opens up and is friendly. When Youbaraj arrives, we gather around to sing Happy Birthday as Yuyu blows out the candles. Unlike in Nepal or India, we wait to eat the cake *after* dinner, not before. We enjoy appetizers and drinks, having a good time bantering back and forth in a light-hearted way. It is easy to connect with these young people after they got to know me. Now they are loosening up. Yuyu especially seems to enjoy my presence. We take a series of group photos and talk about my returning to Japan next time. They tell me I should come in April for the cherry blossoms. Youbaraj promises to take a week off if I come so we can travel around Japan.

It is a good evening with this wonderful family. I will miss them when I leave. When it is time for bed, I pack my things for my flight home. We will get up at 4:00 a.m. so I can catch the train to the airport.

Distant Lands

Sayanora Japan!
Youbaraj accompanies me to the train station and rides with me to make sure I make the right transfer to the express train to the airport, which takes two hours to the airport. At the transition station, we hurry to the train and he makes sure I get the right seat. We bid each other a hasty good-bye for the train is already moving. The train by-passes downtown Tokyo and moves across a channel and out into the country. Narita Airport is quite some distance from the city.

I've enjoyed my sojourn in Japan and hope to return. It's a long flight to Dallas. I pass through intense security in Dallas and hurry to make my connection to Oklahoma City. TSA workers yell at passengers and a trainee stalls screening luggage making everything back up. They tell me I have something in my pockets when I go through the screener, but I do not, turning my pockets inside out to convince them. They just scowl. Passengers are treated with polite dignity in airports throughout the world; it is a shock to encounter rude treatment coming home. I can only imagine how it impacts the mild-mannered Japanese passengers.

I barely make my connection. My friend Hap picks me up in Oklahoma City and we head to my house in the cold. An extreme cold snap has gripped the state. As usual, I return to extreme weather—blizzards, tornadoes and such. This one proves no exception.

It is good to be home at last! Soon it will be Thanksgiving and my daughter Tammy and family are coming from Wyoming and I must get ready. There's no food in the house. My neighbor Sandra shows up at my door with containers of prepared food, enough to last me three days! What good neighbors I have.

Hap has put an electric blanket on my bed. I will have a warm bed later to welcome me home from this my fourth trip around the world. All is well.

Part Six
2015 Holi Festival and Earthquake

"Wandering re-establishes the original harmony which once existed between man and the universe." –Anatole France

1

Bangalore in the South to Manali in the North

My friends in India have begged for some time for me to attend the Indian festival called Holi which seemed like a fun thing to do. From photos I had seen, it looked a bit on the wild side, but I reasoned why not? I yielded to their requests and made a plan for a trip in 2015 to experience that festival. This time I included a trip to southern India, to begin with Bangalore.

16 February 2015

My 11th trip to India is primarily to see friends I have made there. I keep thinking maybe this will be a final trip—at least for a while. I need a financial breather to see what to do next as far as travel is concerned.

I turned 75 on my last trip leaving me with fewer years remaining for me to be gadding about the world, who knows? I want to keep my options open. My trips to India have grown a bit burdensome by obligations to see this friend and that friend, to visit all the relatives and participate in all the family events—like weddings, birthdays, funerals, and festivals. Though they have given me great joy, they have also restricted some of the spontaneity of travel. I'd like to discover some new things. It is for that reason I am flying first to Bangalore on this trip, making my first venture into south India.

Distant Lands

The weather in Oklahoma rises to the occasion by producing an ice storm. I awake to an ice-covered wonderland. Fortunately, my flight is not until late afternoon, so the roads should be navigable by then. The ever-patient Hap comes from his city to take me to the airport through the slush.

I've had to cram both warm and cool clothes this time into the small bag I carry. A check with the weather in India reveals it to be in the 90s in Bangalore, but I also I plan to go to the Manali in the mountains of north India, where it is below freezing and snowing. It looks a little funny taking a coat to south India! I think Hap doesn't understand my need to travel, being super-cautious about it for himself. Nevertheless, I appreciate his friendship over the past fifteen years.

I am lucky this time! I have empty seats on my row which allows me to stretch out for a little sleep—a rare treat on these long flights. Little do I know at the time that it will be the cause of losing my mobile phone as it slips out of my pocket and gets hidden under some blankets that the airline issued me for warmth. When I arrive in London, I hasten from the plane, checking my bags, wallet and passport but not my mobile and don't miss it until I had changed terminals and had gone through a second security. By then, it is too late to return to the plane. I call American Airlines but no report for a lost object has yet been made. They tell me to try again later but it is time to board my flight to Bangalore. The loss of the phone is a great loss for me for it had so many photos from the past year and also most of my contact information. I am most upset and even question why I keep traveling.

The flight from London to Bangalore is also a long one crossing Europe, Turkey, Iran, the Persian Gulf, Mumbai and finally into Bangalore arriving at 5:00 a.m. I hire a taxi to my hotel, located in a distant part of the city. Taxi prices from the airport are high due to the time of day. I'm early for check-in but the hotel has a room available. The desk clerk

Bangalore in the South to Manali in the North

kindly allows me the use of his mobile to call Heathrow to see if my missing phone has been found. No luck!

After fitful rest, I awaken around 4:00 p.m. to begin exploring the immediate area around the hotel. I discover a large Catholic church, St. Paul's Cathedral, across the way and a Catholic hospital nearby. The streets are crowded and sidewalks are rough with most people walking in the streets in and among traffic. Crossing a street is dangerous, I quickly discover. I nearly get clipped by a speeding *tuk-tuk*, actually it did clip my arm. Had I been a couple of inches toward it, I would have been injured. It serves as a quick reminder to be careful. I spot a bus station, a Hindu Temple and a mosque nearby. Apparently, this community has strong Muslim and Catholic influences. There is also the Basilica of St. Mary's not far. I see a nice-looking restaurant and consider trying it for dinner later, but now I must shop for an Indian SIM card for a cheap back-up phone I carry. They tell me I must have the necessary documents of passport and visa in order to purchase a card, so I go back to the hotel for the documents and apply for one, costing 300 rupees. At the hotel, I place again calls to Heathrow but to no avail. I thank the clerk for the use of his phone and promise to pay the extra charges. Back at the restaurant for dinner I order chicken coriander with all the trimmings with Indian bread.

I wait until 10:00 p.m. to go exploring again and find a wonderful restaurant called Sumarkind, decorated in the Moghul style with waiters wearing period dress as Moghul conquerors, including conical hats and scarves and looking quite handsome. I enjoy a few snacks there while I attempt to relearn my simple back-up phone with the new Indian SIM card. My friend Prakesh (not his actual name) calls and we speak briefly. I plan to connect with him in Delhi for a trip to Manali. The streets are deserted when I return to the hotel.

Churches and Temples
St. Mary's cathedral is nearby with an early-morning service in progress.

Distant Lands

It is nice, with a ritual befitting the ornate, soaring architecture. About a hundred people are in attendance. I want to visit Bangalore's famous Krishna Temple complex I had read about. The hotel clerk assures me that I will have no problem getting a *tuk-tuk* to take me there, but the one I flag down outside the hotel confuses it with St. Mary's and confuses a second time taking me to a local Hindu Temple. It is clear he has no idea what I've asked for, so I give up on that notion and get out. I spot another *tuk-tuk*. Fortunately he understands but explains that he has already agreed to take two ladies somewhere but promises to be back shortly. He keeps his word and we make the long drive to Krishna as he points out various sites along the way. He delivers me and gives me directions for taking the Metro back.

The Sri Radha Krishna Temple is a huge complex and quite new, actually. A pathway leads through several mazes to a counter where I deposit my shoes and receive a claim check. From there I ascend steps to the main temple, the interior of which is magnificent with gold-plated altars and alcoves. Tickets are purchased for 300 rupees and I join small groups to await special prayers by a Krishna priest, a young smiling chap wearing the traditional *dhoti*. He prays over us and later passes a flame around for us to enfold us with ritual smoke and then clasps our hands and touches our foreheads. Our tickets include some sweets and a chance to visit the book shop to claim two free books on Krishna as we exit. Murals in the main temple are quite dramatic.

I hire a *tuk-tuk* to the nearby mall, as my original driver had suggested and discover they have an electronic section there. I need to purchase a camera since I don't have my phone available for taking photos. I take the Metro to the end of the line and then take a bus back to my hotel area. At the hotel, I try calling London once again but this time the numbers aren't working. Later I discover a website listing found objects at the airport but no listing is made for my phone. I suspect someone, worker or otherwise, has taken it for their own use or to sell. I file a report but never hear anything from it.

Bangalore in the South to Manali in the North

Because of the heat, I rest in the afternoon and venture out only in the evening. As I walk along, a smart-looking *tuk-tuk* driver follows along beside me offering a ride. I refuse, but he continues slowly while chatting a bit and says I can ride without charge, if I like. He tells me he has no passengers and doesn't mind. He is talkative and pleasant and asks about my sight-seeing and suggests that I should really visit the city of Mysore, which is historic and interesting and less than a day's drive from Bangalore. I had had others before to suggest that I visit that particular city. He tells me he has a car and can take me tomorrow for about 7000 rupees, or about $120, including visiting all the sites there. I tell him I will think about it. He then takes me to a KFC to pick up a chicken dinner to take back to my room. He wants to take me to a shop on the way back, "just to look," which is an old saw to get you into something that is hard to get out of without buying, but I consent and end up buying some sandalwood scarves for my daughters. I finally agree to the trip to Mysore for tomorrow.

Trip to Mysore

Irfan calls to tell me to tell me he is on the way to pick me up in twenty minutes for the trip to Mysore. It is more like an hour before he arrives and he apologizes about traffic. He is accompanied by his friend Hahn who will go also and take turns driving. Traffic is heavy, of course, and frightening for the uninitiated and even for me after eleven visits to India. It's a long drive, but we begin to make some stops before we reach Mysore. Our first is at a famous shrine to a Muslim family of great importance. It was built in the 1700s, built with black basalt imported from Iran and contains the crypts of family members. It is set in a beautiful garden somewhat akin to the Taj Mahal. In Mysore, we visit St. Joseph's Cathedral. From there we tour the Grand Palace of Mysore where the ruling Maharajas of the time lived. What a spectacle it is, grand in design and dimensions and one of the largest palaces I've ever visited, and I've been in a few. I take my time wandering through its magnificent rooms and outside around the perimeter. Later, we stop for a lunch of chicken biryani. The day is getting hot from the bright tropical sunshine. Irfan takes me to several shops to look and to deal with shop keepers who insist I buy something. I hate going to these places and finally tell Irfan, no more! He is upset because he has agreements with them to bring in potential customers, for which he receives a fee. It is the common practice. I apologize and tell him that I do not mean to embarrass him but find it exhausting to deal with and I don't want to buy anything. Our final stop is at a large reservoir outside the city where there are botanical gardens. It is a beautiful place with fountains and flowers and even an aquarium. The sun is setting and makes it a more pleasant walk. We rest on some steps near a fountain and shoot some photos and joke around a bit. I like Irfan. On our return, we drive through small rural villages and stop at a café for dinner. Irfan goes to the kitchen and talks with the owner and orders Japanese quail, freshly caught from the forest. They are not on the menu. We enjoy snacks while our quail are being prepared. The quail is delicious to eat with special seasonings. It is ten when I arrive back at the hotel, quite satisfied with the trip.

I check out early and wait for Irfan to come for me at ten to give me a trip around Bangalore. We tour the Botanical Gardens adjacent to large granite outcroppings similar but not as tall as Stone Mountain in Georgia. It is surrounded by groves of trees and gardens. A pavilion in the center, called the Crystal Palace, is used for special events such as dinners for visiting dignitaries. We tour Bangalore's Palace which is not quite on the scale of the Grand Palace of Mysore but interesting nonetheless. These palaces are filled with the glories of an earlier day when the maharajahs reigned supreme. Works of art included paintings of nudes which surprised me in this land of modesty. Irfan is still keen for me to visit shops which I do only to appease him. I do buy a couple of rings at one but succeed in making the owner at the second quite angry when I don't buy after which Irfan rushes me to the airport so I can board my flight to Delhi. He has been a good travel companion for these past few days.

When I arrive at the Hotel Piorko in New Delhi they have no record of my reservation nor of the transaction and deposit I had made. They tell me also they are booked full. Hotels nearby are also booked. I return to my old standby at the Prince Polonia, even though I had an issue with them from before.

22 February

Unhappy in Manali
Prakesh arrives at six from an overnight bus trip and I greet him in the lobby to get him checked in. We spend most of the day in the room, ordering room service and he gets some sleep. He's works in a city several hours' bus ride away. Late in the afternoon, we go to the Hotel Piorko to claim the refund on my deposit. The bookkeeper finally determines that my payment had been received and refunds it to my account, but has no explanation as to why it did not show up on hotel reservation records.

We spend the rest of the evening relaxing with the hotel staff who pop in from time to time to visit and check on our needs. They all know me since I have stayed with them so many times before.

At a nearby chowk and I buy Prakesh jeans and shirt, which is getting to be a problem for me because many Indians expect gifts from me and are quite explicit about it, which grates me the wrong way. We walk a ways to catch the bus to Manali to ride through the night traversing some of the roughest mountainous terrain. I had been skeptical about going there at this time of year but Prakesh was all keen to go. It is a super-duper Volvo tour bus with reclining seats, one of those buses with cushioned air suspension to ease passengers over the bumps of the road but has a tendency to sway from side to side, which makes one queasy. It's a long night's ride over some very dangerous passes. Prakesh is able to sleep but I find it impossible. We don't arrive until 9:15 a.m. which has made this a 15-hour bus ride due to the wintry weather.

Distant Lands

The room we check into at the Hotel Dilbru is plain with a worn carpet and is freezing cold. I pay extra for a couple of space heaters to give us at least a little warmth. By now, I'm ready for sleep but Prakesh wants to talk, telling me he is already unhappy with Manali. I think he envisioned some kind of luxury resort instead of a small wintry village suitable for skiing. I tell him to give it a chance. I had warned him earlier about how cold it would be at this time of year and had suggested we choose another destination but he was insistent. Prakesh suddenly announces that he is missing his family and wants to go back, which doesn't set well with me at all, having just paid for three nights at the hotel and making a 15 hour bus trip. He is revealing a very immature side which is disconcerting. This trip has already taken a lot of effort to work out details. After I get some rest, we walk around while the sun is out in the afternoon. Prakesh asks me to buy a camera for him, which I refuse, thinking that surely he is joking, but I find that he is not. I tell him my resources are already over-burdened. He begins to pout, saying it would only be a small matter for me to buy the camera. How has this come about I wonder. Had I been so mistaken about the young man's character?

We walk to a forest of large trees near a stream where I had stayed before with Suresh during India's hottest season in the month of May. Now it is quite cold. We obtain a *tuk-tuk* to take us farther up in altitude to a temple to look around. Young ladies are spinning and weaving and we chat with them for a time after visiting the temple. I had taken morning walks here before. Prakesh begins to talk with them making me think he is adjusting somewhat.

Most of the shops are closed at this time of the year leaving little else to see. Back in the room, Prakesh tells me he is upset that I did not buy the camera for him. Communication issues and cultural differences can be difficult at times. He expects many things from me and seems unconcerned about my circumstances. It is a problem I've had before with others, usually without this extreme. He threatens to leave and return home on his own, which I am almost tempted to let him do. We had been here only a few hours. It does not bode well for the rest of our visit. I had hoped to go out for dinner but he wants to stay in and order from the hotel. I had not had much sleep and hoped that things might be clearer in the morning.

A storm hits during the night with both thunder and snow. By morning, there is ice, snow and rain, leaving a blanket of wet snow covering the city. My mind is clearer this morning after a night's sleep. I decide that we should indeed return on the evening bus even though I've paid for three nights at the hotel. Maybe it will give me an opportunity to visit my friend Mike Hatfield, who tells me he might be in Delhi soon, so possibly we can get together. I could use his counsel.

We venture out into the slushy mess for lunch as the snow turns to rain. Power keeps going on and off. I somewhat reluctantly give him a gift I had bought for him in Bangalore. I'm not sure where we are on the camera issue. I offer him the use of my camera, but he refuses. I do not understand the mentality of expecting a gift. He works at a bank and should be a person who knows the issues of finance. It is not just Prakesh. I've encountered the same issue with others in both Nepal and India. I fail to see the difference between this and what beggars do on the streets. After all, he is fully employed.

We leave for Delhi at 4:30 p.m. and it is well into the night by the time we make it down from the mountains over the difficult roads and onto the flat lowlands. A Hindi movie keeps the passengers entertained and distracted from the treacherous roads, but doesn't work for me. Some of the movies are just plain silly, which can be said also for some Hollywood movies.

We arrive early the next morning at the Krishna Gate in Delhi.

At the nearest Metro station we catch the train to the RamaKrishna station near the hotel. Prakesh makes a transfer before we reach there, so he can head to his small village to visit his family in Utter Pradesh, which will take him another four hours to reach. We say a crisp and quick good-bye. I return to the Prince Polonia. Mintu of the staff arranges a massage for me at a nearby barber shop which is welcome after all the ordeal I've been through.

I stay in and order dinner to my room.

Traffic is already building when I walk about this morning. Walking in Delhi is like playing dodge ball. I check on a train reservation for Jaipur and am able to book one for tomorrow morning and send a message to Neeraj. He has a bad news/good news message for me. Bad news is that he has been laid off from his job. Good news is that it now gives him time to show me around Jaipur. I finish the day walking the streets, looking at the shops and stop for a lassi at a street vendor that Neeraj had introduced me to once before. The air is fairly clear today, much in contrast with the usual smog that envelops Delhi. They say being in Delhi is like smoking a pack of cigarettes every day. Construction workers are especially vulnerable to the open dust. With small wiry bodies, I see them at work for long hours enshrouded in dust, breaking up old concrete.

Redeeming Myself
India's congested train stations are always a challenge, especially trying to identify the proper car and seat when boarding. Signs are not obvious. Neeraj greets me on arrival in Jaipur and I check into the Diana Palace Hotel. He brings his friend Vikas later to meet me and we have lunch at the Mohan restaurant, a favorite of locals. Vikas tells us he also has been relieved of his job in a dispute with his boss. He works in child services. So now, I am hanging out with two guys who have just given their walking papers. Vikas decides it's time for whiskey, obtained from somewhere down the street, so they can drown their job loss sorrows, while smoking cigarettes, making my nose to stop up.

Bangalore in the South to Manali in the North

Today is a dreary from cold and rain and I stay in most of the day. Neeraj comes later and we listen to music on his computer. The hotel's WiFi is not working. A lady friend of Neeraj's invites us for lunch, so we go in the rain to her house on the other side of town, stopping to buy chocolates for her three children. She tells me that she comes from Kolkata and is living with her mother and father. I meet the children and her sister as well. After lunch, we take her to buy gifts for her sister's boyfriend whose birthday party is being held at a McDonalds. When we reach there, we do the birthday cake routine, singing Happy Birthday, blowing out the candles and eating and smearing cake on the celebrant's face after which we eat some of the snacks and spend the rest of the afternoon at my room before Neeraj takes her back and we go to Neeraj's house for dinner, allowing me to redeem myself from the terrible episode last time when I threw up upon being welcomed to their house for dinner. We joke about it now and fortunately I do not repeat the offense. We eat the dinner without mishap. Neeraj returns me to the hotel by motorbike and stays the night.

2

Holi Celebration and My Hair turns Pink!

2 March

The hotels in Pushkar are filling for the upcoming Holi Festival celebration. Suresh has reserved a room in the Mona Lisa next to his house. Pushkar is becoming a favorite destination for Holi.

Suresh and his wife Deepika have been trying to have a baby but she has experienced multiple miscarriages, but has news that she is now pregnant once again. She is staying close to home and in bed a lot during these critical months.

Suresh shows me a small piece of property he recently purchased on which he hopes to build a small house. It is in a peaceful spot fairly close in to the main part of Pushkar. Land prices have dramatically increased in Pushkar. We call on Navneet at his shop and visit Mohit's shop, only to find him away helping his mother-in-law host some school children, who have come to visit Pushkar. His younger brother Summit is there to receive us and he invites us to dinner. I accept, but Suresh is fasting once again and cannot eat. Summit brings his young son out for me to see. I had attended Summit's wedding last year. Summit teaches school and assists with the family business that his brother Mohit operates.

Holi Celebration and My Hair turns Pink!

Later at the market plaza we watch a stick dance being performed, leading up to the Holi celebration. It is quite interesting to watch. I return to the Mona Lisa Hotel to my simple room with a shared bath on the lobby. The sounds of the hotel can be quite noisy as they reverberate through the concrete structure.

I stop for chai this morning with Suresh and friends after completing my walk. Mohit comes along and invites me to meet his mother-in-law and her large group of students. I had met her before at Mohit's wedding in their home village. I take photos of the students who are dressed in their school uniforms. There are about a hundred of them making a challenge to for the sponsors to keep them in tow as they move around Pushkar, which is why Mohit is assisting. We agree to meet him for a dinner of pizza at "Doctor Alone's Garden Restuarant." Yes, the guy who runs it is known as Doctor and he attaches the word "Alone" to his enterprises. I have no explanation for it. Navneet joins us in the garden but Mohit is typically late in coming. When he comes he wants to explore with me the idea of going into politics. Over these years, I have become a confidant, counselor and general guru to a number of these friends. I don't know what wisdom I have to impart.

Since the Mona Lisa is such a noisy place, I walk a few blocks over to the Mama Luna, which has a quiet place upstairs restaurant with beautiful green plants, psychedelic art and welcoming quiet. I spend time reading one of the Krishna books that I had received in Bangalore. Along the way I stop at Navneet's shop. He is taking a break and gives me a lift to the hotel and hangs out with me for a time. Suresh also comes. It's never easy to be alone, but these are good friends. Suresh prepares a *bhang lassi* of dried fruit and curd for me to try as traditional preparation for Holi. I sip on it and find it tastes quite good. We will have to wait to see what effects, if any, it has. Ok, so it's a bit of "when in Rome..." Suresh leaves to check on his wife Deepika who is to have a weekly injection. At night we watch again the stick dance performances in the plaza. I've had little or no side effects from the very mild version of the *lassi* I tried earlier.

Pushkar's Holi Celebration

The Holi Festival—Things Go Wild!

Today marks the beginning of Holi. The first day includes a more traditional set of family observances. The wild color powder-throwing takes place tomorrow. Neeraj has come from Jaipur and hangs out with his cousins Saurav and Gaurav. Gaurav is the dentist I have mentioned before. They both live in Pushkar with their parents. It is also the day for the traditional lassi and Suresh makes arrangements for some to be prepared at the hotel including one for me of very mild potency. Neeraj quickly finishes his and is readily consumes a second one. The stronger versions tend to make for a lethargic relaxation. On the days of Holi, many of the men of the city can

Holi Celebration and My Hair turns Pink!

be observed sitting around quietly with resigned peaceful expressions on their faces. For me, it is more fruit than *bhang*. Neeraj has also brought other drinks. The hotel owner joins us and we have a peaceful afternoon in anticipation of tomorrow's more frenzied celebration. The final stick dance is performed at the market area along with a rock concert held at another market plaza with little sleep to be had in Pushkar. Neeraj, Saurav and Gaurav spend most of the day and take in the stick dance before they return to their home later.

Thoroughly exhausted, we return to my room at the Mona Lisa for a break. Neeraj invites Pepe to join us. We are a mess. My face, hair and body are well plastered with multiple colors and I can barely see. We take turns washing the powder from our eyes, hands and faces, but most of them just flop across my bed, having smeared some off with the single towel I have with me in the room. The room is a mess of color, as is the hotel lobby. It will be a job to clean it all up. We drink water and lounge around for a time, still shirtless for the most part, and our jeans are a mess. We laugh about our experiences and Neeraj teases the shirtless Pepe, who is barely covered by his sagging pants, which sends Gaurav and Saurav into spasms of laughter. Once we are refreshed, we return for another round at the plaza. I slip on another T-shirt but that one is ripped from me almost immediately. The crowds have grown even larger. More powder is thrown.

We have had enough and return to the room. What a day! I head for the shower as soon as it becomes available. I wash and scrub and do multiple shampoos. All the brightly colored powders wash away, but when I emerge and look in a mirror, I am shocked to find that my hair has turned pink! I shampoo some more, but it stubbornly remains pink. Apparently my white hair has absorbed all the pigments. My Indian friends with their dark hair and use of gels and oil are able to get their color to wash out. I will be stuck with pink hair nearly three months before it grows out.

Gaurav, Saurav, and Neeraj stay some time at my room and we get some rest on my bed. At night, we go to an Indian restaurant for dinner. Suresh receives news that his cousin from Jethana has been severely beaten as the result of a traffic issue, giving him a gash on his head which require stitches. Suresh goes there to see about him. He is a nice young man and I can't believe anyone could become so angry, but small village rivalries do flare up. I hope he will be o.k. I sleep the sleep of total exhaustion.

The morning breaks bright and clear and I do feel a bit rested. I have the entire room cleaned and sheets changed on the bed. It takes some time to get all the color up but finally the room is restored to its former self. I upload photos from yesterday and check emails. My friend Hap tells me that cold weather has persisted back home. Saurav and Gaurav invite me for lunch at their house and Neeraj comes for me to go there. Gaurav is busy with the dental clinic, while Saurav serves a delicious and filling meal. Afterwards, Gaurav insists that I play the role of a visiting American dentist. He outfits me with a smock and gloves and lets me examine the mouth of a patient, a swarthy-looking older Indian guy. Two extractions are deemed necessary and Gaurav proceeds with pliers to loosen the teeth but wants me to make the final extraction. I feel awkward and am reluctant to do this, but he insists, so I give one of the teeth a remaining tug and out it comes. The patient seems pleased to have had such an important doctor to assist. No doubt he tells tales back in his small village. I tell Gaurav that this would not be proper back home, but he passes it off telling me it only enhances the image of his business. I don't like doing it.

They take me to the edge of town to visit a friend of Gaurav's who farms small fields of wheat and vegetables. He is a young man about their age and quite bright. He takes us on a tour of the small farm to show us the various crops he raises and we discuss the dynamics of farming. I am impressed by him.

Holi Celebration and My Hair turns Pink!

When we return to my hotel room, Neeraj wants to hang out longer, but I need some peace and quiet. The guys have the habit of gathering around me on all sides, talking at the same time getting louder and louder as they go. Since I have no idea of what is being said, I just hear the increasing volume of noise. I recognize that I have once again reached a breaking point of acculturation, so I insist that I need some rest and they finally go. I turn out the light and crawl into bed. Within two minutes, Neeraj is back knocking at my door, telling me he has forgotten his jacket. I turn out the light again and crawl back into bed. Within another two minutes, Gaurav comes knocking at the door. He has come to find Neeraj's jacket. I tell him Neeraj has been here and has found it. I turn out the light a third time and crawl back in bed. Within two minutes Suresh is knocking at the door. He has come back from Jethana to tell me about Aman and when he leaves I turn out the light once again and crawl into bed. Within two minutes, a noisy group of tourists gather outside my room, laughing and talking loudly and carrying on. I give up! I get up, get dressed and walk the streets. At least I am by myself in the crowd, but I soon bump into Neeraj and company bringing snacks and drinks, insisting that we go to my room to enjoy them. It is impossible to carve out peace and quiet in India! I tell them that they must keep their voices down if they are to stay in my room. Suresh shows up and they try their best to speak quietly and for a time they succeed, and we have normal-volume conversations, but I can tell that it is an unnatural for them. I begin to get tickled by their attempts to accommodate me in this manner and begin to laugh about it, which melts the ice and the strain disappears. I am once again okay with them and we enjoy the rest of the time together. There are times in travel when I hit a wall and have to back off.

The sky becomes hazy with dust and a bit cooler. A weak cold front has come, stirring dust into the atmosphere. I walk to seek out a quiet spot on the opposite side of the lake for my Sunday morning meditation. Two dogs come to nuzzle against me as I sit and they seem unwilling to leave my side. If I were Hindu, I could easily believe that they were friends from a former life, craving my affection.

Suresh prepares fruit, curd, and cheese toast for my breakfast. I declare today to be a day of rest. The recent Holi celebration has really taken it out of me. Deepika's family sends some food by a young boy for us to enjoy, along with a chess set, so Suresh and I play a round of chess. Mostly I just walk around observing the tourists who remain following Holi. After dinner, we pop popcorn and sit and talk about friendship and the future. I tell him that I must scale back my frequent trips to India. I've been averaging two trips per year and I must reduce it to no more than one. Back at the hotel tonight, the crowd goes on all night talking and laughing quite loudly until 4:00 a.m., making it impossible for me to sleep.

I tell Suresh that I must change hotels. Each night has been difficult enough, but this is ridiculous. I take a walk out of town near where we had visited yesterday with the young farmer and spot a nice-looking hotel next to his place, so I stop to inquire. It is a newly-built luxury hotel called the Green Haveli and they are offering a very low rate for people to try it. They promise a rate of 600 rupees (about $10) which is a third of the cost of the plain place where I've been staying! I can't believe it. They show me a spacious room on the second floor that has a large, clean bathroom and shower. A balcony looks out over the farmland and they have use of a swimming pool at the owner's other hotel next door. I quiz the young clerk to be sure I've understood the price correctly and he assures me it is correct. I book the room.

When I describe it to Suresh, he is also skeptical and doesn't believe it. We move my things immediately and he is quite amazed by the room. After breakfast, I hit the bed for some much-needed sleep but Suresh comes also to sleep, and is soon snoring quite loudly. It's a conspiracy! I get up and walk out onto the balcony and sit in a chair to relax when I hear loud pounding from a door across the hall. It goes on for some

Holi Celebration and My Hair turns Pink!

time and I decide someone must be in trouble, so I go out to check and a voice begs me to tell the clerk downstairs to open the room. It seems that a long-term resident has somehow locked himself inside, and misplaced his keys. The clerk gets the door open for him. The man tells me that his phone had gone dead and he had no way to get in touch with the hotel. I wake Suresh and tell him that his snoring isn't helping me get any rest. He looks a bit hurt, but leaves and finally I'm able to sleep for a time. The more I try to avoid noise, the more it follows me. This is India!

I manage to enjoy a peaceful day today in the new place. I still have breakfast at Suresh's which is bit of a walk, but I like it here. Tonight Suresh and I accept a dinner invitation from Manu, Mohit's uncle who owns psychedelic art shops here and in Goa and Kasol. Goa, a former Portugese Colony, is in southwest India and Kasol is in the mountains of the north near Manali. He divides time among the three locations according to the seasons with the help of Nikki another cousin who operates the shops in his absence. Manu tells us that he has recently purchased a piece of land outside Pushkar some distance and hopes to build a resort on it someday. He also cautions us about Pushkar society, which he says is very closed and prone to jealousies among people, especially when if they become successful. It is a small-town phenomenon involving the differences between castes and even within the same caste. I've noticed how carefully Suresh protects his and his family's reputation in the community.

We eat Israeli food. Israeli tourists are becoming more and more prominent here and there are many restaurant options that reflect it.

A trip to Nimaj is on our agenda for today, stopping first in Ajmer for a doctor's appointment for Deepika. The doctor reports that the baby is intact and growing. It is good news. He advises her against travel, so she is not able to accompany us for the visit with her family in Nimaj. She hopes after some time that she will be able to make the journey and spend the remaining months of pregnancy there. We have hired a car for our trip. Once again the family there has arranged for me to stay in Nimaj Palace. I will stay in the palace one night and then transfer to their Palace Garden unit for the remainder. It is located in a wooded area just to the edge of town. These were the residences of the former King of Nimaj.

The fair, marking the end of Holi, is in full swing in Nimaj. I take my morning walk all the way to the temple outside of town and back, accompanied by excited school children on their way to school. They pose for photos and walk along with me. I have breakfast at the hotel and check out before noon to make the transfer to the other unit. Several of us spend a fun day at the fair. I think the whole village has turned out. There are rides and goodies to buy, cotton candy and sweets. Vicky, Prashant, Suresh and Rohit have joined us to ride the rides. The Ferris wheel is a bit primitive and quite rickety, swaying from side to side, but it is a small town fair and quite fun. I have dinner in my room at the Garden Unit. Friends come to spend the evening before returning to their homes. We have a good time. My room there is quite large and a bit quaint.

Vicky comes to my room early and lounges around with me and I have breakfast there, after which I pack for checkout. Suresh has said we will leave by 11, but that turns into 12:30 then 2:00. We are gathered back at Prashant's house. Prashant's father tells me about his upcoming retirement which is set for May 31, 2016. They invite me to come. We leave Nimaj after two o'clock with Vicky, Prashant and Rohit accompanying us to Jethana. Prashant has some water business there to take care of. He has started a new business supplying filtered water to area businesses.

We are greeted warmly and always with great curiosity in the village of Jethana. We drop our things at his uncle's house and go on to another uncle's house for chai. Chiki, the dog, barks at us. I've known Chiki for some time now. We walk around town to call on various relatives. One

Holi Celebration and My Hair turns Pink!

has a business in Mysore and I tell him about my trip there three weeks ago. It is a granite business. Neighborhood boys are playing an impromptu game of cricket in the narrow street and Suresh joins in. They ask if I can climb stairs, which seems an odd request, until I find out that we are climbing over some buildings to get to a vacant grassy area, boxed in by the structures. They want to continue their cricket match there. It is fun to watch them, young boys and some older. There are a few course obstructions, but no one seems to mind. Suresh is having a good time. The owner comes out and grabs one of the boys, telling them they are trespassing and tells us all to leave. Suresh gets involved and a heated argument follows. We scamper back over the buildings and down to the street. I'm a bit upset, but they tell me not to worry, that this is normal in the village.

We spend the night at the uncle's house. They give the main bed for Suresh and me to use. The uncle comes and joins us for a time with me sandwiched between the two. The fan is going full speed and bothers my allergies, so I ask Suresh to change positions so I can be on the outside away from the direct flow of the fan.

It is raining when we return to Pushkar. This time I check into the Mama Luna Hotel, just before it begins to hail larger stones than many remember here. I take some time to visit with Navneet who has complained that I have not spent enough time with him. For most of the day, I stay in at the hotel because of the rain.

Suresh is after me to move to Pushkar. He envisions a room for me at his house and expects my help in building it. These expectations are another reason I should limit my trips here.

More rain and hail fall during the night making it cool out. The streets are a mess of mud, puddles of water and soft cow manure along with the usual litter. One wonders if India will ever be able to lift itself from the environmental mire it is creating.

There is no hot water for showers at the hotel. I should have returned to the Green Haveli that I enjoyed before located at the edge of town, but Suresh wanted me closer in. I asked Suresh to show me his house site again. I am anxious to see if it drains properly after a rain and also to ask about sewage. Most of the houses here just let sewage from kitchens and showers flow into the street creating a stinking mess and making it ripe for mosquitos. It appears to drain well. Suresh keeps after me to move here.

For our lunch, Suresh prepares potato sandwiches, trying something new for him. It is good. Gaurav arrives with his friend, the young farmer we had visited before. They are fun to be with. Gaurav is always a little crazy with me.

This morning there is no water, not even for the toilet. Fortunately, I have a small amount of water to make do. I kick myself for not returning to the Green Haveli. As I return from my walk, sparks suddenly shoot out from an overhead power line. I'm sure that it has knocked out our electricity for the rest of the day.

Manu, Mohit's uncle, wants to show me his land out of town. It is about nine kilometers out of town and comprised of a sandy field sloping down from a paved road. He envisions building a secluded resort for tourists there and a place for others to be away from town, which I think means being away from prying eyes. He wants to construct a swimming pool and a few rooms in a farm house to begin with. The land being sandy would be fairly easy to deal with. There are fields behind and on either side of the property. He takes us next to a "colony," which means a housing area marked by plots. He tells us he owns two of them. These plots are destined to become building sites for houses in a cluster away from town. Last he shows us a plot closer to town on which he hopes to build a house for his family.

In the afternoon, I sit for a time in Jonti's Freedom Café. I had not

Holi Celebration and My Hair turns Pink!

been there this time and he is always a fun host with interesting young people frequenting his café. Today he is looking after a very precocious Italian boy about age 5, the son of one of his guests who is away at the moment. The little guy is definitely in charge. Jonti's helper Rahul prepares something for me to have while I relax there.

Mohit has invited us for dinner. We stop on the way to visit another of Suresh's uncles who has been seriously ill. He has been moved out of the multifamily dwelling to the house of one of his sons, Rakesh, which has better access to a bathroom. He is suffering from kidney failure and eczema of the skin. Dialysis is very expensive for the family. I think he is taking only medications and is not likely to live long. He is only about 55, but appears older. He has always been quiet spoken and friendly to me. We move on to Mohit's house for a wonderful dinner and time together upstairs at the rooftop.

On my final trek around the lake this morning, I meet the little old elfin-like sadhu who I greet and give a few coins. How he continues to live is a puzzle to me, but he is always at a certain spot. We say nothing. I just clasp his small hands, say Namaste and slip the coins or small bills into his hands.

I'm ready for my clandestine omelet at the Om Shiva Garden, so I go for breakfast there. It is not on the menu, but they offer it if you ask. Eggs are considered non-vegetarian in this strict vegetarian town. Later I wash out my clothes and go to a cyber café to check emails, and discover a series of urgent messages from my children, telling me that my brother has been taken to jail for murder! I am sure they are mistaken. He had been in trouble for firing a gun at someone and was under indictment for shooting, but had not faced trial as yet and was out on bail. I was sure they were referring to that incident. I think maybe he has had to return to jail on that charge after being out on bail. I send a message to correct their misconception the charges concerning his crime occurring over a year ago. I was half-way expecting that he would be brought to trial and if convicted, would have to serve jail time. My brother, just over a year younger than me, has periods of being delusional, imagining himself as being a citizen policeman or a secret agent on assignment by the president to stop terrorists. It is a bi-polar condition. The messages worry me, but surely they didn't mean murder! I will check on him when I get home.

I spend time with Kamal, Suresh's brother enjoying fresh juice from a street vendor and visit with LotoGuru at the lake. He asks me to bring shoes from America. People are always asking for gifts! We gather at Suresh's house. Mohit comes from an exam that he feels he has done well with. They all try to assist me in packing my suitcase only complicating matters, making it hard to get everything in. I give Deepika one of the sandalwood scarves that I bought in Bangalore. Suresh's mother prepares my favorite snack for me, fried chilies, potato and onions. I eat way too many. We hire a car to take us to the train station in Ajmer where we board the *Shabuti* Express to New Delhi. At a brief stop in Jaipur, Neeraj and his girlfriend are there to greet me. He tells us he is coming to Delhi for some work and will join us there. Suresh and I get a nice room at the Hari Piorko Hotel, where I had tried to stay before, when the reservation got messed up.

18 March Delhi

Sad News from Home

Today my mind is on a brother who died on this day many years ago, only 29 years of age. It was so long ago and such a short life. His sons were ages 3 and 2 at the time. Late in the afternoon I am able to check Facebook and emails at a cyber connection at the adjacent hotel. There are urgent messages from my children telling me that I was the one mistaken, that my younger brother had indeed shot and killed a man and is now in jail, charged with the first degree murder of a 46 year-old man, following an argument of some sort. The details are sketchy but the news devastates me. What I thought to have been the conclusion of another trial, now turns out to be much worse. I immediately think

Holi Celebration and My Hair turns Pink!

of his three sons who are also devastated by the news. We had feared his behavior might lead to something like this, due to several previous episodes of delusion which had kept escalating. His family had warned the police but they said they could do nothing until he had committed a crime, and now this has happened. The pending trial on the first charge had been delayed multiple times, else he might have been in jail and unable to commit a more serious crime. I send messages back to my daughters and a message to his ex-wife as well. I will have to wait until I get home to get the full details. There is little else I can do from here, except pray for the family and the family of the victim as well. I tell Suresh and Neeraj, who express their sympathy.

A friend takes me to an uncle's house for a promised chicken dinner tonight. The friend had stayed with him before whenever he made trips to Delhi. We are soon joined by another man employed by a travel agency who comes bearing drinks, of which he has already liberally partaken. By the time we leave, the two guys are three-sheets to the wind. Because the dinner will take some time to be prepare, we return to the hotel lobby briefly. One of the inebriated guys gets into the personal space of a foreign female guest, who warns him sharply to "Get away!" I grab him by the arm and pull him outside to the street, apologizing to the lady. It's all I need tonight; a couple of drunk friends to look after.

We hire a rickshaw to return us to the uncle's house, located in a medical compound protected by security control at the entrance. It is obvious to the guard that the two guys are nearly drunk and he's not willing to let them pass, whereupon one of them starts hugging the man, making matters worse. The friend tells the man he's related to the uncle and the guard relents and lets the two stagger toward the house, where they remain loud and boisterous, even though the uncle tries to quiet them because the rest of the family are sleeping by now. The other guy takes a liking to me and invites me to visit his family in Haryana the next time I come. He is all over me with man hugs and the overly friendly adoration of a drunk person, repeating the only phrase in English he

Distant Lands

knows "My friend. My friend!" We somehow get through the dinner. At least, the chicken is delicious.

Back on the street, the two want more to drink. Before I know it they have bought beers from a shop to take back to the hotel, but I put my foot down about that and tell them they are not bringing any back to the hotel, so they just start drinking openly on the street instead! Oh, Lord, why am I in this situation! Hasn't this day been bizarre enough for me already? I begin to imagine the police coming and rounding up the lot of us. The friend tells me not to worry about the police, that he knows everyone including the magistrate. Maybe so, but I move away from them as quickly as possible, putting as much distance between me and them as they finish their beers, so we can hire a rickshaw back to the hotel. The other man goes on his way. Suresh has returned by now from shopping and I tell him to get this friend into the room and keep him there, so I can check emails once more to see if there is more news about my brother, stopping at the cyber café of a hotel nearby, only to discover that I don't have enough money to pay the fee for the use of the computer but the manager kindly waives the charges for me. I read more about the troubling news from home. I start back to the hotel to find that Suresh and the friend out to the street despite my warning, saying they were hungry. Perhaps it is better to keep him out on the street for a time than to go back into the hotel, so we walk around. I need some chai anyway, still trying to absorb the news about my brother. We stop at a small Indian café. As we return, the friend wants to smoke and lifts a couple of cigarettes from a vendor without paying for them, causing a ruckus. Suresh quickly slips the vendor the money and we hustle the guy back to the room. This has been a most bizarre day!

Suresh wants to visit his friend Manu, Mohit's brother who lives in the Dwarka area of Delhi. Neeraj and I go for juice at a nearby place. The friend from last night shows up as we return to the hotel, carrying socks filled with snacks for us to share, still overly friendly, evidence that he's been in the sauce again before arriving. There's no place to go but

Holi Celebration and My Hair turns Pink!

to the hotel. I give him strict warnings as we pass through the lobby. In the room, he unrolls a stash of food goodies, including a delicious chicken roll he has brought for our lunch. As we nibble on the snacks, he pulls out a bottle of whiskey from his pants. Oh Lord! Here we go again. The more he gets into the whiskey, the more friendly he gets, exclaiming over and over "My friend! My friend!" Fortunately, we get through the episode better this time.

Mercifully he leaves and I finish packing. My suitcase has broken so I buy a canvas bag from a vendor on the street to replace it. Suresh takes my old bag back with him to use for storing clothes. Suresh returns by now and he and Neeraj get quite weepy about my leaving. I tell them, please no drama. I have reached my limit on drama these past two days. We check out before midnight and they accompany me to the airport showering me with hugs as I take my leave. I am relieved to be leaving for this has turned into a difficult trip for me.

The flight departs on time at 3:40 a.m. with my allergies in full mode and the plane is packed making it a long miserable night. London is cool and cloudy when I make the transition for Dallas. I am totally exhausted. There is a two hour delay due to mechanical problems and I have no way of letting Hap know since I am still without a phone. He tells me later that he had made three trips to the airport to get me.

Sleep is fitful at best. During the night, I dream of sleeping in a house somewhere in India and need to use the bathroom in the worst way, but I am unable to find a toilet and wander around in the dark trying to figure out what to do. I am disoriented and can't find my way back to my room, until I happen to stumble over a bed in the dark, hitting my shins, but I don't know whose bed it is nor where I am.

Was it a dream or had I been sleepwalking?

Who knows…

3

Nepal's Earthquake Leads to Return Visits

25 April 2015

Nepal's Devastating Earthquake

On April 25, 2015 a major earthquake strikes Nepal. The epicenter is located in the Ghorka District to the west of Kathmandu. It strikes just before noon. Within seconds and in the following hours with numerous strong aftershocks, 9000 people lose their lives and thousands more find themselves homeless with the collapse of their houses. It takes nearly six weeks for me to get word concerning the status of my many friends. Fortunately, when I do, I learn that all of them were spared though most of them lost their houses or their family's homes in the mountain villages, which are especially hard hit. My friend Mike is there on assignment and he survives the quake while staying at a hotel in Kathmandu being forced to stay outside for some nights. Thousands seek shelter in the subsequent weeks and months to follow, staying in tents and under flimsy plastic tarps set up in parks and open areas. The devastation affects Nepal's economy in devastating ways with the collapse of tourism which directly affects most of my friends. With these concerns in mind, I decide to return to Nepal to see about my friends. I gather funds from friends at church and from some of my neighbors. On the way I plan to stop first to visit Turkey and after Nepal, I plan to visit India.

Nepal's Earthquake Leads to Return Visits

28 September 2015 Istanbul
My friend Nurettin Unal greets me upon arrival in Istanbul from Chicago. The traffic of Istanbul is thick as we move toward his home, stopping first for a dinner of fish at a restaurant located by the sea just below where he lives. His wife Sibel greets us at their apartment and they provide a room for me upstairs for sleep after the long flight.

I accompany Nurettin to his place of work at the fire station. I have brought a patch I obtained from my local fire station at Deer Creek near my house to present to the crew there. Nurettin introduces me to his chief who welcomes me and serves tea. I present the patch as a gift from his counterparts in the USA and he presents me with a commemorative plate and a cap with an Istanbul firefighter logo on it, after which I eat lunch with the crew. Nurettin gives me a tour of the facility, showing me the various fire trucks and tankers used to fight fires. The crew receives me with a great deal of interest and makes sure I'm well cared for as they bring me snacks and juices to drink. We sit outside and I listen as they share stories with each other, sprinkled with occasional laughter at some joke or other. Occasionally Nuri translates for me.

I have promised to spend time with Atalay, aother friend in Istanbul who operates a print shop. Nurettin takes me to his shop by motorcycle to meet Atalay and his crew. I meet a young man there by the name of Tarik, who is one of the recent Syrian refugees. He had made it to Istanbul along with his brother and they both are working in the print shops housed in the large warehouse where Atalay has his shop. The work is temporary as they hope to make their way to Europe as part of the mass migration there. At the shop, I reconnect with several friends I've made on my previous visits as they come to share lunch and snacks in the afternoon. Atalay has a small bed in his office which he offers for my stay, which will save hotel costs for me, so I take up residence in the print shop. When Atalay leaves work at night, he locks up and leaves a key for my use to use the toilet facilities located in the warehouse. It is a little spooky staying overnight in a print shop, although there is usually another person or two around in the large warehouse.

Atalay comes early to open the shop and we have coffee and later breakfast before he does some work with the presses. Today he plans to take a trip to a city some distance away on the European side of Turkey along with a friend of his and me. Once there we connect with another friend who treats us to a fantastic lunch of a variety of meats and other dishes. It is a relief for me to get out of the big city, though return traffic presents a problem. Later we pick up his son Ozgur from his school. He is a fine and handsome boy of thirteen and knows his English fairly well, so it is always good to visit with him.

My days are spent taking the tram into Sultanahmet to visit the historic district of Istanbul which I love. My fascination with the ancient church *Hagias Sophia* never wanes, so I purchase a ticket and spend several hours touring the historic facility built in the 600s and still standing after these years. There are beautiful mosaics in the process of restoration and always the massive architecture to marvel. The *Hagias Sophia* is the top tourist destination of Istanbul. I visit also a favorite book shop and spend time strolling around the area to see again its many historical wonders. I visit a Turkish coffee shop for some authentic Turkish coffee, much like drinking sludge and quite strong. It takes developing a taste for it to appreciate it. I visit with the owner who treats me to a piece of lemon cake. I buy a bag Turkish coffee to take home with me.

It is Sunday and Atalay is off work. We visit his sister and his mother who lives with her along with some of Ozgur's cousins in an upstairs apartment. His mother is a stately and pleasant Turkish woman. Atalay's father, a Kurdish man, died years ago when Atalay was but ten years of age. A portrait of his father is proudly displayed on the wall above the dining table, a very handsome man, born the same year as I was. They serve a sumptuous dinner which I enjoy and we spend the afternoon with much talking and laughter. Ozgur and his cousin spend time on their mobile phones, like most youth today.

Nurettin comes to the print shop to take me to the airport for my trip to Nepal. It's always a joy to visit him. One of guys operating another print shop pulls a large map of Turkey and one of the world to present to me. We wrap the maps with brown paper so I can take them to with me on the plane. My visit to Turkey is a brief one but enjoyable and I hope to return again next year to spend more time.

6 October Nepal: Earthquake Aftermath
I arrive at the Aryatara Hotel in Kathmandu which my friend Tara arranged for me. It is the one where he works and the same hotel where Mike survived the earthquake in April. I hasten to walk around to survey local earthquake damage in Kathmandu. Brick walls are crumpled near the hotel and buildings in Thamel with braces prop up walls that have a definite lean to them. There are gaps between several buildings where buildings have collapsed into piles of rubble, the debris still remaining. Kathmandu was not as severely damaged as most of the villages of the mountainous areas although the historic old temples, especially those in Durbar Square and nearby in Bahktipur, were devastated. Repair work is in progress but mostly it is still in the cleanup stage, with some of the structures remaining to be torn down. Most debris is removed by hand.

I enjoy meals at the hotel and get to know the staff and spend time visiting with Tara who works there. We visit his grandfather who lives with a son in an area beyond Thamel and have tea, joined by his cousin Sachin, a young man quite active with sports. We receive a blessing with the *tikka* applied to the forehead signaling the beginning of the Dashain festival season. The grandfather is one year my senior.

My plan is to connect with friends who work at the Pashupatinath Temple but the problem is that there is virtually no fuel to be had because India has shut off all imports of petrol, throwing Nepal into a further crisis. Getting a taxi proves nearly impossible and quite costly. I pay triple the price for the taxi there but at least I get to meet my friend Raju and his friends, who each relate their stories of surviving the earthquake. Most had been outside at the time, yet were terrified as people ran from buildings to escape. The earthquake happened just minutes before noon.

I spend the afternoon with them, enjoying tea and eating lunch from a small shop there. I meet Gopal Nagarkoti, a professional golfer unusual to find in Nepal. Raju walks with me to the site where cremations are taking place, still quite busy. He tells me that they were operating at full force following the earthquake. Smoke from the fires blanket the valley along the river. Ashes are scraped into the stream and eventually flow to the Ganges in India. The guys talk about taking a trek tomorrow to Chisopani, a small village in the mountains above Kathmandu and press for me to accompany them for an overnight trek. I tell them that I have just arrived and not sure about my fitness to make such a trek, given a recent diagnosis of an arterial fibrillation issue with my heart. I am afraid that I might slow them down too much but they assure me they are happy to go slowly and don't mind making frequent stops when needed. A young man comes along by the name of Ramesh. I ask him if he is going and he says he is not sure. I tell the others that if Ramesh can go and carry my backpack, I will try it. They agree to that and tell me to meet here tomorrow morning at 9:00.

After dinner back at the hotel, I prepare for the trek tomorrow packing for a one-night stay over on the mountain. I also have a good time catching up with Tara and his friends there.

Tara arranges a car for me for the trip to Pashupatinath for departure on our trek. It is pouring rain which does not bode well for our trek, but perhaps the rain will let up by the time I get there. We arrive to a torrential downpour. None of the other guys have arrived so I wait in

Nepal's Earthquake Leads to Return Visits

the shelter of one of the shops for them. Finally Raju comes walking through the rain now beginning to slacken a bit. Eventually Gopal arrives and Ramesh. Ramesh persuades another young man to join us but he must first get his things. His name is Umes. By the time we have all gathered it is already well into the morning. We are not able to find a taxi to take us to the far side of Kathmandu to our launching point. Instead, we pile into a van for a short distance in hopes of finding a bus to ride. With few buses still running, buses are hopelessly overloaded. The only space available is on top of the bus, so the guys push me up to a high ladder at the back so I can get to the top with them. Perhaps you've seen pictures of buses fully packed with people riding on top and hanging from doors. That would be us! They tell me to hang on tightly and do not rise up as power lines barely clear the bus. We make our way over the rough streets of Kathmandu to the launching point. Several power lines give us close calls. My hands become numb from hanging on to a small rail with all my might to keep from being thrown from the bus on sharp turns and sudden stops. We arrive at the site of departure about noon, quite late to be starting a trek, which will go straight up the mountain. They stop to buy food for us to carry, including a fresh chicken to skewer, while Ramesh and I start ahead. The ascent consists of a series of steps leading by the water source for Kathmandu near waterfalls. I had been this far before with Manish, but we keep going up and soon the others catch up with us. It is hard for me at first because I haven't been in Nepal long enough to acclimate to the altitude, having just left Istanbul at sea level. We stop a few times for me to catch my breath. I begin to set a slow, steady pace which suits me, and they are good to respect it. The group discusses taking an alternate route to avoid the steeper grade, but it is a much longer way around. We opt to do it and cut off on a trail leading through a jungle-like area on a path still slippery from the rain. We stop often, first at a place which is built into a rock formation sheltering a small room with a platform built on wood poles, where we climb all hunched over to drink a featured local soup served in clay bowls along with tastes of the local sour wine.

Distant Lands

Raju spots plants of a special kind which grow fairly abundantly and he harvests some for his smokes and we rest while he prepares it, giving me a chance to catch my breath. On we go, eating up time with more stops than I require. We follow a dirt road for some time listening to the sounds of nature. Umes has brought a radio which plays music most of the time, drowning out the sounds of nature, until I ask him to turn it off. Umes is an interesting young man. He keeps up a steady conversation with me about various girlfriends and tales his experiences. Ramesh and I stop at a rock structure for rest and I learn more about him. I like Ramesh and we become good friends. He is good to help me along. We stop at a small café for lunch and meet the owner who cooks for us and brings me a traditional Nepali hat to put on for photos. Sometimes we stretch out on grassy areas for short naps. Umes takes to calling me his grandfather. As darkness approaches, we are still a long ways from Chisopani but we stop to build a fire and skewer the chicken we have brought with us, taking up much too much time getting the fire going and it is pitch dark when we proceed. None of us carry a flashlight, a major oversight on our part, and have only our mobile phones for lights to navigate our way through the darkness, which sometimes involves steep climbs or sharp descents. We use only the lights occasionally for we must preserve the batteries. By now, we have been trekking for over seven hours and I am reaching a state of near exhaustion. I stop for rest but try again. Still we are not there. I tell them I can't go any farther for I've reached my limit. What to do? I ask if they could go for help and come back for me but give it one last try and we finally arrive at Chisopani about 10:00 p.m. at the guest house we have reserved. The owners are asleep by now and we awaken them. The group is hungry so the lady fires up a cooker to cook rice and dahl for them but I want only a little soup and just want to crash. The original guest house had been destroyed by the quake with only this small kitchen surviving. They built a small group of shed-like rooms out back of bamboo topped with corrugated tin roofs for guests. They take us to a room with several beds which we share and hunker down under the blankets for the night air has gotten quite cold. I sleep with Raju. I check my phone app for the distance of our trek and discover that we have trekked nearly twelve miles mostly up. That I made it so far is a miracle but it has left me totally exhausted.

Earthquake Claims Nepal Guest House

Distant Lands

We wake to a cold morning and omelets for breakfast after which we walk around the village to see the devastation left by the earthquake. A four-story guest house tilts at a 45 degree angle, the bottom floor having been collapsed by the quake with people killed there. A table and chairs still set at an exposed third floor room, as if waiting for guests. Other buildings are mere rubble. Others have facades broken away exposing empty rooms. We stop at a place for tea, open amid the destruction. Residents have constructed sheds of bamboo or corrugated metal. In the distance we see the high peaks of the Himalayas and evidence of major landslides.

Back at our place, we build a fire outside for warmth and sit around it. Umes decides that I need to spike my hair like his and offers to do it for me. I let him, which delights him. He puts gel on my thin hair and sweeps it into a spike and we take photos together. He thinks I'm a cool grandfather.

They tell me that we are staying two nights here instead of the one night that I had anticipated. I did not bring medicines enough for two nights and worry about my condition, but there is little I can do about it at this stage. We cook our dinner at the campfire and enjoy the rest of the time together.

Walking around the village the next day, we inspect additional earthquake damage. It's sad to see how much damage these mountain villages sustained. Families are slowly clearing and rebuilding.

I'm anxious to get back down so we start back at my insistence. We are a little short of money paying out and I give what I have and they match the rest. We stop at a beautiful lake on the way down where we rest and take a bunch of photos, spending a great deal of time there, more than necessary. They have been good to stop often for me but more than I require and staying longer than needed. As a result, we are late getting back. I had promised to meet another young friend today but hadn't anticipated that we would still be trekking. It is almost dark by the time we return and load onto a bus, inside this time. A fight breaks out among the ones on top and the bus stops and the police are called, delaying things even further. Raju and I get off near the Boudhinath Stupa so he can help me get a taxi back to Thamel, but none are available and instead he finds a bus for me and instructs the driver to let me off at an appropriate stop near Thamel, but I don't really know where I am when I get off the bus. I hire a bicycle rickshaw to take me toward my hotel but he doesn't know the way. After several stops and conflicting directions, we eventually come to a landmark that I recognize and we are able to make it back. I miss the meet-up with my young friend and haven't been able to call him. I later learn that he had dressed up to meet me and was quite perplexed and disappointed that I didn't show.

I book a flight to Pokhara, one of my favorite places with its beautiful lake. I check into the Crystal Palace Hotel and in the afternoon and rent a row boat with an oarsman provided to take me out on the lake. It's a beautiful and relaxing time as we move along overhanging branches on the far side and listen to the singing insects in the trees. With so few tourists because of the quake and the fuel crisis, the boat operators are quite hungry for business. I give my oarsman a good tip which he appreciates.

After a couple of days, I return to Kathmandu where I had promised to hook up with my friend Manish. Gopal meets me at the airport and we walk together from the airport to Pashupatinath , cutting through the golf course. Gopal is a professional golfer and tells me the fairways were covered with makeshift tents some three months after the quake by people who had fled their houses. I meet up with Manish who shows me the new apartment he has rented after the other one had been destroyed by the quake. His father barely escaped the falling building. He tells me the new rent has almost doubled. Pinkey and Vicky are growing up, especially Vicky who has now grown taller than his sister. I

Distant Lands

spend a couple of nights with them. Manish wants me to visit a village to see more damage but with the shortage of fuel and has no way to get there. We find a source of fuel, arranged by a guy on the street, costing about $30 for a couple of liters, about a gallon, outrageous but there is no other possibility. The village we visit was completely devastated with large piles of rubble are heaped up from houses and temples completely destroyed or left with crumbling exposed walls. A man invites us into his house, still standing, but once inside we see that the back half has fallen away. Nevertheless we climb steps carefully to the second floor where he serves us chai, showing me photos of his family including a daughter in college. He points to a journal of people who have made donations and asks for one which I give. He tells me that most of the victims of the village had been women, children and the elderly, who happened to be inside their houses when the earthquake hit; most of the men were in the fields or away at work. Manish explains that for a couple of months you could still smell the corpses as the rubble was being cleared away. It was a sad scene.

Back at Pashupati, I walk to the Boudhinath Temple some distance away. The huge stupa has lost its top, a tower representing the stairway to heaven. Other buildings surrounding the stupa were also severely damaged.

Returning to the Aryatara Hotel, I accompany Tara to the airport where we receive his brother arriving from Japan, along with the brother's father-in-law, a Japanese man. Youbaraj married a Japanese woman and they live near Tokyo. It has been three years since he has been home to see his parents. At dinner together on a balcony we get better acquainted and talk about plans for a trip to Tara's home village. The problem is transportation due to the fuel outages. Tara is able to obtain a four-wheel drive vehicle, necessary to make the steep ascent but costing nearly $600 USD, way beyond their reach. I promise to help, using some funds provided by a study group back home. I'd hate for Youbaraj to have travelled all this way and not be able to see his parents. Their

Nepal's Earthquake Leads to Return Visits

farm house, the one I've stayed in before, has been damaged by the quake. The parents have lived outside under a tarp for some time.

We go to Baktipur loading up supplies to take, including tents if necessary, and buy a supply of food and water to sustain us while there, making the vehicle crowded, including us and another brother's wife and children, along with the supplies we are carrying. Once we reach the vicinity of the home village, we turn off the paved road, taking a road newly carved up the mountain, steep and rough in places but the vehicle is in good condition and we make it, unlike the last time we tried this. The parents are happy to see their son after a long absence and they meet the father-in-law as well, who has little conversation since he doesn't speak English, though Youbaraj is careful to include him as much as possible. We see farm houses in the village with walls torn away. At their farm house, large cracks mar the walls, but we determine that the house is still livable, so we choose to stay inside. A cousin's house nearby had been completely destroyed and is now in the process of rebuilding, using improved building techniques, incorporating wooden planks in the stone walls to allow more flexibility in quakes.

It is the beginning of Dashain, so we immediately go into preparation mode, the first order of business being the slaughter a goat for our food, which we do ceremonially as I've described elsewhere. Everyone gets involved as the sacrifice is made and the carcass cut into small pieces. We spread a tarp connected to the house to make a shelter under which to eat. They ask me how I like to eat my goat, as if it is a part of my normal diet, but I tell them how I like to skewer meat over an open fire making shish kabobs, with meat, onions and peppers, explaining how it works. They decide to try it with the goat meat. We build a fire and make skewers from strips of bamboo. Youbaraj has brought some special spices from Japan and we use those to season the pieces of goat meat, along with onions and chilies and skewer them over the fire. It is a hit with the group, which by now includes several cousins who have come. They find it all quite delicious. Even the skeptical father tries it and is pleased, saying it is better than the usual way of boiling the goat. Youbaraj shares soup with us he has brought from Japan, along some special drinks making for an enjoyable evening.

The next day we move to the cousin's house, nearing completion, for the major ceremony related to Dashain. An altar is prepared in the yard and the chants begin amid the sound of blowing horns. The father-in-law and I observe from the side. The ceremony concludes with the sacrifice of the goat and the eating of the food offerings. It has begun to rain.

Nepal Family Dashain Festival Tikka Markings

We sleep downstairs on pallets spread on the floor side by side, instead of up as before, putting us next to the goats. We listen to the goats munching on their cut vegetation all night, accompanied by sounds of passing gas. Yet, it is a good family time. The guys compete in card playing during times of leisure. We each receive the large *tikka* blessing smeared across our foreheads. After a few days, we return by trekking down the mountain to return to Baktipur. I've enjoyed time

Nepal's Earthquake Leads to Return Visits

with Youbaraj. He invites me to visit him in Japan, which I hope to do next year. I stop by Pashupati for a final visit and Gopal at a room he arranges for me in a small hotel nearby for one night.

Leaving Nepal for Delhi, I feel much sympathy for these friends in Nepal as they deal with the multiple crises facing them. It is very difficult time for them.

4

Surprise Birthday Trip

27 October Delhi

76th Birthday Mystery Trip

I reach Delhi in time to celebrate yet another birthday in India. This one is my 76th and as usual Suresh and Neeraj have arrived to make it a big deal. Suresh hints at a major surprise for me, involving a trip somewhere. It is all a mystery. My Australian friend Brad is there as well to join us for a mutual birthday celebration. Suresh spreads a table decorated with rose petals and presents a cake with candles. They sing Happy Birthday and proceed to smear cake on our faces for good measure.

The next day we leave for the airport to begin the mystery trip. Suresh won't tell me where we are going; only that it is to be a four-day trip to a destination that I don't learn until we check in at the domestic terminal and receive a ticket to Goa on the west coast of India. Goa is the former Portuguese Colony and a favorite resort destination for the winter months. What a surprise!

Reaching Goa, we hire a car to take us to the Bagh Beach area. The beachfront hotel recommended to Suresh is out of our league, so we settle for a cheaper one in a small village a short walk from the beach.

Surprise Birthday Trip

Goa is a touristy area and the village where we are staying is lined with restaurants and bars, obviously focusing on the night life, remaining open and lively into the wee hours of the morning, not a quiet place. After a little rest, we head to the beach where a few people are playing in the water. I get in too and enjoy the feel of waves crashing over me from the Indian Ocean. After a tasty lunch at a nearby restaurant we walk around until evening as things liven up. Suresh orders snacks for us to enjoy while we sit on lounge chairs looking out to the beach. He is shocked when he gets the bill, quite expensive. Boys come with fire displays and various souvenirs to ply the beach enticing tourists to buy. A canopy is set up for dancing at dark, with active participants quickly working up sweat from the humid air. Suresh and Neeraj join in and pull me into the crowd a few times, but it is much too hot and humid for me to last long.

The historic old city of Goa is filled with large colonial-era cathedrals. The Portuguese established churches, along with monasteries to propagate the faith. Goa remained a colony until after India declared its independence from Britain in 1947. A museum presents the history of the colony.

Suresh begins fasting for one of his series of fasting days. We stop at a restaurant but he remains vigilant while Neeraj and I enjoy snacks before our meal is served. Suresh must wait until moonrise to eat. He checks his clock for the time and it is now the proper time to begin, but the requirement is that he has to be able to actually see the moon before he can eat. The moon is hidden from view by large trees. I get up from the table and move to one side of the restaurant, where the moon is visible and motion for him to come to see it. He is grateful and hastens back to the table to hungrily devour his food. Suresh is always the most diligent in keeping the specific rules of his faith, but he loves eating too.

We visit another beach some miles from ours; this one is popular with

Indian visitors and is much more crowded, with the usual cows on the beach. However, we do meet a couple of Russians who tell us they are here to make documentary films.

Jaipur

We enjoy our days at Goa, but we are ready to go because our expenses are mounting by the day. We return to Delhi and book a train to Jaipur to stay a few days with Neeraj, while Suresh goes on to Pushkar. Neeraj and his friend Vikas take me for a ride on the motorcycle without telling me where we are going. This is turning into a trip of surprises! We travel about 60 kilometers outside Jaipur to what is billed as an authentic Rajasthani Village, a re-creation of village life of another era, sort of a Disneyesque version. We pay the fee to enter a compound of huts on dirt streets. Native girls are dancing traditional dances and offer photo shoots with us, for tips of course. I do my best with dancing, dubbing my efforts as the Rajasthani Mash. We sit on pillows to be served tea and a traditional dinner, after which we visit compounds exhibiting differing styles of village homes, from the humblest to the elaborate style of the Raj. We even witness a sword fight staged by young men showing the prowess of the military of that day.

Pushkar New Baby and Diwali

Neeraj helps me book bus travel to Ajmer and Pushkar. This time I stay at the Doctor Alone Garden Hotel in a nice room. It is during Diwali once again with all the ceremonies connected with this most important festival, including beautiful displays of fireworks which I view from the roof above my room at the hotel. They go on all night.

We make another trip to Nimaj. The treat this time is that I get to see Suresh's new daughter for the first time, born just a month ago on October 7! Deepika has been staying in Nimaj with her parents. The baby's name is Aria but they call her Debbie, maybe for my benefit in honor of my daughter by that name. She is a beautiful child and an answer to their prayers. Suresh takes a picture of me holding her in my

Surprise Birthday Trip

arms which they now display on the wall of their room in Pushkar so little Debbie can remember me when she looks at the picture. I stay at Nimaj Palace and attend the obligatory volleyball matches involving the young men of Nimaj, where Vicky and Tony usually play. On the way back, we stop in Jethana to visit Suresh's uncle and family and two sons Mitty and Keshaw, Mitty now a young lad of fifteen and little Keshaw always a delight. I am "Keith Uncle" to them.

Delhi Friends and Family
It is time to return home. I book a train to Delhi to visit my niece's family and to visit with my friend Mike, who happens to be there as well. I spend a few days in Delhi before flying toward home through Amsterdam. It is Thanksgiving time in America, so after four days at home I fly to Pittsburgh to be with my family there.

My world family has grown quite large these past few years, spanning time, cultures and nations. How blessed I am!

Part Seven
2016 Turkey, Terror and Turning 77

"Travel is fatal to prejudice, bigotry, and narrow-mindedness, and many of our people need it sorely on these accounts. Broad, wholesome, charitable views of men and things cannot be acquired by vegetating in one little corner of the earth all one's lifetime."
–Mark Twain

For the final part of this narrative, I share travel experiences in 2016 covering time in Turkey, visiting my friend Atalay and his extended family in the extreme eastern part of the country, near the borders of Armenia and Iran toward the end of Ramadan. It was a delightful experience, but the trip took a darker turn in the political upheaval breaking out in Turkey. Later in the year, I made one more visit to Nepal to see how my friends were making with earthquake recovery, and to India where I celebrated birthday number 77.

1

Ramadan with Family in East Turkey

28 June 2016

Terror in Turkey

Atalay in Istanbul and I still at my home chat excitedly about my coming to Istanbul tomorrow. We are planning to travel to the city of Kagizman in far eastern Turkey for a week with his relatives. Kagizman is his boyhood home and is located near the border with Armenia and Iran. I had already booked flights for three of us to fly to Kars in east Turkey—Atalay, his son Ozgur and myself. Relatives are to meet us in Kars for the trip to Kagizman. It is toward the end of Ramadan (Ramazan in Turkish), which means that the family will still be fasting when we arrive but with the end of it there will be feasting. After chatting with Atalay, I return to the business of last-minute preparations. I had voted this morning in one of our state's primary elections. Sometime in the afternoon, I pick up my phone to check messages and a news flash hits the screen, reporting shootings and bomb explosions happening now at the Istanbul Airport! I immediately switch on the television in time to see all hell breaking loose in the attack on the airport. Video feeds show terrorists detonating bombs near the departure entrance to the airport. At least three terrorists are identified exploding bombs and shooting people. This airport is quite familiar to me and I recognize where the action is taking place. My heart sinks.

Distant Lands

My phone starts buzzing as people call and message to tell me what is happening and ask if I am still going. I watch the television screen transfixed and horrified. It looks doubtful that I can travel to Turkey. The U. S. State Department announces that all direct flights from the U.S. to Istanbul are being cancelled. Mine is a connecting flight through London. I have already bought tickets, plus the three tickets for the trip on to Kars and think about all the penalties if I make changes. I contact Atalay through Facebook and he assures me that his family is safe.

There is nothing to do but wait. I go about my business for the rest of the day. My yard needs mowing before I leave. I have put it off until this afternoon. The evening news shows additional photos of the horror taking place there.

In the midst of this, I receive an urgent message from a friend in Nepal, whose father is seriously ill in the hospital and is facing a critical surgery. Without the necessary funds for the surgery, it will not be done, unless he can guarantee payment. I don't have the kind of money he needs but I check with my friend Hap and we are able to pool $300, so I quickly arrange to send that.

Members of my class at church call and my daughter calls from Wyoming, all wondering what I am going to do. I don't know as yet. I cobble together a dinner of sorts. Later, messages come through saying that they plan to re-open the Istanbul airport the day after tomorrow, the day of my scheduled arrival. Perhaps it can be a "go" for me, provided that I am willing to take the risk. As doubtful as it looks, I decide that I should go ahead as planned. If I get half-way and issues continue to develop, I'll deal with that along the way.

Hap arrives later in the evening to take me to the airport in the morning, which he does. I check my bags all the way to Istanbul. So far; so good. I make it to Dallas. In Dallas, just before I board my flight to

Ramadan with Family in East Turkey

London, I receive a call from a group wanting me to lead a seminar. My mind is scrambled with the urgency of the moment but I give them a tentative yes telling them of my situation. They promise to get back with me about particulars later. It seems that they had remembered something I had published a long time back and want me to talk about it in a conference setting.

As soon as I finish this conversation, I receive a message from one of the ladies in my group at church, who tells me she is willing to provide additional funds for my Nepali friend to cover the father's surgery. I ponder how she can get the money to me while I'm traveling? We discuss some possibilities. If it works, I can forward it to my friend, once I arrive in east Turkey. Her offer touches me deeply.

So much is happening at once!

Our flight is delayed over an hour due to unspecified mechanical issues and is overbooked with $800 vouchers being offered to reschedule, but I feel I must go on. Too bad, for the voucher would have been nice.

London airport security is a zoo with lines backed up and the process grinding forward at snail's pace. I board the flight to Istanbul with mostly Turkish passengers who are making up for the flights missed because of the attack.

On the plus side, my seatmate turns out to be a university professor from Muenster, Texas, south of Gainesville below the Texas-Oklahoma border, teaching in Istanbul in various universities over the last twenty years. Dr. Clifford Enes is a 74 years old professor of literature, an engaging conversationalist. We talk about Orhan Pamuk's work whose novel *Snow* is set in Kars, where we intend to fly after Istanbul. He explains what is behind the growing conservative-fundamentalist movement in Turkey and his fears for the future of education there, telling me there are already firings of those perceived to be in opposition to Erdogen,

Distant Lands

the Prime Minister and those who are simply branded as intellectuals. Little do we know how soon events will engulf the nation to put Western-oriented education in jeopardy.

The lines are long at the Istanbul airport but I am able to obtain the necessary visa. Atalay is outside waiting but the line takes over an hour to process before I can get to baggage claim for my bag. When I do, the bag has not shown up. I wait and check. Finally a trace is made and they tell me the bag never left London and will not arrive until late tonight. Since we plan to leave in the morning for Kars, I will wait to retrieve it then. It is the second time this has happened on a flight to Istanbul. I go outside where I meet Atalay, walking past bullet riddled glass and workmen busy reinstalling plate glass panels that were blown out less than 48 hours earlier by the terrorists. Welcome to Istanbul! Atalay greets me warmly and we hurry to exit, only to get caught up in heavy Istanbul traffic. We stop at his print shop. The air is hot and heavy with humidity and I am feeling weary from the travel, so we relax there with cold drinks and peanuts and later drive to his home, where we are welcomed by his wife Ulku and her mother, who is living with them. Ozgur, like a dear grandson to me, also greets me. They offer the use of their shower while dinner is being prepared. I change into shorts and a t-shirt and we catch up on events as best we can, with limited English. Dinner is Mediterranean-style vegetarian served with traditional bread for Ramadan. We talk awhile but I find it difficult to stay awake. They offer a pull-down couch where I sleep soundly until light from the next morning spreads across my face.

A full breakfast of bread, boiled egg, pastries and fruits energizes me for the day. We drive to the print shop to pick up our driver to drop us at the airport. He is a bearded young man, wearing the traditional Islamic dress of white and quite devout to observe all the regimens of Ramadan, Atalay tells me. He seems pleasant enough, but airport security being as tight as it is, stops us because he fits a profile of suspicion following the attack. Security officers order us to exit the car for a thorough search including my carry-on bag. Satisfied, they pass us through. Atalay and I get off to search for my lost luggage, while Ozgur and the driver park to meet us at the domestic terminal on the other side of the airport. On the way in, we encounter again the areas blasted out by the terrorist's bombs with hasty repairs being made. News cameras are rolling at a crowd surrounding a Member of Parliament giving a press conference concerning the attack. We see more bullet-riddled glass nearby. Inside, I am able to retrieve my lost luggage and we hasten to the domestic terminal to meet up with Ozgur and our driver. The driver says good-bye and returns to the print shop with the car as we check into the flight to Kars, with enough time to spare to sit and enjoy some tea.

Our flight takes us east over most of Turkey to the outpost city of Kars, about a two hour flight from Istanbul to this remote airport. Atalay's cousin Su'at and his family are on hand to greet us. We load our things into a van and head south from the airport bypassing the town. The terrain is rolling, with volcanic hills and escarpments reminding me of Wyoming in many ways. Fields of clover are in bloom to give the area a fragrance. We stop by a small stream and take a few photos before heading up in elevation over a pass to descend on the other side toward a river in the distance. There are herds of cattle, sheep and goats grazing alongside the road. We see the ruins of a castle fortification perches on the cleft of a rock outcropping. As we approach the valley with its stream heading for the river below, we pass through multiple orchards laden with ripening apricots. Once we reach the river, we cross and ascend a volcanic gorge carved by another stream to reach the city of Kagizman, which sets on the slope. We continue through the small city, down a gorge and back up on the other side to a cemetery located there. Atalay wants to visit his father's grave. His father had died at age 42 when Atalay was only 10. We locate a hand-painted stone with his father's name with a barely-discernable date of birth and death. Atalay and his sisters hope to replace the stone and make a grave frame, with a more proper set of

Distant Lands

stones, while we are here. After the cemetery, we stop at a paradisiacal orchard of fruit trees and pluck fresh apricots, sweet mulberries and other fruits from heavily-burdened trees. A cousin cooks mulberries in a large pot over an open fire, turning them into a paste. Back in the village, we stop at Su'at's house, an apartment on an upper floor in a concrete building to be welcomed warmly and served tea. The cousin's elderly mother lives with them, along with the son U'mut and two younger daughters.

Because of Ramazan (Ramadan), we eat lightly during the day. Our hosts have abstained from all daytime eating, including the little girls who are finding it quite difficult. Children have permission to eat during this fast, but one of the girls really wants to imitate her parents and joins in the fast. Atalay engages with his cousin and Ozgur with his cousin U'mut, as they catch up in Turkish, with me just listening and observing, letting the family go on with their re-uniting. The grandmother is surprised that I cannot speak Turkish. They give me a small bedroom for the night. We plan to relocate to a vacant house when Atalay's sisters and his mother arrive tomorrow from Istanbul.

A small balcony gives a great view of the volcanic mountain in the near distance. We enjoy the open air as we prepare for sunset, marking the end of the daily fast. Plates of food are brought but everyone must wait until the sun drops behind the horizon, and then not wasting a second after the sun sets, the hungry family plunge in to eat bread, vegetables and Mediterranean-style foods such as olives, tomatoes, cucumbers. There is fresh honey from area beehives. The little girls are ravished and eagerly dig in, with everyone happy now and the start to talk with great animation. It is fun to watch this family enjoy the meal.

Following the meal, Su'at invites us to join him for a walk downtown. A walk sounds good to me after the full meal. It turns into a social event as we stop at various outdoor cafes to chit-chat with the local population, who have all turned out for the evening, and drink multiple cups of tea as we move about from one place to another. I am introduced, to much curiosity, for it is rare for someone from America to visit here. They have received refugees from nearby Syria because of the wars there and according to Atalay, the men are discussing their presence, as he interprets for me the nature of the discussions going on. Atalay's cousin is a business man in the town who knows most everyone and they know him. Many are related in one way or another. I meet the one remaining uncle, brother to Atalay's deceased father. Though mostly it is men who are out, there are also groups of women in the public areas. The city is small enough for everybody to know everybody else. We stop for ice cream as well.

Abandoned City
It is a beautiful morning. The climate here is most refreshing. Again, we enjoy bread and fresh honey for breakfast while the others fast. We plan to visit the abandoned city of Ani today. It is site I wanted to explore when I found out that we were coming to this area. Ani has been abandoned for centuries in this fought-over border land. After we go there, we plan to pick up Atalay's mother, sisters and one of their young sons Cem, flying in from Istanbul. Also, we plan to visit a variety of bee farms in order to retrieve honey for the cousin's business. It promises to be a full day.

One of the guys we met last night shows up with the van for our trip. He is quite pleasant. We load up—Atalay, his cousin Su'at, Ozgur and U'mut who is Su'at's 12 years old son. The road ascends through the hills toward Kars. Before we get there, we turn off on a side trail leading through fields of clover over rocky ground to a camp near a series of bee hives. The keeper stays in a small tent there to tend the bees. While we watch, the guys retrieve honey from the hives, using smoke to calm the bees.

Distant Lands

Ancient Abandoned Cathedral in Ani, Turkey

We continue on past Kars some 60 kilometers until we come to the abandoned city. For a thousand years, it was an important stop on the silk route to China. Who knows, maybe Marco Polo stopped here on

Ramadan with Family in East Turkey

his journeys. At one time the city boasted of a thousand churches, built during the long reign of the Byzantine Empire and peopled by the ancestors of today's Armenians, who now live just across a nearby gorge separating Turkey from Armenia. The region came next under control of the Ottoman Turks, who in turn lost it to Czarist Russia, only to regain it, and now it is part of Turkey. Each occupancy resulted in purges and brutalities, with one faction winning over the other. After a long series of battles, the city was abandoned. We purchase tickets to visit as it is considered an historical site. A part of the wall still remains. Once we enter through a gate in the crumbling wall, we see before us an expanse of grass, populated only by crumbled ruins, parts and pieces of cathedrals and churches standing forlorn in the distance. Trails lead to the various ruins. Few buildings remain intact. We stop at an abandoned mosque, which was built later during the Turkish occupancy. Its chambers echo with the sounds of our footsteps and voices. While the others continue talking inside I venture outside to a bluff over the river and look across to Armenia where I see military towers which give Armenian security forces the ability to see what we are doing. Tensions still remain. I continue along a trail toward an abandoned cathedral, filled with pigeon droppings and scarred with graffiti. Steel braces support parts of the structure from further collapse. Long ago, priests and worshippers offered prayers and incense here to the Virgin Mary and lit candles and confessed sins in this place that they considered holy.

I get separated from the group but continue exploring. Another site, I discover the remnant of an ancient Zoroastrian Temple dating from the time of Christ. Some speculate that the Magi who visited the boy Jesus might have been Zoroastrians, astute in the astrology of the day. Who knows? I stop at several other cathedral remnants marveling at how many there are and wonder what this city might have sounded, smelled and looked like in its day. There are remnants of military garrisons, but mostly the area is reclaimed by grasses growing among littered stones.

A trail leads to a lower area and on to the remaining wall. I emerge

Distant Lands

there and return along it to the entrance to wait for the group, who has taken a different path. I climb to the top of the wall to see if I can spot them. I can't. After some time, they appear along one of the trails heading my way.

Once gathered, we stop at the nearby the small village, consisting of a few mud-constructed buildings next to the ruins, where there is a small shop selling cold drinks and snacks and we load up on them.

Our driver turns off onto a side road a short distance, then entering a path leading through the fields of clover, toward another beehive which is quite some distance, if you can imagine our driving thirty or so kilometers through pastures and fields of wheat and clover, encountering a herd of cattle and wending our way through to a dirt road leading to a remote village, where we stop there to visit an elderly man and his family—whether friends or relatives, I do not know, to exchange some goods. The elderly man serves the village of less than a hundred as its mayor, well into his 90s, alert, stately with moustache, and hospitable as he welcomes us to his home where he lives with his family. There is a young mother with baby, probably his great-grandchild. I take some photos with him.

We stop at a thriving beehive not far from a major road, bees swarming toward our van when we enter. These are aggressive bees and require special suits to be worn for protection. Su'at, the driver and Atalay suit up, with the rest of us remaining in the van. The bees attack furiously, sometimes catching exposed places to sting as the guys extract the honey. When they return to the van and try to take off their suits before getting in, the bees attack again forcing us to back the van some distance to get away from the hives, so the transfer can be made, yet there are still some that get in the van and go after us! Atalay has been stung on his eyelid, which begins to swell, making him looks like a prize fighter after a match. We drive away to the main road toward Kars to meet his arriving family at the airport. We are late. They have waited an hour for us.

Ramadan with Family in East Turkey

We load people, luggage, containers of honey and water, which makes a tight fit in the van but we make it. It's a jolly group riding back toward Kagizman, stopping once to sample mineral water flowing from a fountain. Clouds gather on the horizon giving a dramatic dimension to the landscape. It begins raining as we approach Kagizman.

Dinner again is a sumptuous feast, lively with animated conversation by the reunited family. Late in the evening we make a walk, crossing a gorge to visit another relative's house for more tea and lengthy conversations. My energy is depleted by now. We return after midnight and I shower and go to bed, but the family talks until 2:00 a.m.

3 July Sunday

Meditation

The morning is bright, clear and sunny and the air refreshing. With the family still asleep I get up and seek some time alone for personal meditation and worship. It is a wonderful family and I'm enjoying the experience of being with them. As I sit alone on the balcony, I look down on the orchards of fruit-bearing trees below, a veritable Garden of Eden here. The trees are watered from streams flowing down the mountain, with plenty of water for irrigation, channeled along the streets in small aqueducts. As I meditate, the message of Psalm 23 plays out in my mind, remembering that from our travels yesterday we had seen flocks of sheep and traveled through fields of wheat and clover, resting along still waters and plucking fruit from abundant orchards. I begin to recite from Scripture *"The Lord is my Shephard, I shall not want. He makes me lie down in green pastures, he leads me beside quiet waters, he restores my soul. He guides me in paths of righteousness for His name's sake. Even though I walk through the valley of the shadow of death, I will fear no evil, for you are with me; your rod and your staff, they comfort me. You prepare a table before me in the presence of my enemies. You anoint my head with oil; my cup overflows. Surely goodness and love will follow me all the days of my life, and I will dwell in the house of the Lord forever." Psalm 23 NIV.* In addition to the thoughts about the green pastures and still

Distant Lands

waters, I reflect about eating at tables prepared for me among, not enemies, but new friends and family. Our visits to the cemetery and to historic places where death and destruction had reigned remind me of life's mortality. On this Sunday morning, I am left with a new confidence that my journey has been a good one, leading along a good path surrounded by love and embrace. I have witnessed the bonds of family and the hospitality, that included a stranger—me! Surely boundaries of nationality, religion and intolerance disappear when goodness and love prevail. I thank God for His grace and mercy!

Feasting at End of Ramadan in Turkey

Feast begins again at the touch of sunset. Sumptuous fare served on a low table—soup, bread, beans, mutton, chicken, fresh salads, green beans, eating with passion, after having fasted the day, hardest for the 10-year-old girl, trying her best to stay committed to the regimen. After dinner, we walk to a relative's empty house, being cleaned for us to move into tomorrow, so we will have plenty of room. We return after midnight and sit around the kitchen table, grandmother and everyone talking at once with great animation, drinking coffee and munching on sweet breads and fresh cherries picked from the orchard. It is 2:00 a.m. and the conversations are still going full throttle.

I bow out after then and shower before bed. Tomorrow marks the end of the thirty-day fast. It is July 4 also. No telling what we are in for.

4 July

End of Ramazan

I greet the day with a Happy 240th Birthday thought for my country on a bright, beautiful morning in Kagizman, Turkey. I have celebrated our country's founding from outside a couple of times before, once at the American embassy in Harare, Zimbabwe at a picnic and cruise on the Zambesi River, and once in London.

Sunset marks the end of Ramazan. I anticipate no fireworks or parades but do expect the feasting to be over the top! It is hard to imagine more than what we've already experienced each night. This trip has been a delightful experience for me so far and I've fallen in love with this wonderful family. Back home, I'm sure my next-door neighbor is busy with his usual fireworks extravaganza he and friends put on every year in our neighborhood.

Another bountiful, and I do mean bountiful, breakfast awaits us, after which we walk downtown to a bank which is open for only half a day today. I want to complete the transfer to my friend in Nepal to help with his father's surgery. Filling out the necessary forms proves laborious, even with Atalay translating for me. Our teller is pleasant and patient, but she has not handled this kind of transaction before, so we are careful with everything. Finally, we get the transfer made and I notify my friend that the money is available for pick-up.

Distant Lands

We gather our things and transfer to the house in the orchard, which is nice for the additional space in provides for all of us, but convenient for picking and plucking all manner of fruit from the orchard. We set up a small wading pool for the kids that Atalay has brought from Istanbul. They delight in splashing around in the summer heat, even inviting me to join. Rains come in the afternoon, more rumbling thunder than rain. The rains have brought a sudden coolness and we gather under a porch on couches with the kids. Ozgur dozes close to me in a contented nap.

Feasting begins again at sunset, this time in a leisurely manner to go on most of the night. Relatives come and go in a steady procession, sitting, chatting, drinking tea, eating, smoking and telling stories. Smoking is common throughout Turkey, which I must endure. The local family is quite traditional in dress, most of the women wearing the traditional head gear, though Atalay's sisters are more modern, leaving their heads uncovered. Some of the relatives even slip in a nip or two, despite the usual ban. It is a typical family and all are welcomed. The reverie goes on well past midnight. I sleep on one of the couches that folds down into a bed located in a hallway between the rooms where Atalay's family with sisters and grandmother and the kids all sleep.

5 July

After tea and light snacks, Atalay and I take a brisk walk toward the mountain. We meet a group of boys along the way who beg to be photographed with me. Back at the compound, we indulge ourselves in a serious breakfast. Relatives drop by all day, a tradition of this first day after the fasts. At times, I think we have received at least half of this city's population of 18,000! Each visit requires snacks, tea or coffee. I drink enough tea to float Noah's ark, minus the elephants! It is fun to watch the interactions and observe the respect and affection shown. The kids happily play in the pool most of the day. Atalay and I take a couple of walks to work off the excesses of our eating. Late in the afternoon, the rains come again with lightning and thunder. I check

Ramadan with Family in East Turkey

Facebook and learn that Kevin Durant, our team's star player, is leaving the Oklahoma City Thunder team. What a loss! However, I am not too surprised by it.

By 9:00 p.m. I feel the effects of the day, with so many visits, so much food, conversation that I can't understand, constantly smiling and greeting and trying to participate as best I can, but letting the family just be themselves without feeling obligated to translate everything for me. It becomes a bit overwhelming. With permission, I return to my bed about ten, way early, but I need the time alone.

While everyone sleeps, I steal away for a brisk walk alone early in the morning toward the mountain. Our house is at the edge of town, so it doesn't take long to be in the open area along a dirt road. I encounter shepherds with small flocks of long, wooly sheep. When Atalay awakes, we have coffee and go once again for a walk, joined by one of his sisters and her son Cem (pronounced Jim) and Ozgur. It is fun and the weather is nice. We hear thunder across the valley. Every afternoon brings thunder and rain. We return to a bountiful breakfast served around noontime. Before we finish our breakfast, workers come and spread plastic tarps around mulberry trees, which they then climb, shaking the branches and raining sweet mulberries down. These are the largest and sweetest mulberries I've ever seen or tasted. I shower, washing out some underwear to hang outside, but the rain comes and I have to move them to hang them on the porch in front of a trio of carefully-scarfed, traditional women relatives visiting from Kars, a bit embarrassed because the wind keeps blowing them down into the mud. I re-wash them and move them inside to my room. I feel a little faint, which sometimes happen when my system gets too low in magnesium due my A-fib heart condition. All the comings and goings have thrown me a little off schedule. Atalay suggests that I should have a good shot of whiskey to calm my system. Visitors continue to show up during the day and into the night. Dinner is eaten in shifts away from the visiting guests and finish with watermelon.

Distant Lands

At night, we turn the tables and become guests ourselves, visiting a couple of different uncles and their families, with tea and snacks served at each place. Along the way we encounter a wedding in progress with spirited dancing. We spend long times at each house. I try not to act bored and a bit put off by so many smokers, who universally always manage to get upwind from non-smokers, flooding us with smoke. Some of the conversations get quite loud and boisterous with a few family issues related to an inheritance. When we return, a taxi is ordered for the grandmother and I ride too, which I am glad to do as I am about walked out for the day.

The days spent with the extended family remind me of the days growing up in a large extended family. We also had large family gatherings at holidays, with aunts, uncles, cousins by dozens, loud, boisterous, busy talking, cooking, eating, joking, laughing, discussions of crops, weather, automobiles, household chores and neighborhood gossip thrown in. Then as now, I was always the shy, quiet observer.

It has been quite a ride for me. I've been greeted, kissed on both cheeks and fed the fare of the land. Elders get multiple kisses and the kids as well. Fathers kiss their children often, both sons and daughters. We gather at tables, set up outside under the orchard trees, where conversations rise in volume as all speak at once with excited tones. Occasionally, Atalay tells me what is being said, especially if it relates to me, as it sometimes does.

Atalay tells me that we will be going to Kars to attend a wedding. A van comes and we all load up, except for grandmother, and head for Kars. On the way, one of the girls gets motion sickness and we stop a couple of time for her to throw up. We arrive in Kars. It is the first time for me to actually be in that city. Kars is a historic old city, which has for centuries served as a military outpost with a garrison and a large fort on the bluffs protecting a key river juncture through which an invading army might pass. There are shops and restaurants lining the

Ramadan with Family in East Turkey

ancient streets. We stop at a relative's house for tea. Since we have time before the wedding starts, we drive along the river between opposing bluffs to a bridge that leads back on the other side, then up to the old fort above. We explore the fort on foot making our way up steep steps to view its walls and the valley below. If these stones could talk, there would be stories of invasions and battles won and lost. Orhan Pamuk's novel describes an attempted coup during the snows of one winter in which a military take-over clamps down on dissidents. In a way, it is prophetic about what is soon to happen back in Istanbul, but I don't know that at this time.

It is time for the wedding. We go back into town to a wedding venue located over a shopping mall, being held in a large room already filled with guests with music playing. We have some difficulty finding a table off to one side. Cokes and snacks are available at the tables. The wedding dances begin with the bride and groom appearing for a dance surrounded by shooting candles going off all around them. The parents of both bride and groom take to the floor for a dance. After that, a large dance circle is formed and traditional dancing begins, men and women locking arms and dancing in a circular motion around the floor. It is quite lively. Our host joins in as do a number of others. At one point, they even pull me in where I join the children but obviously, to my embarrassment, I am not as skilled as the others. A couple of young men perform a lively dance, which is not unlike the Celtic dances of Ireland. It is all fun. There must be a thousand people present. The hosts are obviously wealthy and have invited us because of Su'at's business connections. I am the only Westerner present.

We return to Kagizman late at night, tired and exhausted but happy for the trip.

Installing Grave Marker for Atalay's Father

Today we go to the cemetery on the hillside to install the new grave stone and frame for Atalay's father's grave. We had earlier gone with his sisters to select and purchase it. We assist the workmen as the grave is cleared of weeds and the new frame is put into place and filled with dirt and stones. I take pictures as Atalay and each of the grandchildren shovel dirt onto the grave. The top of the grave is left to remain uncovered. A new head stone is dropped into place in the slot provided and sealed. On it is transcribed words to tell of Mustafa Pakir, son of Joseph Pakir, who was born in the year of my birth and died on the 25th of October, 1982 at the age of 42, just two days before my 42nd birthday. Atalay and his two sisters look on the grave in silent respect for a moment before we take our leave. A storm is fast approaching from across the valley. The mission to honor their father is almost complete. We clear away the debris and head down the hill just as the rain hits. We are wet by the time we reach home and must change into dry clothes. There remains one more thing to do to fully complete their mission. When the rain lets up, we go downtown to purchase food to be distributed among the poor of the city in their father's honor.

Returning, we visit a few shops, greeting and kissing friends and former classmates of Atalay's along the way. With Su'at and some of the others, we make a trip to visit the waterfalls, following a road along the narrow cliffs until the road becomes too difficult for the van. We must walk the final distance to the waterfall which flows over a small dam. Edging our way out onto the top of the dam to the falls, we must take care as the stones are slippery and we must be careful not to fall. There we take photos as the day darkens and we return. The grandmother is having oxygen and seems to be short of breath. I worry for her health.

For my early morning hike, I walk again up the hill to the cemetery. After breakfast, Atalay and I return to remove the plastic laid over the fresh concrete. It is time to leave Kagizman, but first there are multitudes of good-byes to be said and relatives to visit, hugs and kisses to be given and received all around. It has been a good week, though a bit overwhelming at times. They invite me to return. I have been the subject of proposals for arranged marriages with various widowed relatives, whether serious or not, I don't know. It was some of the subjects

Distant Lands

of conversation over these past few days without my knowledge at the time. I am now being teased by some of the guys about becoming a step-dad to them. Su'at gives me the gift of a large jar of honey to take home.

At the airport in Kars we clear security, after I am stopped concerning a small rustic cross that Ozgur had picked up in the dirt while in Ani. They are careful about artifacts being taken out. After spirited discussions with a supervisor, I am cleared to proceed. The flight to Istanbul leaves on time. From my window seat, I observe the terrain below, interesting especially as we approach Istanbul coming in low over the shore of the Black Sea. I clearly see the Bosporus below and a new bridge spanning it. In a matter of days, that bridge will be one of the ones taken over by tanks, but that is still unknown to me as we approach.

Our driver gets searched once again by the airport security when he approaches by car. His look triggers the profile of a terrorist, we think. We arrive safely at Atalay's house where Ulku and her mother are waiting. She has prepared a nice dinner with more normal proportions than we had been having in Kagizman. A reality show on television is playing, and the family excitedly draws my attention to it for it is featuring my friend Nurettin participating in one of the rigorous contests. It is a re-run from last season. Ozgur kindly gives up his room for me to use while I am here. The air in Istanbul is decidedly warmer than we had grown accustomed to in east Turkey.

2

Days of Calm before the Storm

10 July

Atalay and I take a long walk along the Marmara Sea and later go to Atalay's shop. I visit again the historic part of the old city and a favorite book shop to purchase a couple of books—Orhan Pamuk's "Snow," set in Kars that we have just visited and Ayse Kulin's "Last Train to Istanbul," a World War II thriller about rescuing Turkish Jews from France. I like to purchase such books by local authors while I visit their home turf. Back at the print shop, I find Atalay and Ozgur sleeping but they wake and we have lunch. In the afternoon we take Ozgur to enroll him in an English course. I get to meet the officials of the private school. One of them turns out to be an American from Kansas City married to a Turkish wife. We enjoy discussing various cultures and sharing our experiences while in Turkey. When we finish, we go back home and pick up Ulku and her mother so they can visit with some friends in another part of the city, one of whom is a former classmate of Ulku's and the lady's sister, mother and father, who is in poor health, both in their mid-80s. After tea and chocolates and a good visit, we return home.

Nurettin is on duty at the Begoglu/Taksim Fire Station. I take a mini-van to Taksim and walk from there quite some distance to the station, which also includes a police station. The complex is in the heart of the city near Taksim Square, which is the site of many demonstrations and public gatherings. Nurettin has now become Fire Chief. Unfortunately when I get there, I am told that he has been called away for a fire. I tell the group that I will return later and decide to spend time walking around and have lunch before returning late in the afternoon. I return just after he and the crews returned from a difficult fire. I am told he is taking a shower. They invite me to sit outside with a group of other fire fighters and policemen, many of whom look quite weary as well. Nurettin emerges and joins me. In spite of the shower, he still smells of fire. He tells me about the fire as he takes me inside to show me his spacious office. We chat for a time before he takes me upstairs so he can have lunch. Since I had already eaten, I take some juice to sip on. He introduces me around to the other firemen. I had spent the night with him at his previous fire station during my last trip to Istanbul. A bearded young man appears and Nurettin introduces him as the Iman (chaplain) of the fire station. We talk about his studies leading up to becoming Iman. He says he had spent four years at a Madrassa and four years of Islamic studies at the university level. I ask if he was familiar with the *Jaleel*, the Gospels, which I understand Muslims are encouraged to read. He says that he had not spent time studying them. In turn he asks me if I have read the Qu'ran, which I have only a little. Nurettin quips that I should make a believer of our friend Atalay since he is a secular man. Sensing Nurettin's exhaustion, I do not prolong my stay. It is good to see him and I take my leave. Nurettin sees me out offering directions for my return by the metro, which is a bit confusing to find. When I seek to make a transfer to the proper line, the metro card is declined for it has run out of cash. Unfortunately the cash machine used to add money fails to work. A businessman spots my dilemma and offers to swipe his card for me so I can board the tram. In the hubbub of transfers and heat, I am beginning to feel faint. The tram is also quite crowded causing me to worry about passing out. A passenger sees my discomfort and offers a seat and watches to tell me when the tram arrives at my stop. People are caring.

Days of Calm before the Storm

The episode passes in the fresh air as I walk back to Atalay's print shop and we return home. Tonight is scheduled for Atalay and Ozgur's martial arts class across the bay in Kadikoy. It is a long walk to catch the train that goes under the sea to reach there. By the time we make it, I am feeling quite exhausted for I have been walking most all day, up and down the hills of Istanbul. The train takes us across and we emerge for more walking to the site of the lessons. I sit and observe the fighting techniques as they practice and are quite good at. Ozgur gets matched with adults at times and is able to hold his own. It is late by the time we reach home. I am one tired puppy! When I check my phone app which monitors my steps, I discover that I had walked nearly twenty miles today.

13 July

Ozgur too is tired and chooses to stay home today. They want me to stay too, but I choose to go with Atalay to the print shop. I am feeling better, except that my legs and feet are sore from all the walking yesterday. A friend, Umet, arrives and cooks up a nice lunch. He routinely brings vegetables and meats to cook at Atalay's shop and we have a good time cooking onions, meat, and peppers followed by tomatoes with garlic. I assist where I can. It is really good food. If that weren't enough, Atalay's young friend Huseyin brings drinks snacks and drinks in the afternoon. He is 27 and a most likeable sort who seems to enjoy my company. After work, we join with some of his friends on the roof of the parking lot to discuss the day while we avoid the rush hour traffic. It is a favorite gathering place. We enjoy some time listening to music on his mobile before driving home.

Today at the shop, I make coffee while Atalay starts the presses. At mid-morning, I break away and take the tram back to Sultanahmet to walk around the old city and to the Tophane area as well. For a change, I get touristy and have lunch at a KFC which I found near the wharfs of Serkeci where ferries ply across the Marmara. I purchase a ticket for a ferry to the Bosporus leaving at mid-afternoon. It is billed

Distant Lands

as a two-hour cruise. Sea breezes are refreshingly cool once we reach the open water and the sun is bright making in necessary to get under a canopy, but most of the time I spend topside viewing the scenery along the shore. Being on the ferry provides me a great vantage point for viewing the skyline of historic Istanbul with its surrounding suburbs. It is not crowded and there are only a few us who are foreigners. Mostly we see mothers with children and families out for an afternoon. Hawkers sell water, snacks and ice cream.

Making a couple of stops at ports on the way up we take on more passengers. The Bosporus is the historic and fabled waterway separating Europe and Asia. These are international waters which allow passage of ships from Russia, Ukraine and others from the Black Sea to the Mediterranean. Several modern suspension bridges span the bay, loaded with traffic. Along the banks we see large mansions of built by the wealthy. They are made of concrete which replaced the older wooden structures of old which were vulnerable to fires. These were the setting of other Orhan Pamuk's novels in which he wrote of life in the waning days of the Ottoman Empire. Large government and corporate buildings also dot the shore, although limits have been placed on the height of such buildings.

About mid-way up the Bosporus, we turn around and start back, stopping once at a pier under one of the major bridges near a restaurant. Diners watch from their tables as passengers are exchanged. In a few hours, tanks will control all these bridges, but I do not know about that at this time. Rather, I enjoy a relaxing afternoon outing on the waters of the Marmara and the Bosporus.

I return by tram to the Cevilizabagh, the metro stop near Atalay's shop.

Talip arrives this evening at Atalay's house bringing with him his 17 year-old son Boron for a visit. Talip is a business friend of Atalay's with whom I have spent some time at the shop. Ozgur breaks out his traditional Turkish guitar to play for us. Boron and I also spend some time practicing English together. The young man hopes to enroll in the university this year in computer science. He is handsome like his father and bright. We enjoy the evening with tea and a traditional Ottoman-style sweet made with clabbered milk. It was quite good. Later we also have watermelon.

15 July

Caught in a Coup Attempt!
I have little idea what is in store for the country, as well as for myself, in the next several hours when I agree to spend the evening in the city, while Atalay and Ozgur go again across the bay to Asia for their martial arts class. We agree on a place to meet by 11:30 p.m. after they finish. We plan to meet in front of a hospital; in fact it is the hospital where Ozgur was born, easily accessible for me by tram.

The day is spent at the print shop, which I find particularly noisy from construction of a large mosque being built next to it, which seems a bit of overkill to me, since there is another one just a few meters away. Muslim prayer calls from the loud speakers mounted on minarets can get quite loud at times, especially this close. Jack-hammers bang away like mechanical woodpeckers. All their noise is piled on top of a myriad of printing presses operating at full force in Atalay's shop downstairs, above us and next to us in the other shops. The shops are housed in sections of a large warehouse. I hear the "harrumph harrumph" of a big paper cutter above us, along with the clicks, clacks, clangs of the other presses. It is enough to give one a headache. I decide it's time to clear out for Sultanahmet, where I envision a quiet restaurant where I can enjoy tea and maybe even the fabled water pipe, just sitting and watching people come and go as I write in my journal. While waiting for the next tram, a young man from Tunisia strikes up a conversation with me. He is one of the many refugees who have fled to Turkey, jobless and homeless. It isn't long before he asks for money for lodging and food. I give him a little which leaves me short of money. When

I check to see if I have enough for the water pipe and a nice dinner, I discover that I have only enough to buy a small burger from a Burger King, disappointing since I have hours to kill until 11:30.

Istanbul's Blue Mosque on the Eve of the Coup Attempt

I spend time walking around, feeling quite contented as I watch evening draw nigh and the lights of historic Istanbul go up. It is beautiful and serene scene, with not many people about. The lighted historic buildings are their most impressive at night. I sit quietly in front of the lighted fountain

Days of Calm before the Storm

and simply watch, happy to have chosen to come to Turkey at this time. I take a few photos until the appointed hour when I hop on the tram and head for the hospital to meet up with Atalay and Ozgur. The area there is filled with people visiting small neighborhood shops and walking the streets. I cross the street to a waiting area in front of the hospital. Since I am a little early, I expect to have to wait some time. The air is cool.

After a few minutes, I begin to notice a change in the people. Where before, they had seemed relaxed, busy and jovial as they hastened about their shopping, they now look anxious, holding mobile phones close to their ears. The pace quickens. The trams stop running. I think that perhaps they usually stop at this hour of the night, I didn't know. Overhead I hear a helicopter or two *thump thump* by. A couple of ambulances leave the hospital and others arrive, but again I think maybe it is a normal occurrence for the hospital. By now, 11:30 has come and gone and I do not see Atalay anywhere. He is always prompt. I check my phone, but there are no messages. I wait, thinking he has just been delayed. People begin hurrying faster, looking ever more worried. Perhaps there has been a tragedy somewhere, perhaps a fire or bad automobile accident. More helicopters appear. A military jet screams low overhead. It is midnight by now and still no Atalay. Now, I am beginning to get anxious. The streets thin out. Twelve becomes 12:30. What should I do? Messaging doesn't result in anything. Something has happened, but what? Where can I stay if he doesn't come for me? Maybe I should walk to find a hotel and get a room for the rest of the night, but I don't know of any hotels located in this area. I hate to leave this spot, in case he does come. If I leave, how will he ever find me?

I even consider walking into the hospital and feigning a heart attack. They would give me a place, but I quickly cancel that thought. More ambulances have arrived. It is no time for games. Just as I'm about to walk away, to start my search for a place to stay, I hear my name called out from somewhere within a small crowd behind me. I turn around to see. It is a lady I do not know, shouting my name. She calls again

Distant Lands

and I move toward her. She motions for me to follow her. Obviously, she knows who I am, so I follow her. She tries to explain, but does not know English. I understand enough that Atalay isn't coming. We walk for a couple of blocks and turn onto a side street. She motions me toward a car that is parked indicating I should get in. Inside the car, I find Ulku who is waiting for me. She explains that the lady who called my name is her sister, that Atalay had called her to come to get me, that a military coup is in progress and he has been blocked by soldiers and tanks from coming. We drive away, careful to take only the remote back streets, as we wind our way back to their house. We avoid intersections controlled by soldiers. Arriving at the house, we hasten up the steps. The TV is on with news reports showing scenes of tanks and gunfights between soldiers and police. No one knows where the Prime Minister is. Has the military captured or killed him? Atalay and Ozgur arrive about thirty minutes later, after having walked a great distance because access to their car had been blocked by soldiers. We embrace, glad that he is ok. By now, a few F-15 fighter jets scream loudly overhead, creating sonic booms, loud enough to shatter glass in nearby windows. The loud roar frightens us. What is going on? Will soldiers come here? We don't know. A curfew is in place on the streets and most of the television stations are shut off the air. A lone station still broadcasts. Soon, it shows a man holding a mobile phone on which he has the Prime Minister. Holding the phone in front of the TV camera he is able to provide a link for the Prime Minister to broadcast to the nation, calling for his followers to hit the streets in protest, despite the military curfew. Thousands respond and begin confronting the soldiers and the tanks controlling the bridges. All hell breaks loose. I can only hint at the anxiety we are feeling. Though Atalay dislikes the Prime Minister, he is against the coup. We don't yet know the outcome. It is between 4 and 5:00 a.m. before it looks like the coup is falling apart. Most if the soldiers refuse to fire on civilians and begin surrendering some of the tanks leading to a frenzy of reprisals as soldiers are seized by the angry crowds and beaten. Scenes of protest are shown from Taksim Square, a place I had been just a few days ago. Crowds of protestors proclaim victory. The coup has failed!

Days of Calm before the Storm

A little after five, we hear a loud speaker on the street, which makes me anxious. Are we being evacuated or about to face something awful? I rush to ask Atalay who calms me by saying it is only a street vendor. I am on edge for sure! My phone lights up with messages from friends in America asking if I am okay. News of the coup attempt hit there almost immediately. Church members begin praying for me. I hasten to get access on Facebook to send a message that I have indeed survived and am safe.

As the news unfolds in the early morning hours, we are shown scenes of confrontation and death, both in Istanbul and in the capital Ankara. The Prime Minister announces that all connected with the coup will be sought out and severely punished. There will be major repercussions. It happens almost immediately and in the days to follow when soldiers, journalists, teachers and anyone who has expressed opposition is rounded up and imprisoned. It is a sad turning point in Turkey.

Post-Coup Demonstration

We are exhausted by the ordeal, of course. In the afternoon, we go for a walk to relieve our tension. As we walk along the streets, we see places where there had been fighting just a few hours before. The police headquarters is nearby and near there we see blood in the streets where police and soldiers had been shot and killed. People begin bringing flowers as memorials. We run into a large demonstration now forming, blocking the streets with trucks and other vehicles. Everyone is waving Turkish flags. There is an immediate and large outpouring of support for the government. I thread my way past the news cameras and the hordes of demonstrators just to get past. Loud speakers rally the crowds for a show of support. Cars with youths waving flags from their windows zip by us, shouting as they go. We hasten away from the crowds as quickly as possible. All Istanbul is on an adrenaline rush! We return home to watch more footage of the violence from last night.

17 July Sunday

Turkish Haman

It is time to break away emotionally from the events of the weekend. Sunday morning brings a bright sunny day. Atalay had promised earlier that we would visit a particular *haman* when we talked about before the coup. Atalay stays glued to the TV listening to all the speeches, so I do not bring it up. Being a guest this long can become a burden, so I don't want to add to his during this time. In the distance I can hear church bells ringing reminding me that this is Sunday morning. It is a welcome sound for me. I miss my church. We eat breakfast late and I want to walk early, but everyone was asleep and they don't want me to go out alone now.

After some time, Atalay tells me that we should visit the historic *haman* as promised. It is located next to a mosque, as most are, which was built in the 1500s. We check in and receive a towel with a pair of baggy shorts to wear. It is a large and clean facility. The three of us, Atalay, Ozgur and I, make our way to the basins to soap and clean ourselves, rinsing with hot water we pour over ourselves from dippers. There is

Days of Calm before the Storm

a large oval slab in the center of the room. When you lie on your back and look up, you can see open portals in a domed ceiling, giving the effect of looking at stars at night. There is a nice indoor swimming pool and we enjoy the cool water there. Atalay chats with some of the men who are asking about me, being a foreigner, while Ozgur and I swim and splash water playfully at each other.

After swimming, we return to the big slab, where to endure a Turkish scrubbing, which is done with an abrasive glove used by an attendant who scours the soapy body with it. Atalay is done first and goes to lie on the slab for his massage given by a guy about his age. I am assigned for my scrubbing and massage to be done by a big burly Turk who looks like he could butcher beef, which might be me. However he seems pleasant enough as he takes control immediately. He begins the scrub showing me the residue of my skin being peeled away by the glove. I just hope he leaves some still intact. I sit as he thoroughly works my legs with downward motions. He bends me forward like a potter slapping clay around for a new shape and works on my back, then bends me back the other way to scour my front torso. In English, I tell him to go easy, but it only serves to encourage him. I feel like a snake shedding its skin! When he is finished scrubbing, I am thoroughly doused with water washing off the soap. He motions me to move toward the slab where Atalaly is being beaten and pummeled with his massage. Atalay gives me a mirthful look, knowing full well what is about to descend on me. "Ok, buddy, it's your turn." I stretch out on the marble slab. Mr. Burly begins beating and pummeling me with abandon. Ozgur sits next to me, watching, totally amused by my ordeal. Burly Bob rubs, punches, making loud slaps on my body as he proceeds to knead muscles into a soft putty. I feel like a rag doll. After he finishes both sides, he pulls me up and motions for me to go wash at the basins, which I do, glad to still to be alive. It was hard, but I admit it was also good. After our ordeals, we return to the pool, but by now it is closed to men and opened for the ladies, so we return for more soaking and heating before we shower to return to the reception area. We are met by attendants there and covered with large towels and served juice. The television is on and everyone sits glued watching the latest developments on the coup attempt.

Afterwards, we walk to a flat some distance away to visit again the sisters and parents of Ulku's friend. Atalay and I are still hot from our time in the Haman and it is a very warm day. I begin feeling overheated, so Atalay trades places in the warm room so I can sit by a window, which is the only place the air is stirring. We are served Turkish coffee which is like drinking sludge, but is good once you develop a taste for it, and some sweets. A few neighbor ladies arrive. I soon get the sense they are talking about me. Atalay explains that they are talking about my being single, leaving me with the feeling that I'm being sized up as marriage material, with Atalay devilishly leading them on.

It is time to move on! We visit the famous *Chora* Museum, the remains of a monastery from the 1500s. Since the others had been before, only Ozgur and I go in. Mosaics on the walls depict events in the life of Jesus. I explain to Ozgur the story behind each one. I love being with Ozgur. He is not only a handsome boy, well-mannered; he is intellectually curious. I call him my Turkish grandson.

Back home, we see television interviews of various politicians suddenly positioning themselves in support of the government. More videos of the night of violence are shown. At my insistence, we go for a walk in the evening along the Marmara Sea and the whole family goes along. We need a break from the news reports. We visit the remains of an old tower anchoring the wall which surrounded historic Constantinople. In gardens nearby there are flowers in bloom. It is a nice evening. We take photos as the moon rise.

It is Monday after one of the most turbulent weekends in Turkish history. The country is still reeling from the coup attempt. Recriminations are being felt on a wide scale. The Prime Minister Erdogen moves quickly to suppress independent thought and begins to eviscerate his opposition. Freedom of expression will be the real victim of this coup attempt.

Large scale funerals take place for the victims, with much mourning as crowds wail in agony. Emotions run high. When we return to the print shop, one of the guys shows a photo of a fellow shop owner in his 50s who was killed. I don't know the circumstances.

I return once again to Sultanahmet by tram. Fares on public transportation have been declared free today and tomorrow in celebration of the victory over the coup. It is a means of garnering public support. As I walk by the Blue Mosque, I turn to see a man running toward me, shouting. It is a friend that I had made seven years ago on my first trip to Istanbul, now 30 years old. How he recognized me from a distance, I don't know. His job is to meet tourists to lure into visiting a relative's carpet shop by offering tea. I thought he was no longer in Istanbul, but here he is. How he remembered me from that time, I don't know. I tell him that I was on my way to get some lunch, so he accompanies me to an Arab café nearby. He tells me he had opened his own carpet business last year, but it had gone under. He then invites me for tea at his cousin's shop, assuring me that I can just look and not buy. It is the old ruse. I reluctantly go out of friendship, knowing full well that I am in deep trouble. It is nearly impossible to get away from these guys without buying something. Sure enough, we go through the whole routine—tea is served, casual and pleasant conversation follows, a workman begins to lay out carpets, you are asked to pick a favorite one by size or color and you go through a process narrowing them down to two or three. They let you catch your breath at that point as you try to find reasons to leave, but they are not through. You must make an offer, no matter how ridiculous. The bargaining thus begins until in desperation you buy something. So it goes. I end up with two more carpets, small ones that I don't need. My friend is pleased and takes me for coffee and we visit a friend's apartment but he is away at the time. Servet, his name, comes from Sirrit in east Turkey and wants me to visit there sometime. It is in an area of southeast Turkey where our State Department warns about Americans visiting because of its close proximity with Syria and Iraq. He presses me to make a donation for a friend in his village who wants to marry. All my refusals are in vain, and I give him something just to get him off my back. He has succeeded once again!

I beat a hasty retreat and return to the print shop.

With work there finished, we go to rooftop parking for the car, but traffic is at a standstill. Our friend Huseyin comes again and we hang out again with a few friends. What better place to escape both traffic and the overbearing news of the coup than on the rooftop. They listen to music and even begin to dance together. I have come to love these friends. After some time, we drop Huseyin at his home, sitting for a time in a parking lot just to enjoy a little more time together.

This is my last full day in Istanbul. I'm looking forward to getting home and relieved that the airport is open once again. I is time to escape the eye of the storm that I have flown into on this trip. Certain friends of mine back home comment that I have the knack of stirring up trouble wherever I go! This has been by far the most "on edge" experience in my travels. I fear for Turkey with the reactions taking place. One report says that 15,000 educators have been detained or removed from their jobs. It is worrisome. The U.S. is under pressure to return one of the chief opponents to the Prime Minister from his refuge in the U.S. He is being accused of masterminding the coup which he vigorously denies.

Before I leave, I ask for time to spend with Ozgur and get permission to take him with me for one final trip to Sultanahmet, where I treat him to lunch and ice cream as we sit in a small café and enjoy chatting. As we walk around, I do not see a single Western tourist. I must be the only one! There are numerous locals about due to free fares on public transportation. Turkey's tourism is at a total standstill. We shop for gifts for my grandkids and I buy a small gift for Ozgur as well.

Atalay is running late finishing his print work. We encounter impossible traffic going home, trying alternate routes. We arrive with just enough time for Ozgur to run upstairs to retrieve their workout duds, so we can catch the train for the trip to the martial arts class across the bay in Kadikoy. Tonight is Kung Fu night. I accompany them for one last time. The fighting is interesting to watch, but also quite energetic as opponents slam each other to the floor. Ozgur holds his own quite well. They are practicing how to defend themselves against multiple attackers. The techniques are quite interesting to watch, and effective. At the conclusion, I meet their trainer and we take some photos together. He has become good friends with both Atalay and Ozgur. It is late by the time we get home and have dinner. I finish packing and set my alarm for four hours from now, making for a short night before we go to the airport in the morning.

20 July

The alarm goes off at 5:00 a.m. Ulku is already up preparing breakfast for us. I say good-byes with hugs and kisses. We head for the airport where we find security tight and the lines moving slowly. I have an extra bag with the carpets to handle. In London, I have to change terminals, which requires clearing security once again. On my flight from London, I am stuck with middle seats all the way. After I get buckled in, I casually joke with my seat-mate sitting on the aisle that I would readily give a quarter to exchange seats with him. He just smiles at me in return. No one comes to claim the window seat next to me, so I claim it. Once airborne, the guy on the aisle starts chatting with me, telling me he is from Brussels heading for Colombia with plans to spend some days in Dallas. He plans to visit Bogota and Cartagena in Colombia. I learn that he is also a member of Belgium's parliament, at age 31. As we chat, I relate my experiences in Turkey with the coup attempt and about my travel to east Turkey before. We hit it off and soon

Distant Lands

begin discussing politics, telling me he is shocked by Trump's outbursts and by England's Brexit. We discuss economics, religion, everything, especially about travel experiences. He, like me, enjoys travel to observe local cultures. He is single, a Social Democrat, who represents the Flemish people of Brussels in the Belgian Parliament. He gives me his card and we exchange Facebook addresses. The food is good which we both enjoy. We are also both tired and manage to get a little sleep on the 10-hour flight. A new friendship is formed in this lucky encounter.

After I clear immigration in Dallas, I go to retrieve my baggage but it does not come! Once again I am faced with lost luggage. They give me a receipt and I go through security to board the domestic flight. The security lines are a zoo, with TSA people yelling gruffly at everyone. The lines are slow because they are not allowing trays to put personal items in. People have to stuff their bags with keys and coins, etc. K-9 dogs are sniffing at us too.

I reach home safely, but my luggage takes four more days to arrive.

My luggage may be lost but my memories will always be with me.

3

Nepal's Mountain Villages and a Tale of Indian Villages Abandoned by Love

Once again, I return to Nepal and India after a year's absence. Mainly, so I can check on friends in Nepal, still recovering from the earthquake. Being close to India, I will make another visit there also.

2016 Nepal and India

Trekking and Celebrating
This is my eleventh trip to Nepal and twelfth to India. It had been a year and I am anxious to see my friends once again. Nepal is still rebounding from the earthquake of 2015 and some of my friends are in need of help. I want to see about them.

Since I've traveled there so many times, I won't detail flights and connections. My first contact there is with a new friend Ramesh, who I met last time when we trekked together to Chisopani. He is on hand to receive me at the airport and to accompany me to a hotel which Tara has arranged for me at the Backyard Hotel, literally off the street in a backyard area. Typically I am ready for sleep after two days' worth of flying but Ramesh has other ideas. We walk around Thamel while catching up and eventually he spends the rest of the night with me at the hotel.

Distant Lands

Tara connects later and introduces me to a young lady he met at a Japanese language class and wants me to go with them for dinner and a night out, which makes a long evening since I still haven't caught up on sleep. The next morning I meet Bishwas to help him deal with a bothersome tooth that needs extracting. He had earlier sent photos of his teeth to me while I happened to be at my dentist. I used the opportunity to show the pictures to my dentist who recommended the extraction. We find a dentist nearby and have the offending tooth pulled and cavities filled. He repays me by inviting several friends to my room for snacks.

Friends Gopal and Raju insist I take a trek to the mountain village of Chisopani, as we did last time. We take off on my third day here, before I have adequately acclimated, joined by a friend of Gopal's who is a fellow golfer Krishna whose name and Raju, another friend of mine. The trek is a major challenge for me because of the thousands of steps required to get up the mountain. I clock 18,000 steps to the crest with more to add by the time we reach Chisopani. One doesn't think about leeches being a problem in the Himalayas, but I learned I was wrong. Leeches fling themselves from the wet undergrowth to pants legs and work their way to the inner parts of clothing. When I look down, I discover that one of my socks is red with blood. Later discover that one had even made it into my underwear. Because I take a blood thinner, these leeches were having a bloody good time of it. It is 8:00 p.m. before we reach our destination, having started at 9:00 in the morning. I dream only of a nice shower and bed for rest when at the guest house which we had stayed the last time, but it is completely in the dark without power and no toilet or running water, and cold by now, so we hunker down under heavy blankets to sleep. The next morning, we seek another place to stay and gratefully get a proper shower. The buildings of Chisopani are still damaged by the earthquake and many remain in their former positions of tilt and damage that we had observed last year. We poke around the ruins for a couple of days before setting out on the trail toward Nagarkot and descend to a village below to meet up with some of their friends, who serve us a meal including wild boar that one of the men had shot in the mountains. It is pouring rain when we start toward Kathmandu in a car we have hired.

The next day I take the scenic flight to Pokhara over rugged terrain and check in at the Crystal Palace Hotel where a young friend of mine named Shyam works, enjoying time together over the next few days, rowing on beautiful Lake Fewa, celebrating his birthday and taking a motorbike trip to the mountain village of Dhampus. I meet the guitar player there I had met last year. Pokhara is noted for its good food, which I enjoy. Otherwise I take walks along the lake and get a couple of good massages from local barbers while there.

Upon return to Kathmandu, I meet my friend Manish whose father has been quite ill and give him some money to assist, as well as a few small gifts for his niece and nephew. Nearly all the friends I have mentioned in this narrative had lost houses in the earthquake last year. Manish treats me to a visit to historic Kirtipur for dinner together at a traditional Newari restaurant sitting on the floor. When I return to my hotel, I learn that young Shyam has lost his job just after I left Pokhara over some issues with his manager and is now on his way to Kathmandu to visit a friend. Life is seldom simple for these guys. Tara and his friend Tej also come to visit me, along with the Bishwas who is feeling better by now from his tooth extraction. Tara spends the night before I leave Nepal.

Reuniting with Friends in India
I reunite with a friend Piyush, and Mike who is working in India and happens to be in Delhi for a couple of days before returning home. Piyush is the young man I met while visiting his native village three years ago, after he had given us a ride to a neighboring village on his motorcycle. We enjoy a limited time together joining Ratan, another recent friend who had come to spend a couple of nights in Delhi. Mike is staying at a hotel in Connaught Place and Piyush and I drop by to visit him for about an hour. I joke with Mike that the only time we ever see each other is in India.

Distant Lands

After a train ride to Jaipur, I hook up with Neeraj who greets me with smiles and a big hug. Neeraj introduces me to a friend Ram and suggests that I should accompany Ram to visit his farm the next day some distance from Jaipur, "an amazing place" Neeraj tells me. Ram and I travel some distance to get there and it is indeed an amazing place. The unique thing about the farm is its use of a pioneering technology developed in Israel for growing crops in desert settings, using hot-house structures with careful monitoring of water which is saved from rain and applied by drip irrigation techniques carefully regulated by computers. We explore the cavernous structures on the main farm, which at this season are growing cucumbers. His family operates five other such farms as well. Returning to Jaipur, we hang out with Neeraj and his cousin Saurav the remainder of the afternoon enjoying the camaraderie of good friends. Ram hopes to come to America next summer, he tells me. After he leaves us, Neeraj and Saurav take me to Neeraj's family home for dinner, where the family talks about Neeraj's upcoming marriage set for February, asking me to attend. Neeraj confides some misgivings about the proposed marriage which is later called off.

I catch the train to Ajmer to visit Suresh and his wife Deepika in Pushkar and to see their little girl Aria. They treat me to a ride together on the new cable cars to the summit of Savrati Temple, to which I had climbed twice before and believe me the cable car is much easier.

Over the course of the next several days, I meet up with old friends, including Yuvraj back from work in Abu Dhabi, and we celebrate little Aria's first birthday in a big way at the Aroma Palace with cake, balloons and many guests. I resume morning walks around Pushkar and take meals at Suresh's house and enjoy evenings at Jonti's Freedom Café, hanging out with several young backpackers from Israel and Australia. Rahul and Jonti take good care of me there and I enjoy the chit chat with these young men and women. Among others I meet is Rishi, an independent film maker from Mumbai. We hit it off immediately. When he finds out that I have done some writing, he suggests that we should collaborate on some short films. He has made films with the actor Dev Patel of "Slumdog Millionaire" and "Best Exotic Marigold Hotel" fame, both favorite movies of mine.

There are side trips to Nimaj and Jethana to visit Deepika's family and to celebrate the Dusserha festival in a neighboring village. My friend Vicky announces plans for his marriage in February and invites me to attend. We hang out with Suresh's brother-in-law Prashant and several of his friends each evening after dinner. In Jethana we visit Suresh's uncle and other relatives and his uncle accompanies us back to Ajmer, inviting us to his new "second" house and we visit a life-long friend for tea. They both invite me to stay there next time.

On several of my previous trips, Suresh had wanted me to meet one of his professors from the university and this time we make arrangements to do so. The professor is tall and stately, and now retired. We enjoy tea and conversation as guests at his nice house in Ajmer after which he treats us at a jungle-themed restaurant for lunch. It's quite a place.

Suresh is hosting a couple of visiting Australian ladies and asks me to join them for special ceremonies at the lake. The following day we make a trip outside town with them to a special temple where the guru Aloo Baba's holds forth. Aloo Baba is an icon of the area. For years he existed only on a diet of potatoes. The Hindi word *aloo* means potato. We spend the evening there and eat a *dahl bhoti* dinner supplied by a caterer that Suresh had arranged for us. I notice that one of the Australian ladies speaks with a very strange cadence to her voice. She later tells me her incredible story. Over a year ago, she and her 80 year-old husband were attacked brutally at a friend's home where they were home-sitting while the friends were away on vacation. Intruders broke in, robbed and beat them, almost killing her husband. She had fought them vigorously like a mad woman and was nearly strangled to death by one of the attackers, accounting for her manner of speech. She and her husband managed to survive, though barely. Being a chain-smoker had also given her a husky voice.

Distant Lands

Jaisalmer Desert Outpost
The Abandoned Village called Kuldhara

Abandoned Village of Kuldhara, India

Nepal's Mountain Villages and a Tale of Indian Villages Abandoned by Love

The desert city of Jaisalmer is located at the western edge of the state of Rajasthan. I had wanted to visit there for many years and was determined this time to do so. We had contacted a hotel owner here who is a friend of one of Suresh's friends and he had agreed to host me. Since his luxury hotel is fully booked he had arranged for me to stay at a cheaper hotel nearby, which better fit my budget. I am met at the station upon my arrival at midnight and taken to the hotel he has selected, built into the wall surrounding the imposing fortified old city, which commands the heights above the city of Jaisalmer. Manu, the friend, met me each day to take me by motorbike visiting places in and around Jaisalmer. We visit the lake, watch a sunset from a look-out point and eat at an open air restaurant on the far side of the city. One evening, as a surprise, he takes me on his motorbike fifteen kilometers beyond the city into the desert to visit the fabled abandoned village of Kuldhara. He has a friend there who runs the only shop operating in the abandoned village and lives there alone among the ghosts of Kuldhara. We walk among the ruins of the village, abandoned overnight some 200 years ago. The villagers were Paliwal Brahmins and had lived in the area for 700 years, farming the arid terrain and subsisting on flocks of sheep and goats with some success. The ruler of Jaisalmer came regularly to extract duty from the villages. During one of his visits, he spotted a beautiful girl and demanded that the village give her to him to become one of his wives. The village elders took counsel and refused, mainly because he was not Brahmin. The powerful ruler became so angered by their refusal that he demanded that the girl be turned over to him within 48 hours. The elders took counsel among themselves and with the other villages of their caste, decided their only alternative was to leave. The 84 villages were abandoned in the course of one night! I envisioned a scene like that of the movie "Exodus" when the Israelites of Biblical fame abandoned their homes in Egypt, a scene of chaotic haste, with oxen pulling carts burdened with quickly-gathered household and farm items, herds of livestock and whole families following on a journey into the night without a specific destination. These villagers scattered themselves over the breadth of India. Descendants can still be found in other parts of the country today. It was rumored that they had pronounced a curse on the villages when they left. Many believe to this day that the villages are inhabited by ghosts, which have allowed them to remain little disturbed over the centuries out of the fear to decay slowly, disturbed only from the ravages of nature. Indeed, the villagers had left in such a hurry that some of them even forgot where they had buried their treasures of gold and silver. A few years ago, a couple of Westerners came with metal detectors and discovered caches of treasure buried in the floor of one of the dwellings, one which we visited. The police were alerted by locals and the men were arrested. The state then determined that the village should be preserved and are now turning it into a tourist attraction. It makes for quite a story, the stuff of legends, all to protect a young girl from the humiliation of a bad marriage.

Manu invites me for tea every day. This morning I sit with a retired army officer friend of his. There is a strong military presence in Jaisalmer since it is located not far from the Pakistani border. It is common to see military planes flying over. I meet people as I wander about, one of whom is a deaf shoe-shine boy, who happily gives me a shoe shine and even polishes my well-worn Aussie leather hat. I meet the owner of a nearby restaurant, who invites me to dinner. The manager of the hotel where I am staying is also quite friendly, and allows me an extra stay in a room when I have to check out on my last day, before catching the train at midnight. I hope to return to Jaisalmer.

27 October

Seven Seven—Celebrating with Style
It is a long journey by train back to Ajmer with the train making a number of stops, some in remote areas of the desert to wait for oncoming freight trains to pass. Back in Pushkar, Suresh and I join a cousin preparing a pasta dinner for the guys in the family. We sit on the floor and enjoy the pasta along with the cousins.

I hang out on the street over the next couple of days. Families arrive daily in the city carrying small boxes of ashes, the remains of recently-deceased family members. Pushkar Lake is a sacred stop for them. Many have made the pilgrimage to the Ganges and return here for one final ceremony. I count twenty such groups walking by in a matter of minutes one day as I sit on one of the streets.

Keith's 77th Birthday Party in Pushkar

My birthday approaches and as usual Suresh is busy making plans for a celebration. I keep telling him to keep it simple but my words dissipate in the wind. When the appointed evening arrives, I am outfitted in all-white Indian attire and escorted by his brother to the Hotel Aroma, where arrangements have been made in an open-air room fully decorated with banners and balloons. People gather around and I am seated before a rose petal-strewn table on which candles are burning and a birthday cake presented. It is my 77th birthday. As I lean forward to blow out the candles, when one candle ignites a part of my kurta and quickly flames up. I slap the flame immediately and extinguish it, saved from a burn only by my undershirt which has protected me. The crowd sings Happy Birthday and feeds me slices of cake, each approaching to put a piece in my mouth according to custom and then smear some

Distant Lands

on my face. Immediately fireworks are set off and glitter is thrown everywhere. One of the guests arriving a little late tells us he wasn't sure where the party was taking place until he saw the fireworks and knew that this must be it. I am treated like a celebrity. An Australian couple who happens to be in the restaurant at the time is invited to join in the celebration. They marvel at the elaborate preparations made for me. So much for my request for a simple birthday!

Diwali has come and I join the family on the night of celebration in the multi-family dwelling. An altar is prepared and chants and incense are made to mark the occasion. We go through the ritual ceremonies, first in the presence of the parents and then by Suresh, his wife and me. The city is aglow with lights and fireworks during the night.

It is time for me to go. I leave a weeping Suresh at the train station in Ajmer and arrive in New Delhi at midnight. Fortunately my hotel is within walking distance of the train station. The next night I board the flight for home returning via Amsterdam across the Atlantic to Atlanta and finally to home, arriving on November 4. It is election time in America. Millions of votes are cast the next Tuesday. The majority of votes go to the candidate who loses, but because in our system, the votes allocated through the Electoral College are the ones that actually elect a president. What America's future will be under a Donald Trump presidency remains to be seen.

For now, I am happy to close my travel journals, wiser and richer by the many experiences of a solo wanderer. It is a story I tell with a sigh of the road less traveled.

> *"I shall be telling this with a sigh*
> *Somewhere ages and ages hence:*
> *Two roads diverged in a wood, and I—*
> *I took the one less traveled by,*
> *And that has made all the difference."*
> *– Robert Frost*

Acknowledgements

My circle of friendship has expanded exponentially with each journey. I acknowledge a host of friends who have welcomed me into their homes, their hearts and shared adventures with me. These names may not ring a bell with most readers, but they have an everlasting place in my heart. Without them, my travel would have been far different, more sight-seeing and less exploring. From Nepal: Manish Kumar Singh, his niece and nephew Pinkey and Bickey, his brother Sonu and their father and friend Raju. Tara Mainali, his brothers Gopal, Kumar, Youbaraj, parents and "cousin-brothers" Tej and friend Bishwas Asitis, whose tales of trekking need telling. Also from Nepal: friend and golfer Gopal Nagarkoti, his friend Krishna, young Ramesh Chetri who has become like a son, and his family, Umes, now working in Dubai, who calls me "Grandpa," Lokman Shrestha and his dear family of many years. From India, my dearest and best friend Suresh Parashar and his entire family—mother, father, sister Bebu and brother Kamal, their aunts and uncles and cousins, Suresh's dear wife Deepika and little Aria, a new granddaughter to me. Nimaj villagers: Vicky, Prashant, Tony and their lovely parents, friends Ajay, Ravi and Bablu. In Pushkar, dear friend Mohit Parashar and his entire family, Jonty and Rahul at the Freedom Café who invite me to meet many young, free-spirited back-packers, Rishi from Mumbai, a creative independent film maker I met there.

Distant Lands

There are many other friends from Pushkar, too numerous to mention but very much in my thoughts. From Jaipur: my close friend Neeraj with whom I have shared much time and spiritual connection; his family who welcomed me despite my throwing up upon greeting them. From Delhi, my new relatives Anita David, her daughter Janetta and, of course, daughter Jennifer, married to my grandnephew Christopher, who are now living in Gorgoan near Delhi along with their precious son, my great grandnephew Luther Rishon. From Bangalore: Irfan who drove me all over the place and shared delicious quail from the forest for dinner one night. From Meerut: translating buddy Rahul. From Utter Pradesh: Piyush, a friendship started in a small village with a lift on his motorcycle. From Turkey: my long-time friend and firefighter, hero and champion swimmer Nurettin Unal and his wife Sibel. Also from Turkey: Atalay, his wife Ulku and son Ozgur, who I consider my Turkish grandson, and Atalay's extended family in east Turkey who welcomed me during Ramadan and following. Add to the Turkish list, my funny and good-natured friend Hoseyin who works at the print shop complex, and Atalay's business friends Talip and Inaj. From Egypt: Karim and his family at el Fayoum and Giza, Hamid, Ibrahim and Adam who escorted me around and saw that I got through Tahrir Square safely. From Yemen: Khaled, whose family and friends are now enduring a brutal civil war with famine sweeping their historic land. From Dubai: Alex and his family who hosted me for a brief visit and is also part of my extended family through my niece Jennifer of Delhi. From Malaysia: George and Wendy Liew who hosted me in church and beyond one day in Kuala Lampur. From Hong Kong: Louis Lui who took time to show me around a busy city. From Germany, friends Hank and Honjoerg, who graciously welcomed me into their home in Koblenz.

I acknowledge, from this side of the planet, my friend Hap who patiently looked after my things and retrieved me from the airport each time upon my return, driving some distance from the city where he lives, his aunt Tari, who encouraged me to "write it down." Fellow

Acknowledgements

church members: for prayers during various scrapes and their generous assistance to some friends in need. My family, who wonder about my sanity but allow me to venture forth anyway. Each of these has made a deep imprint on my life, character and my soul.

Quotations in the headings were garnered online from various "Quotations About Travel and Wanderlust" sites.

Postscript

My friend, 92-year-old Tari Wood asked me recently what my "take-a-ways" from the travel I've done over these years. "You should include them in your book." It's a good question, but not that easy to answer. These are the things I have learned:

Travel is one of the best ways to discover the world. Reading about it is good and recommended. Experiencing it is far better.

Age is no excuse to stop living.

Love is not bound by time, location or convention.

Evil and danger harm us only when we fear them.

Each discovery opens the door to a new one.

Certitude is the opposite of faith. Only with humility does the journey of faith lead to truth, which surprisingly is found all around us.

It is not about "me" or "we, it is about "us." We are part of the human family and must learn, not only to live together, but seek to understand one another. Isolation and intolerance are our greatest threats.

CPSIA information can be obtained
at www.ICGtesting.com
Printed in the USA
BVHW030156280422
635614BV00005B/28